NICAEA

NICAEA

THE COUNCIL AND CREED THAT DEFINED CHRISTIANITY

Edited by Don Thorsen

Friendship Press™

Nicaea

The Council and Creed That Defined Christianity

ISBN: 978-1-961088-28-3

Cover design by Laurie Ingram Art + Design. Cover photograph: Mosaic floor of a Roman-era structure in Incesu, central Turkey from the 4th century. Photo by Sercan Küçükahin for Anadolu Ajansı. Used by permission.

Table of Contents

Part 3
Creed and Community: Unity, Formation, and Worship

Contributors

Editor
Don Thorsen

Associate Editors
Jeanette Bouknight
Michael Reid Trice
Robby Waddell

BISHOP ANTHONY (ANTON CHRIS VRAME [AVRAMOPOULOS]) OF SYNADA is Director of Holy Cross Orthodox Press and Adjunct Associate Professor of Religious Education at Holy Cross Greek Orthodox School of Theology. He was a member of Faith and Order of the National Council of Churches from 2005 to 2019, and Chair of Faith and Order from 2008 to 2013. He currently serves on the Table for Christian Education, Faith Formation and Leadership of the National Council of Churches, and as a Board Member for Friendship Press. He is a Bishop of the Greek Orthodox Archdiocese of America (Ecumenical Patriarchate of Constantinople).

THE REV. DR. SANDRA BEARDSALL is an ordained minister in the United Church of Canada. Originally from Brampton, Ontario, she served congregations in Newfoundland and Labrador, then, following completion of a ThD from the Toronto School of Theology, spent twenty-four years as Professor of Church History and Ecumenics at St. Andrew's College, Saskatoon. In retirement Sandra remains engaged in ecumenical work locally and nationally. She is active in Palestine solidarity movements and is a member of the Faith and Order Commission of the WCC, where she assists with Nicaea 2025 projects and enjoys a foretaste of visible Christian unity.

The Rev. Dr. John Chryssavgis is Professor of Theology at Holy Cross School of Theology, where he also serves as founding Executive Director of the Huffington Ecumenical Institute.

Anthony Chvala-Smith, PhD, is Paul E. Morden Seminary Chair and Associate Professor of Religion at Community of Christ Seminary and Graceland University. Trained as a historical theologian and New Testament scholar, his academic interests include the Augustinian tradition, Trinitarian thought, and modern European theology. Dr. Chvala-Smith also serves Community of Christ as a theological consultant and represents the denomination on the Faith and Order Convening Table of the National Council of Churches. Tony and his partner Charmaine are both ordained ministers and regularly work together in their varied roles for the seminary, Graceland, and the church.

The Rev. Elizabeth A. Eaton is the fourth presiding bishop of the Evangelical Lutheran Church in America (ELCA) and chair of the Governing Board of the National Council of the Churches of Christ in the USA. Eaton earned a Master of Divinity degree from Harvard Divinity School and a Bachelor of Music Education degree from the College of Wooster. Her Eaton's four emphases for the ELCA are: We are church; We are Lutheran; We are church together; We are church for the sake of the world.

His Eminence Archbishop Elpidophoros (Lambriniadis) of America, Most Honorable Exarch of the Atlantic and Pacific Oceans, is the eighth Archbishop of America elected since the establishment of the Greek Orthodox Archdiocese in 1922. He has served as the Orthodox Secretary of the Joint International Commission for the Theological Dialogue between the Orthodox Church and the Lutheran World Federation and as a member of the Patriarchal delegations to the General Assemblies of the Conference of European Churches and the World Council of Churches. He was the Secretary of the Pan-Orthodox Synods in Sofia (1998), Istanbul (2005), Geneva (2006), and Istanbul (2008). He has been an active member of the World Council of Churches serving on its Central Committee and also serving on its Faith and Order Commission since 1996.

DAVID N. FIELD is the Ecumenical Staff Officer for Faith and Order and Theological Dialogue for the Council of Bishops of The United Methodist Church and Research Associate of the Research Institute for Theology and Religion at the University of South Africa. He has a PhD from the University of Cape Town and is the co-author of *A Rainbow over the Land: A South African Guide on the Church and Environmental Justice*, and the author of *Bid our Jarring Conflicts Cease: A Wesleyan Theology and Praxis of Church Unity* and *Our Purpose Is Love: The Wesleyan Way to Be the Church*.

DOUGLAS A. FOSTER is Professor Emeritus of church history in the Graduate School of Theology at Abilene (TX) Christian University. He received a PhD in Church History from Vanderbilt University (1986) and an MA in Theology from Scarritt College (1980). His scholarly work has centered on ecumenism, the global Stone-Campbell Movement, and the history of white supremacy and racial oppression in American Christianity. His contribution to the 2024 National Council of Churches Faith and Order book *Confronting Racism and White Supremacy in the US* is titled "The Origins and Anti-Christian Nature of the Great Replacement Theory."

TESSA E. B. FROST is currently serving as representative for the Christian Science Church on the National Council of Church's Faith and Order convening table. She is the Director of Federal Government Affairs for the Church's Committee on Publication. Tessa is also a singer and songwriter, and has published a CD of original inspirational solos for church services called *Soulshine*.

REVD. DR. PHILIP HALIKIÁS, Greek Orthodox Archdiocese of America, is Chief Equity and Compliance Officer and Adjunct Professor for Orthodox-Catholic Relations and Ecumenism at Holy Cross Greek Orthodox School of Theology. He has a Greek/Hispanic background and focuses on Ecumenical and Interfaith work through the National Council of Church's Faith and Order Commission and Muslim Christian Dialogue. He is an active member of the North American Orthodox-Catholic Consultation. Halikiás represents the Orthodox Church on the editing team for the World Council of Churches Week of Prayer for Christian Unity. He is on the boards of the Huffington Ecumenical Institute, Brookline, MA, and North American Academy of Ecumenists.

Dr. Antonios Kireopoulos is Associate General Secretary at the National Council of the Churches of Christ in the USA. An Orthodox Christian theologian, he is the director of Faith and Order, Interreligious Relations and Collaboration, and International Affairs. He has been with the National Council of Churches since 2003.

Amanda Kiser has worked in the public affairs office of the Church of Christ, Scientist, called the Christian Science Committee on Publication, since 2012. She currently serves as the denomination's Lead Representative for Ecumenical and Interfaith Affairs.

Rev. Dr. Jessica Lugo is an educator, pastor, and administrator. Lugo serves as Executive Director of the Association for Hispanic Theological Education (AETH). An ordained American Baptist minister with over 25 years of leadership experience, she is passionate about theological education and forming Hispanic leaders by bridging the church and the academy.

The Rev. Dr. Loida I. Martell is the 18th Vice President of Academic Affairs/Dean and Professor of Constructive Theology at Lexington Theological Seminary. She is a licensed veterinary medical doctor and an ordained minister in the American Baptist Churches/USA. She is a bi-coastal Puerto Rican who has taught in various institutions of higher learning and pastored in New York City. She pioneered the study of evangélica theology, co-edited *Teología en Conjunto: A Collaborative Hispanic Protestant Theology*, and co-authored *Latina Evangélicas: A Theological Survey from the Margins*. She is a co-convener for the National Council of Churches Table of Theological Dialogue and Matters of Faith and Order. Dr. Martell was the Distinguished Fellow for the Baptist Scholars International Roundtable for 2024. She was awarded the Lifetime Achievement Award by La Comunidad of Hispanic Scholars of Religion (of AAR/SBL). The American Baptist Home Missions Societies awarded Dr. Martell the 2015 Richard Hoiland Christian Education Award, its highest recognition for "faithful and effective leadership in Christian education," for her long-standing work in nurturing culturally and racially diverse classrooms and for exceptional leadership.

MATTHEW J. VAN MAASTRICHT is the Pastor and Teacher at the Altamont Reformed Church in Altamont, New York, and the Helderberg Reformed Church in Guilderland Center, New York. He is also an Adjunct Instructor and Fellow of the Reformed Church Center at New Brunswick Theological Seminary in New Brunswick, New Jersey, where he lectures on the Reformed confessions and church polity, and is a PhD candidate at the Theologische Universiteit Utrecht, in the Netherlands.

REV. DR. PAUL A. MCALLISTER is founder and president of Global Leaders in Unity and Evolvement (GLUE), and a member of the Think7 Japan Task Force on Peace, Security and Global Governance, and Think 7 Italy Task Force on Science and Digitalization (2022-2024). He serves on the National Council of Churches' Faith and Order convening table and on the Theology Task Force of the National Council of Churches' Interreligious Relations and Collaboration convening tables. McAllister is a Bonhoeffer Senior Fellow at the Miller Center for Interreligious Learning and Leadership at Hebrew University, and Chair of the Interfaith Caucus of the North Carolina Democratic Party.

BISHOP VASHTI MURPHY MCKENZIE is a trailblazing retired bishop of the African Methodist Episcopal (AME) Church. In 2000, she made history as the first woman to be elected to the episcopacy in the denomination's over 200-year history. Bishop McKenzie further broke barriers by serving as the first woman President of the Council of Bishops and Chair of the General Conference Commission. She has presided over districts in Africa, Tennessee, Kentucky, and Texas, and is the author of six books, including *Not Without a Struggle: Leadership for African American Women in Ministry*. Bishop McKenzie is currently the President and General Secretary of the National Council of the Churches of Christ in the USA (NCC).

REV. KIRSTEN SONKYO OH, PHD, is Professor of Practical Theology at Azusa Pacific University and the Ecclesiastical Associate Professor of United Methodist Studies at Fuller Theological Seminary. She holds a PhD in Theology with an emphasis in Pastoral Care and Counseling and focuses her research on intercultural narrative counseling using multidisciplinary approaches, to address the intersections of Identities. As an ordained elder in The United Methodist Church, she served as a co-convener for the Faith and Order Table of the National Council of Churches (2018-2024) and provides ongoing mentorship and leadership for the United Methodist Women of Color Scholars Program through the General Board of Higher Education and Ministry.

Ann K. Riggs, Friends United Meeting and Friends General Conference, served on the Faith and Order Commission of the National Council of the Churches of Christ in the USA, 1997-2002 and 2008-2009, and she was director of the Commission 2002-2007. Riggs was Principal (President) of Friends Theological College, Kaimosi, Kenya, a ministry of Friends United Meeting, 2009-2014, and she has served on the Christian and Interfaith Relations Committee of Friends General Conference since 1997. Representing Friends, Riggs has served in a variety of roles at the World Council of Churches. She writes on ecumenism, Quakerism, and pastoral care in ecumenical and interreligious settings.

The Rev. Dr. Carmelo Santos-Colón is the Evangelical Lutheran Church in America (ELCA) Director for Theological Diversity and Ecumenical & Interreligious Engagement in the office of the Presiding Bishop. He serves on the commission of Faith and Order of the World Council of Churches and on the convening table on Theological Dialogue and Matters of Faith and Order of the National Council of the Churches of Christ in the USA. He has served as pastor in congregations in the Metropolitan Washington, DC, synod of the ELCA and has been involved in grassroots organizing and advocacy efforts in defense of the dignity and rights of immigrants and minoritized communities. While serving as a parish pastor, Santos-Colón was also a member of Georgetown University's Theology and Religious Studies faculty, where he taught courses in theology and neuroscience, theological ethics, Latinx and Latin American theologies, and "The Problem of God."

James R. Thomas is an ordained pastor in the Evangelical Lutheran Church in America. He is a retired associate professor of church and ministry and worship from Lutheran Theological Southern Seminary of Lenoir-Rhyne University and a visiting professor of church history and ministry at Good News Theological Seminary in Accra, Ghana. Born in Lafayette, Louisiana, he attended Union Theological Seminary in New York and earned a PhD from the University of Minnesota. He is the author of *A Rumor of Black Lutherans: The Formation of Black Leadership in Early American Lutheranism*, published by Fortress Press in 2023.

Don Thorsen, PhD, is Professor of Theology in the Seminary at Azusa Pacific University. He has degrees from Stanford University, Asbury Theological Seminary, Princeton Theological Seminary, and Drew University. Thorsen has published more than twenty books, along with numerous book chapters and journal articles. He lectures, teaches, and preaches nationally and internationally, and has done so in more than a dozen countries. He works ecumenically with the Wesleyan Holiness Connection and Wesleyan Theological Society, serving on Convening Tables for the National Council of Churches, both with Faith and Order and with Interreligious Dialogue and Collaboration.

The Rev. Dr. Ali Tote is the Bishop of the Saskatchewan Synod of the Evangelical Lutheran Church in Canada. Ali has served as bishop since his election in May 2024. In addition to his MDiv from Lutheran Theological Seminary Saskatoon, Ali holds a PhD in epidemiology from the College of Medicine of the University of Saskatchewan, and an MBA from the University of Fredericton with specialization in innovation leadership. Ali serves as the vice-president of the Canadian Black Scientists Network (CBSN). Ali hopes for a church that reflects the diversity of God's creation. Ali is married and has two daughters.

Michael Reid Trice, PhD, EMBA, is Spehar-Halligan Professor and Executive Director, Center for Ecumenical and Interreligious Engagement (CEIE), Seattle University. He teaches in the CEIE Leadership Academy and the Executive Leadership

Program, SU School of Business and Economics. Trice is Parliament of the World's Religions Vice-Chair. He is co-editing two volumes: *Discerning Leadership* and a volume via the Covid-19 Commission, *Vatican Dicastery for Promoting Integral Human Development* (Georgetown University Press). Trice was Associate Executive for the Evangelical Lutheran Church's Ecumenical and Interreligious Office from 2004 to 2011.

ROBBY WADDELL, PHD is professor of New Testament and Early Christianity and Director of the Global Pentecostalism Center at Southeastern University. He is on staff at the Centre for Pentecostal and Charismatic Studies at Bangor University and an Associate Editor of the Journal of Pentecostal Theology. Waddell's areas of specialization include the book of Revelation, the Gospel of Mark, Pentecostalism, ecological hermeneutics, and college pedagogy.

REV. DR. ANGELIQUE WALKER-SMITH is Strategist for Pan African and Orthodox Faith Engagement at Bread for the World in Washington, DC. She brings extensive global, national, and local experience as a faith and public engagement thought leader, journalist, speaker, broadcaster, scholar, preacher, and author. In 2022, she was elected President of World Council of Churches from North America-Turtle Island, becoming the first Baptist World Council of Churches President and the first woman from the US Historic Black Churches elected in this role. She has served as Ecumenical Liaison for the National Baptist Convention USA and is a Board Member of their Home Mission Board.

Welcome! The Nicene Creed 1,700 Years Later

Bishop Vashti Murphy McKenzie

THERE ARE MOMENTS in history when the soul of the Church is called to clarity—not for the sake of certainty alone, but also for the preservation of truth and the proclamation of the Gospel. The First Council of Nicaea in AD 325 was one such moment.

The early church stood on the precipice of deep division and theological uncertainty. Bishops and leaders from across the Christian world, including Africa, Asia, and Europe, came together. What emerged from their deliberation was more than a statement of belief—it was a lifeline to unity and a testament to the living mystery of God. It was the Nicene Creed.

The Creed arose in a context marked by significant controversies, particularly surrounding the nature of Jesus Christ and his relationship to the Father. The Arian Controversy, which denied the full divinity of Jesus, prompted this council and the subsequent formulation of the Nicene Creed.

This historic confession—affirming that Jesus Christ is "God from God, Light from Light, true God from true God"—proclaimed the full divinity of Christ. It settled disputes that risked splintering the early Church, and in doing so, preserved the integrity of the Gospel message. The Creed remains a bold witness to the shared belief in the God who is, the Christ who is, and the Holy Spirit who is moving within and among us.

Beyond its historical significance, the Nicene Creed also underscores key theological concepts that have shaped Christian worship and practice for centuries. It encapsulates the essence of Christian identity, providing a concise summary of essential beliefs regarding God, Jesus Christ, the Holy Spirit, and the Church. As congregations recite the Creed, it fosters a sense of belonging and continuity with the universal Church, bridging divides across time and culture.

Moreover, the legacy of the Nicene Creed extends to its role in ecumenical dialogue. Its emphasis on core beliefs serves as a common ground for diverse Christian traditions to engage in meaningful conversation, striving for unity amidst differences. In our contemporary world, where theological fragmentation often poses challenges, the Creed acts as a reminder of the shared foundation upon which many Christians stand.

This Nicene Creed lifted the Church from the ashes of division and breathed into it a holy unity. It reminded believers then, as it reminds us now, that in Jesus Christ we are bound not by culture or language or empire, but rather by a shared belief in the God who was, who is, and who shall always be.

As the Church approaches the 1700th anniversary of the Council of Nicaea, we find ourselves again in a world shaken. We are being shaken by discord, distortion, and division. The challenges may have different names—ideological extremism, exclusionary theologies, racial, economic, and environmental injustices—but the call is familiar: Return to the core of our confession and remember the One in whom all things bind together.

This book invites you to explore the profound impact of this ancient declaration of belief and its enduring legacy in the spiritual journeys of many. It is hoped that you will take time to remember, reflect, reimagine, and experience a renewed motivation to reengage the meaning of ecumenical solidarity:

Remember the Nicene Creed's original context, a time of passionate debate about truth, unity, and identity.

Reflect on its profound language, each phrase carrying centuries of meaning and spiritual weight.

Reimagine its power in our present, how this ancient declaration still speaks, still centers, still gathers the people of God into one body.

Renewed engagement with visible unity that honors Indigenous culture, marginalized people, and ecumenical solidarity.

As you read the various perspectives presented in these pages, may you be inspired to dig deeper in your own life of faith and gain a deeper understanding of the traditions that bind us.

Special thanks to the leadership and membership of the Faith and Order Convening Table of our National Council of the Churches of Christ in the USA for spearheading the development of this book: General Editor, Don Thorsen, Wesleyan Theological Society; Associate Editors, Jeanette L. Bouknight, Christian Methodist Episcopal Church, Michael Reid Trice, Evangelical Lutheran Church in America, and Robby Waddell, Society for Pentecostal Studies; the various contributors for their scholarship; and Tony Kireopoulos, convening table coordinator.

To every pastor and preacher, evangelist and lay member, theologian and Bible scholar, student and seeker—Welcome! Engage this Nicene Creed, not as a relic of the past, but rather as a living testimony that still breathes through the Church today. Let its words interrogate our witness. This season may be our Sankofa moment, where we look back to our past for the strength to move forward at a time when the Church Universal is again called to speak clearly and stand boldly, lovingly, deeply.

By the grace of God,

Bishop Vashti Murphy McKenzie
President/General Secretary
National Council of the Churches
of Christ in the USA (NCC)
May 2025

Foreword

An Invitation to Renew Our Vocation to Visible Unity

Bishop Elizabeth A. Eaton

SEVENTEEN HUNDRED YEARS ago, the First Ecumenical Council was convened in Nicaea. Christian bishops, clergy, theologians, and staff from throughout the Roman Empire gathered to discern matters central to the Christian faith, namely: *How do we understand Jesus Christ?*

Specifically, the Council sought to end disputes about the divine nature of Jesus and his relationship to God in an attempt to unify all of Christendom. Naturally, debates arose, and different schools of thought emerged. In the end, near-consensus was reached—and later expanded in 381—resulting in the Nicene-Constantinopolitan Creed.

Ever since, Christians have articulated the complexity of the faith in clear and simple terms:

> We believe in one Lord, Jesus Christ,
> the only Son of God,
> eternally begotten of the Father;
> God from God, Light from Light,
> true God from true God,
> begotten, not made, of one being with the Father;
> through him all things are made.[1]

This articulation has stood the test of time and has been translated into countless languages and contextualized in Christian communities around the world. This anniversary is an opportunity to celebrate the God-given gift of our visible unity, and an invitation to share that more fully. It is also an occasion to claim our place in the 1700-year-old conciliar ecumenical movement that began with a common affirmation of our faith "so that the world may believe" (John 17:21b).

At the same time, this anniversary invites further reflection, and even self-critique. The First Ecumenical Council is a reminder of how Christians—then and now—remain divided. The history surrounding it also raises questions that resonate for us today: on the collusion of church and empire, on the forced exclusion of Jews and religious minorities, and on the diminished role of women in the early church, to name a few. In our context of rising Christian nationalism, racism, hatred, and inequity, there is plenty of grappling for us to do as churches.

Even so, I would posit that this anniversary calls us to two critical actions. The first is to refocus on our common faith as the primary lens for living out who we are called to be. The Creed has never been about rote recitation of doctrine but affirming our faith within Christian community. The second is to reorient all that we do to focus on bearing common witness to our faith—proclaiming the life, death, and resurrection of Jesus Christ. This ecumenical vocation was, is, and will always be at the heart of our life together until Christ comes again in glory.

For us in the National Council of the Churches of Christ in the USA, the coincidence of this anniversary with our own 75th anniversary—and in a year when all Christians celebrate a common date for Easter—is a reminder that our witness to visible unity is tied across time to all the saints throughout the ages and across space to the vast and vital global Christian fellowship today. Thus, we offer this volume as a contribution to that witness and look forward to receiving the witness of others. We pray that God will enrich us all as ambassadors of Christ's unity, justice, and peace for all, and for the life of the world to come. Amen.

Notes

1 *Evangelical Lutheran Worship* (Minneapolis: Augsburg Fortress Publishers, 2006), 126.

Preface

Don Thorsen

SEVENTEEN HUNDRED YEARS ago, when the Christian church was still quite young, a very important meeting of church leaders took place in the ancient city of Nicaea. The growing faith, though lively, was facing serious disagreements that threatened to break it apart, particularly over the true nature of Jesus Christ. Was he truly God, or something less? Their goal was not just to settle an argument, but to clearly and strongly state the basic truths of the Christian faith, especially about who Jesus Christ truly is—fully God and fully human. The result of their intense discussions, the Nicene Creed, became a lasting sign of Christians' deep commitment to Jesus and his saving work, affirming his divine equality with God the Father.

Today, as we celebrate the 1700th anniversary of this pivotal event, we are asked to think again about how deeply and lastingly the Nicene Creed has affected us. Far from being just an old document from history books, the Creed is still a lively, active statement, spoken aloud in countless churches around the world every week. It crosses different church traditions and countries, acting as a powerful force that brings believers together in a shared declaration of faith. More than just a summary, it is like a spiritual guide that has steadily led generations through complicated beliefs, defining key doctrines like the Trinity (God as Father, Son, and Holy Spirit) and the Incarnation (God becoming human in Jesus). It has kept the faith true and helped us understand God better.

This collection of writings is a serious yet celebrative way to mark this special anniversary. It brings together many different voices, each looking at a unique part of the Nicene Creed's rich history: its detailed background, its deep theological meaning (such as the co-eternality of the Son with the Father, and the Holy Spirit as "Lord and Giver of Life"), how it is still important in today's fast-changing world, and its ongoing call to live as followers of Christ.

Brought to you by the Faith and Order commission of the National Council of Churches, *Nicaea: The Council and Creed That Defined Christianity* invites you to rediscover the profound depth and vibrant power of the Creed that continues to shape the heart of Christian belief. Whether you are a pastor, scholar, or simply someone curious to understand your faith more deeply, this book will inspire a renewed appreciation for the enduring legacy of Nicaea's foundational moment in church history—and its ongoing influence in our lives today.

Bishop Elizabeth A. Eaton provides a Foreword to the book, inviting Christians to renew their vocation to visible unity among churches. John Chryssavgis provides an Afterword, which describes Nicaea as both a watershed moment in church history and a threshold moment for us today in advancing Christians' unity-in-faith.

The book is divided into three parts. *Part 1. Nicaea Then and Now: History, Memory, and Imagination* looks at the Council of Nicaea historically, and then imagines its practical relevance for today. *Part 2. Creedal Theology: Incarnation, Spirit, and the Mystery of God* discusses theological issues related to the nature of God the Father, Son, and Holy Spirit, and how they apply to Christians. *Part 3. Creed and Community: Unity, Formation, and Worship* talks about how the Nicene Creed is used in churches around the world and how it may serve as an instrument of unity as well as worship.

Three chapters in the book appear in both English and Spanish languages. Philip Halikiás, Loida I. Martell, and Carmelo Santos-Rolón provided them to the anthology. The English and Spanish language chapters are a tribute to the worldwide relevance of both the Council of Nicaea and the Nicene Creed.

I want to thank Antonios (Tony) Kireopoulos, who spearheaded this commemoration of the 1700th anniversary of the Nicene Creed, appealing to expertise from the members of Faith and Order for contributions to the book. It is part of

A Faith and Order Book series, sponsored by the National Council of Churches. I also want to thank Brian Sigmon, who provided publishing and editing excellence on behalf of Friendship Press. Finally, I want to thank the Associate Editors—Jeanette Bouknight, Michael Reid Trice, and Robby Waddell—for their editing work and organizational insight in completing this book.

The Nicene Creed[1]

I BELIEVE IN one God, Father Almighty, Creator of heaven and earth, and of all things visible and invisible.

And in one Lord Jesus Christ, the only-begotten Son of God, begotten of the Father before all ages; Light of Light, true God of true God, begotten, not created, of one essence with the Father through Whom all things were made. Who for us men and for our salvation came down from heaven and was incarnate of the Holy Spirit and the Virgin Mary and became man. He was crucified for us under Pontius Pilate, and suffered and was buried; And He rose on the third day, according to the Scriptures. He ascended into heaven and is seated at the right hand of the Father; And He will come again with glory to judge the living and dead. His kingdom shall have no end.

And in the Holy Spirit, the Lord, the Creator of life, Who proceeds from the Father,[2] Who together with the Father and the Son is worshipped and glorified, Who spoke through the prophets.

In one, holy, catholic, and apostolic Church.

I confess one baptism for the forgiveness of sins.

I look for the resurrection of the dead, and the life of the age to come.

Amen.

Notes

1 Nicene Creed, Greek Orthodox Archdiocese of America (GOA), website, official GOA English translation, accessed May 1, 2025, https://www.goarch.org/-/the-nicene-creed.

2 Western churches later added the phrase "and from the Son" (Lat., *filioque*).

PART 1

Nicaea Then and Now: History, Memory, and Imagination

1

The Council of Nicaea: Challenges and Opportunities for the Church Today[1]

Archbishop Elpidophoros

BECAUSE I WAS the Metropolitan of Bursa before my election to be Archbishop of America, a city only seventy-five kilometers from Νίκαια (as it was then known in Greek), I have a special affinity for the place—its spiritual topography as the home of the First and the Seventh Eecumenical Councils recognized by both the Orthodox and Roman Catholic Churches.

Between these two councils in Nicaea—the first in 325 CE, and the second in 787 CE—the spiritual constitution of Christianity was composed over centuries of inquiry, controversy, and the life and death struggles of the empire, known then as "Roman" and now as "Byzantine." The occasion of the seventeen hundredth anniversary of the First Ecumenical Council of Nicaea presents to all Christians both opportunities and challenges, as the very title of this chapter observes. Consider the circumstances surrounding the Council.

Nicaea takes place only fourteen years after the Edict of Toleration that ended the Diocletian Persecution—one of the worst periods of oppression the Church experienced since Nero—and only twelve years after the Edict of Milan that made Christianity a legal religion of the Roman Empire.

Thus, in a single generation, Christianity went from a treasonous and despised faith to the preferred religious tradition of the Roman Empire. When Christianity became the faith of the emperor, it was certainly inviting for those who sought his favor. And remember, at this time, Christianity is estimated to have accounted for perhaps only 10 percent of the population of the empire.

From a time when the emperors of Rome were declared to be gods themselves—beginning with Augustus in whose reign the Lord Jesus was born—we now arrive to the Nicene declaration that the Rabbi of Galilee, Jesus, crucified under Roman Law, is:

> Φῶς ἐκ Φωτός, Θεὸν ἀληθινὸν ἐκ Θεοῦ ἀληθινοῦ, γεννηθέντα, οὐ ποιηθέντα, ὁμοούσιον τῷ Πατρί
>
> Light of Light, True God of True God, begotten, not made, consubstantial with the Father!

This truly amazing and, indeed, miraculous transformation expressed by Nicaea, becomes a mere fifty-five years later—despite the continuing fractiousness over Arianism and the brief reign of Julian the Apostate (the last pagan emperor of Rome)—the official and only legal religion of the Roman Empire. A truly remarkable about-face if there ever was one! The impact of the Council of Nicaea is truly impossible to overstate.

As a hierarch of the Orthodox Christian Church, and especially one born and raised in the region, I feel deeply about this Council, particularly because of the conciliar model that it manifested for the Church. In considering its relevance for today, I see many more opportunities than challenges because of the following. The structural, dogmatic, and institutional fragmentation of Christianity since Nicaea undeniably exists and is well documented. It is counterproductive even to try to reverse the course of the history which has delivered us to this moment. It is the essence of ecumenicity that we accept one another where we are and for who we are.

But the faith expressed by Nicaea, and the remarkable transformation that it witnessed in a mere generation, still demand our attention, now more than ever. For like an inviting hearth that sheds light and warmth, Nicaea can offer to any Christian community the most essential elements that invigorate and nourish the spiritual life. This anniversary of Nicaea presents us with the openings to not merely return to a shared expression of our faith tradition, but also a model for conciliarity that has stood the test of time and is ready to bring us into a renewed sense of unity with one another.

In saying this, I must stress that the Creed as we have it today, in use in our liturgical context, is the product of the formulation offered to the Church at the Second Ecumenical Council in Constantinople. Nevertheless, it is the faith of Nicaea, summed up with laconic elegance by Saint Athanasios the Great:

> Αὐτὸς γὰρ ἐνηνθρώπισεν, ἵνα ἡμεῖς θεοποιηθῶμεν.
>
> For He [the Lord] became a human being, so that we might become divine.[2]

Those who see the controversies around the definition of Nicaea, which is affirmed again and again by the later councils, as mere splitting of hairs, risk missing the greater import of the Nicene Council. By establishing once and for all the fullness of Christ's divinity, and setting the Church on a course of experiencing God as Trinity, Nicaea becomes the standard by which every subsequent experience of the Godhead is not only relatable, but also intelligible—at least to the degree that any human mind can apprehend the uncontainable God.

The plumb line of Nicaea stretches across the centuries of understanding the person of the Lord Jesus Christ. It was an attempt to respond to Christ's question: "But who do you say that I am?" (Matthew 16:15). For it is in the vision of his message, of his meaning and of his Person, that the Church exercises her mission. In the enhanced Nicene-Constantinopolitan Creed, the article that affirms the Church as "one holy catholic and apostolic" also relates to the person of our Savior. He is one person—a definition enhanced through subsequent councils, but fully expressed in the original form of the Creed.

As many of you already know, the form of the Nicene Creed was influenced by the early baptismal creeds. This makes perfect sense, because baptismal creeds could be easily memorized and avail the illiterate classes of society with a comprehensive view of the faith into which they were entering. The Creed's formula encapsulated the fullness of the teaching of the New Testament at a time when the New Testament was still being formed. Even today, the final Nicene-Constantinopolitan Creed is recognized as having twelve articles, one for each of the twelve apostles, and is used in the majority of the world's Christian churches as a baptismal creed once again, coming full circle.

The oneness of the person of the Lord is joined to his holiness issuing forth from his divinity, his applicability to all people (the "catholic" attribute), and finally, the apostolic authenticity of the teaching about him in the authentic tradition of his disciples. All of these characteristics are then imputed to the body of Christ, the Church, because they issue from the head of the body.

These same characteristics not only help to define relationships within ecclesiastical bodies, but their interrelationships as well. The idea of "Oneness" has, for example, led to all kinds of theories about the visibility and invisibility of this characteristic. For the Roman Catholic and Orthodox Churches, we usually maintain that the unity is indeed visible, while at the same time we try not to deny where the Spirit might choose to blow.[3]

In the majority of Protestant traditions, the "oneness" of the Church may not be perceptible by human powers of apprehension, but it is still most definitely One Church! This affirmation alone is a cause for hope in our inter-Church relations, because it takes the declaration of essential oneness and unity and leaves it in place, in spite of any and all apparent evidence to the contrary. Ultimately, if we Christians are to apprehend our fellowship with one another, we have to at least have faith in "the assurance of things hoped for, the conviction of things not seen."[4] In the same vein, his All-Holiness Ecumenical Patriarch Bartholomew stated in his historic opening address to the Holy and Great Council of the Orthodox Church, convened in Crete in June 2016:

> The Church constitutes a single body in the entire world, united in the same faith and the same Divine Eucharist and sacramental life, which is why it also needs synodality on the global level. This need was expressed and is fulfilled by the Ecumenical Councils, which were indeed convened whenever there was a call to secure the unity of all the local Churches on a global level, as well on matters of faith, administration and pastoral concern. These Councils represented all of the Churches in the world and were accepted by all inasmuch as they constituted and constitute the supreme authority in the Church, thereby preserving its unity.[5]

The creedal formula is a call to renewal for all Christians—a basis upon which not only can good ecumenical relationships be built, but also a foundation for re-integration and even re-unification. We must be careful not to press the latter too early and too far, making interested parties reticent to embrace a full-throated embrace of one another.

But the Creed, as we have inherited it, is a starting point on which we can all agree, except a very small minority of Christian bodies. Even this has historical precedent, because just as the Christian church of the first three centuries had divergences—especially with the so-called Gnostic systems of belief—Nicene Christianity became the harmonious composite of intellection and experience. It allowed for the expansion of the faith of the Lord Jesus throughout the empire, eventually leading to its Christianization. There were always variances, as there are today, but they remain a minority position.

The phenomenon of historical factionalism and Christian "denominationalism," now represented by well over forty thousand instantiations, show us that having a single source to which we all can lay claim is a genuine cause for solidarity and spiritual harmony. We are not going to reverse centuries of institutional, dogmatic, and biblical interpretive variation. Yet, despite this degree of fragmentation, the Council of Nicaea of 325 CE is the dominant and inclusive paradigm for our future relationships.

It is important to remember that the ecumenical movement is only a recent phenomenon—a little more than one hundred years in duration thus far. I believe that this is exceedingly important to stress. Although Roman Catholics and Eastern Orthodox Christians (together with the ancient Oriental Churches) represent far and away the majority of the world's Christians, the incredible diversity of the Protestant minority also holds, for the most part, to the Nicaean plumb line of dogmatic formulation expressed in the Nicene Creed. It was later amplified by the Second Ecumenical Council in Constantinople in 381 CE, which happened one year after the legal mandate for Nicene Christianity. This fact alone manifests the merits and value of not only celebrating the impending anniversary but also engaging how the models that emerged from Nicaea are relevant to our ecumenical and inter-Church relationships today.

An exceptional Ecumenical Patriarch of Constantinople, Saint Photios the Great—who faced troubled times and troubled relations with the Western Church in the ninth century—still saw that the universal, ecumenical faith that commences with Nicaea could be maintained while there were differences of all kinds. Photios stated:

> The fact that other customs and laws are kept by others, yet without violating the Faith or departing from common and universally-held decrees, will not lead the discerning observer into thinking either that those who keep them fall into the wrong, or that those who do not accept them violate the law.[6]

Unity in faith and diversity in practice. Well before the ecumenical movement in which we so rightly take pride, the Christians of the first millennium understood what was essential for the Church to hold fast.

The second millennium saw a splintering of the Churches that defies imagination, and yet, the faith expressed by Nicaea abides. And again, that is why this anniversary is such an opportunity for ecumenically-inclined believers.

For we are now at the dawn of the third millennium of our glorious faith in Christ, and sharing a reaffirmation of Nicene Christianity may be the key to unlock many doors that have, heretofore, been shut by historical and even political exigencies.

The passage of time has hardened the perimeters of our respective Churches, making them seem impenetrable to reintegration. But the faith of Nicaea is able to soften these boundaries and make them permeable and flexible, such that we can distinguish the small "customs and laws" from the essentials of the faith. I borrow here the words of Metropolitan Kallistos of Diokleia, of blessed memory: "The Creed belongs only to those who live it."[7]

With this kind of openness and receptivity, we will find ourselves prepared to accept one another without conditions and demands that make impossible the fellowship of the saints to which we are all called. Nicaea is our key, through which we may unlock the closed doors that have been built up through the centuries and open our ecumenical relationships to new possibilities.

The decisions of the Council of Nicaea had tremendous repercussions for the future of the Church and established a model that all Christians practice to this day. Leadership in the Church—any Church—is rarely seen as prophetic (a category usually reserved for unaffiliated communities dependent on individual personalities). Rather, it is conciliar paradigm that brings together the disparate members of the body and unifies them through a process of dialogue, exchange, consultation, and finally, consensus.

This model has been used throughout the centuries, and both preceded and followed the first ecumenical council. Before and after Nicaea, there were local councils that attended to local needs, and their solutions were often adopted by the larger council. The plumb lines that we call "canons" are the most obvious example of this process.

All of Christianity reckons the number of ecumenical councils differently, but everyone starts with Nicaea. This manifests a basic truth that, were we all to embrace it, would easily reveal we have more in common than we hold differently.

Conciliarity will always be the way forward for the Church, irrespective of the issue to be addressed. But we must be willing to approach the issues honestly and in the light of Nicaea, which continues to illuminate the landscape of the Church as it has for the last seventeen hundred years.

Finally, even though there are many avenues that lead from Nicaea, I must mention the teleological model for humanity that the Nicene Creed proposes. For the full divinity of Jesus is the pattern for the divinization (*theosis*) of every human being. We return to Saint Athanasios:

> Αὐτὸς γὰρ ἐνηνθρώπισεν, ἵνα ἡμεῖς θεοποιηθῶμεν.
>
> For the Lord became a human being, so that we might become divine.[8]

The realization of our divinity, ensconced in the image of God in which each of us is created, is based in the total and complete divinity and humanity of the person of our Lord Jesus Christ. All that the Lord attained through his incarnation, ministry, teaching, passion, crucifixion, death, burial, resurrection, and ascension is included in the Nicene definition. Thus, the faith of Nicaea is the faith that leads us heavenward.

As the leader of the Greek Orthodox People of America, a hierarch of the Ecumenical Patriarchate of Constantinople, and as a believer in Nicene Christianity, I see opportunities everywhere in the anniversary of Nicaea. The challenges are already present. We do not need to make them more complicated than they already are. But we all have a responsibility to find ways to elevate what is most essential—what is Nicaea in its simplicity.

Are we willing to trust, to believe, that the seventeen-hundred-year-old affirmation of faith can still be useful in our modern era? Can we see the differentiation in our worship and practice is not enough to overcome the truth of the Nicene-Constantinopolitan Creed?

The substance—the οὐσία—of our faith in Christ is indeed enough to actualize the ὁμοούσιον—the consubstantiality between us. This reality we affirm in the Creed exists from all eternity and all infinity between our Lord and his Heavenly Father, and which extends to the Holy Spirit. This is the very basis for our understanding of the Holy Trinity, a doctrine nowhere explicit in the Gospels, but everywhere implicit in the life and experience of the Church.

May we all be blessed in the year of 2025 to actualize the ὁμοούσιον in our own lives and in the lives of our Church communities. May we ever give all glory, honor, and worship to the all-holy, good, and consubstantial Trinity, Who is forever blessed unto the ages of ages. Amen.

Notes

1 This chapter was originally presented as a lecture by Archbishop Elpidophoros on September 19, 2024, at The Catholic University of America in Washington, D.C. His lecture is published here with revisions; see *Orthodox Observer News*, website, September 19, 2024, https://www.goarch.org/-/lecture-the-council-of-nicaea-challenges-and-opportunities-for-the-church-today-at-catholic-university-of-america.

2 Athanasios (Athanasius), *De Incarnatione Verbi Dei* (Athanasius on the Incarnation), trans. T. Herbert Bindley, Christian Classics Series III (London: Religious Tract Society, n.d.), §54 (p. 153), https://dn790000.ca.archive.org/0/items/deincarnationeve00athauoft/deincarnationeve00athauoft.pdf.

3 Cf. John 3:8, NRSVue.

4 Hebrew 11:1, NRSVue

5 All-Holiness Ecumenical Patriarch Bartholomew, "Inaugural Session of the Holy and Great Council," Holy and Great Council, website, June 20, 2016, https://holycouncil.org/opening-ecumenical-patriarch.

6 Provided is an English translation of Photios, "Letter 290 of Photius to Nicholas I," August/September 861, in *Photii Patriarchae Constantinopolitani Epistulae et Amphilochia,* 3 vols., ed. B. Laourdas and L. G. Westerink (Liepzig: BSB B.G. Teubner Verlagsgesellschaft, 1983), lines 241 and following in vol. 3, p. 131, Internet Archive, website, accessed May 26, 2025, https://archive.org/details/photiipatriarcha0003phot/page/131/mode/1up.

7 Metropolitan Bishop Kallistos (Ware) of Diokleia, excerpts from *The Orthodox Church*, pt. II, 7, quoted by fatheralexander.org, website, accessed May 30, 2025, https://www.fatheralexander.org/booklets/english/history_timothy_ware_2.htm.

8 Athanasios (Athanasius), *De Incarnatione Verbi Dei* (Athanasius on the Incarnation), §54 (p. 153).

2

What If Nicaea Didn't Happen?

Bishop Anthony (Vrame) of Synada

WHILE WE CELEBRATE the achievements of the First Ecumenical Council held at Nicaea in 325 CE, we might for a moment consider what might have happened to Christianity and the Christian church (Christendom) if this germinal event in history had not occurred. What would Christianity look like without Nicaea? After all, there was no assurance that Emperor Constantine would have called the assembly. There was no precedent for imperial involvement in the Christian church at that point, especially taking actions that would resolve debates among Christians and elevate the status of the Church. We should not forget that until Constantine, Christians were more likely to suffer an ill fate at the hands of imperial involvement than to be supported. (Admittedly, Christians who disagreed with Nicaea or other councils were not usually spared.) We may certainly critique the involvement of the Roman Empire with the Church that Constantine unleashed; but if Nicaea had not happened, what might have happened to Christianity and the Christian church?

We often wonder how history would have been different if certain events had or had not happened. Attempting this thought experiment about the Council of Nicaea is both an opportunity to consider the gifts that this ecumenical council gave to Christianity and an opportunity to consider an alternative history. Of course, we cannot change history, but we can and should study it carefully. Through that process of study, a question that should probably be asked is, "What if it hadn't happened that way?"

We Believe

When the Nicene Creed is typically recited today, the opening words are, "I believe." This personal confession of faith recited in many Christian baptismal rites is significant because it joins the individual to the community. The Nicene Creed unites the baptized in each and every place, today and throughout the ages, as a community of believers. When stated in confirmation (chrismation) rituals, the Creed becomes a personal appropriation of the faith of the Church, a sign of growth and maturity, especially for communions that practice infant baptism.

In the Byzantine rite of ordination to the office of bishop, the candidate must first recite the Nicene-Constantinopolitan Creed before the ordaining hierarchs and the community of faith. (He will also later recite additional statements and affirmations of faith.) Having done this just a year or so ago, I can assure the reader of the personal impact of reciting this most familiar of statements so publicly: first, it needed to be recited perfectly (in the original Greek, no pronunciation errors, no omissions), and second, it needed to be recited authoritatively. There could be no doubt in myself or those hearing me about what "I believe."

However, scholars understand that the original text—if one were to be found—of the Nicene Creed begins, "We believe." A generation ago, the ecumenical community in its exploration of the apostolic faith could affirm:

> The confession "we believe in" articulates not only the trust of individuals in God's grace, but it also affirms the trust of the whole Church in God. There is a bond of communion among those who join together in making a common confession of their faith.[1]

When Christians gather ecumenically, reciting the Nicene-Constantinopolitan Creed in its ancient form, that is, without the *filioque* (a later addition), is an act of communal identity as the one, holy, catholic, and apostolic Church.

That the Church's universal affirmation of faith begins "We believe," created a communal identity. (We must recognize that the concept of a personal or private identity is something that will emerge much later in history.) Without a Nicene Creed, even beginning "I believe," Christian faith would have been private and individual, not communal.

The Nicene Creed Provides Continuity

The religious educator Maria Harris, referencing G. K. Chesterton's *Orthodoxy*, writes, "Tradition means giving votes to the most obscure of all classes, *our ancestors*. . . . Tradition refuses to submit to the small and arrogant oligarchy of those who merely happen to be walking about."[2] One of the positive elements of Tradition, with a capital "T," is that it remembers the past, hopefully without idolizing it as a "golden age." A Christianity without Nicaea is a Christianity only of our own, quite possibly self-aggrandizing and triumphalist, era. Nicaea obligates us to face our history and ask what we hope to hand forward—tradition as handing forward, not only what has been inherited. Without Nicaea and its Creed, Christianity might have been unmoored from history and its own history. Without Nicaea there would be no historic or universal reference point for subsequent generations. Jaroslav Pelikan wrote:

> The doctrine of the Trinity (enshrined in the Nicene Creed) has been the unquestioned—and unquestionable—touchstone of truly orthodox faith and teaching. It has given its outline to systematic theologies like the Institutes of John Calvin, to catechisms, and to sermons.[3]

Without a Nicaean definition, any answer to Jesus's question to his disciples, "Who do you say that I am," would be acceptable. Even that exchange pointed to a desire for an answer about which the disciples could all agree:

> Now when Jesus came into the district of Caesarea Philippi, he asked his disciples, "Who do people say that the Son of Man is?" And they said, "Some say John the Baptist but others Elijah and still others Jeremiah or one of the prophets." He said to them, "But who do you say that I am?" Simon Peter answered, "You are the Messiah, the Son of the living God." (Matthew 16:13-16)

Nicaea provided an answer that has stood the test of time. From the beginning, Christians have been interpreting the Bible in order to answer Jesus's own question. Nicaea provided an actual definition of that interpretation, affirming the Lordship of the risen Christ.[4] Over the centuries Christians have debated further questions about the Trinity. For example: Is the Holy Spirit equal to the Father and the Son? How is Christ fully human and divine, "unconfusedly, unchangeably, indivisibly, inseparably"? Was it possible to depict the person of Jesus in images? Yet always, Nicaea is the starting point. Subsequent decrees of ecumenical councils affirm all that had been decreed before, beginning with Nicaea.

Without Nicaea, Christianity could also have become easily subject to changing trends and whims, even political whims. Any power could edit Christianity to fit its current desires, political views, or social agendas because there would be no historic point of universal agreement. Christians relying on the historic Church affirmation of the person of Jesus Christ were able to resist the Nazi attempt to wash away the Jewish identity of Jesus.

Without Nicaea, theology and doctrine might not matter and all Christianity would be local. Christians debating Trinitarian issues, Christology, and so on, might seem unimportant—"professional hairsplitting"—to some. However, Christians discerning who they are, what they believe, about God and God's relationship to humanity is critical to living as the body of Christ. Without Nicaea, there would not be much need for an ecumenical movement because the movement begins from the premise that Christians do not live in the unity of the past. Should Christian unity, full communion, be achieved one day, the ecumenical movement would no longer be needed. However, on what basis would communion be restored? Nicaea provides the reference point for a universal Christian faith, one that brings about communion.

Without a Nicene formula, Christians would continue to celebrate the Resurrection of Christ—the central event of its teaching and life—on different days and dates. (I fully appreciate the irony of this statement as an Orthodox Christian.) The death and resurrection of Jesus Christ form the core of the "Good News" that is to be spread to all people. "[I]f Christ has not been raised, then our proclamation is in vain and your faith is in vain" (1 Corinthians 15:14). Without Nicaea and its universal formula for determining the date for celebrating the Resurrection, Christians would have continued to be divided as to the celebration of their central element of faith, weakening Christian witness. That the late-twentieth-century and current debates about returning to a common Easter date have always pointed to the Nicene formula, there is no need to "reinvent the wheel" or re-litigate the issue. There is a seventeen-century-old formula that worked then and now. What's needed is better astronomical data (essentially an Eastern Orthodox issue to be worked out, but that is a discussion for another presentation).

Conciliar Governance

Without Nicaea, there would not be a process for resolving issues at a large scale. Based on the "Council of Jerusalem," recorded in Acts of the Apostles chapter 15, councils were occurring to manage the life of the Church, but all were local until Nicaea. Any attempt to "impose" or "influence" other local Christian communities were limited. Nicaea gave Christianity a way to function globally or universally (albeit largely due to imperial enforcement ability).

Christianity, beginning with the disciples themselves, has always been addressing issues of its identity, teaching, and practice. Councils have been the preferred method of resolving those issues. The Council of Jerusalem broke through the impasse on receiving Gentiles into a Christian community rooted in the Jewish practice of circumcision. Christianity had to overcome dietary restrictions of Judaism (Acts 10:13). The early Church had to resolve issues of eating foods that had been offered to idols (1 Corinthians 8). St. Paul regularly addressed "errors in Christian communities."[5] How or why else could Paul have written the following?

> For it has been made clear to me by Chloe's people that there are quarrels among you, my brothers and sisters. What I mean is that each of you says, "I belong to Paul," or "I belong to Apollos," or "I belong to Cephas," or "I belong to Christ." Has Christ been divided? (1 Corinthians 1:11-13).

Throughout this essay, other issues of debate have been pointed out. What matters is that Nicaea gave Christianity a process for resolving debates on a grand scale.[6] This conciliar process continues to this day, albeit within a communion, for example, the Holy and Great Council of the Orthodox (Crete 2016), the Second Vatican Council of the Roman Catholic Church, or better yet named Ecumenical Council XXI (1960s), the Lutheran World Federation, and so on. The search for a Nicaea level council eludes Christianity to this day. The anniversary of Nicaea 325 this year raises the question: What are the questions that Christianity faces today that could lead to a council at the scale and impact of Nicaea? The First Ecumenical Council of Nicaea points to a way—a way that we would not have if it had not happened.

All Christians have enjoyed the now seventeen-hundred-year-old gift of the First Ecumenical Council, held at Nicaea in 325 CE, attended according to tradition by 318 bishops, with many more in support. Gifts, especially old gifts, are meant to be cherished, celebrated, and admired. They require attention, telling the usual story of their origins but also clarifying the story as more information about their history becomes available. Anniversaries are good times to put these gifts on display, but also to remind ourselves of what other generations have bequeathed to us and hopefully what we continue to use in our lives. We should not forget these gifts and how much poorer our story would be without them. Nicaea is no exception to this.

Notes

1 *Confessing the One Faith,* Faith and Order Document 153 (Geneva: WCC Publications, 1991), 15.

2 Maria Harris, *Fashion Me a People: Curriculum in the Church* (Louisville: Westminster, John Knox Press, 1989), 8, emphasis added.

3 Jaroslav Pelikan, *Jesus Through the Centuries* (New York: History Book Club, 2005), 58.
4 John Behr, *The Nicene Faith: Part One, True God of True God* (Crestwood, NY: SVS Press, 2004), 66.
5 Behr, 8.
6 Behr, 61.

3

Who Went to the Council of Nicaea and Why Does It Matter Now?

Ann K. Riggs

JOHN S. MBITI was a Kenyan and an Anglican priest. He was director of the World Council of Churches' Ecumenical Institute at Bossey, Switzerland, from 1974 to 1980. Mbiti is sometimes called the father of modern African Christian theology. Mbiti contributed to mutual understanding between the global North and the global South. His books introduced African Traditional Religion (ATR) to the wider world. Mbiti said, "African peoples concentrated their attention on life's journey from before birth to after death. They wanted that journey to be meaningful, happy, safe and satisfied."[1] He continued, "African Religion tries to make the journey of life worthwhile for both the individual and the community of which he was a part."[2] He described religious practices and community rituals that accompany human life from before birth to after death. Using these practices, religious beliefs, values, and virtues are made available and held up for learning and emulation.

The Religious Society of Friends (Quakers) also aspires to an identity between beliefs and life. Friends arose in mid-seventeenth century Britain and are a break off from the Church of England. The name Friends is drawn from John's Gospel, where we hear Jesus saying: "You are my friends if you do what I command you" (15:14).

George Fox, an important leader among Early Friends, wrote in a letter to Quaker ministers in 1656: "Be examples in all countries . . . wherever you come, that your carriage and life may preach among all sorts of people, and to them; then you will come to walk cheerfully over the world, answering that of God in every one."[3] In "The Place of Creeds and Confessions among Friends (Quakers)," in *Ancient Faith and American-Born Churches: Dialogues Between Christian Traditions* from the NCCCUSA Faith and Order Commission, I displayed core Christian Quaker faith claims embedded within John Woolman's autobiographical spiritual Journal.[4]

Friends are not alone among Protestant groups who understand themselves to be noncreedal. The purpose of this essay is to suggest a way that Friends and other noncreedal communities may join with others in learning from the Council of Nicaea. Together we can celebrate the 1700th anniversary of the Council of Nicaea. Through attention to shared spiritual values, behaviors, and virtues shown by the participants in that Council, we can look for greater unity across the Christian community in our time in faith and action.

Some Quaker jurisdictions use classic articulations of Christian doctrine, such as a the "Letter to the Governor of Barbados" by George Fox and others,[5] the "Statement of Essential Truths" written by Rufus Jones and James Wood, for Five Years Meeting,[6] and the "Richmond Declaration"[7] as normative for faith. Others do not. These statements are clearly similar to historical creeds used by the wider Christian community. However, Friends' usual focus is toward lived spiritual experience and toward "walking in the light (1 John 1:7) in the loving obedience of faith" ("Richmond Declaration"),[8] rather than verbal articulation. Distinctive readings and emphasis are evident. Since the seventeenth century, John 1:9, cited in this passage from the "Richmond Declaration," has been called "the Quaker text":

> It is with reverence and thanksgiving that we profess our unwavering allegiance to our Lord and Savior, Jesus Christ. No man hath seen God at any time; the only begotten Son,

> who is in the bosom of the Father, He hath declared Him (John 1:18). In Him was life, (John 1:4) and the life was the light of men (John 1:4). He is the true Light which lighteth every man that cometh into the world (John 1:9); through whom the light of truth in all ages has proceeded from the Father of lights (James 1:17). He is the eternal Word (John 1:1) who was with God and was God, revealing Himself in infinite wisdom and love, both as man's Creator (Col 1:13-16) and Redeemer (Col 1:14); for by Him were all things created that are in heaven and that are on earth, visible and invisible.[9]

Quaker theology and spiritualities valued across a wide diversity of Friends are often apophatic, mystical. Human words and concepts are understood to be unable to capture the mysterious divine reality. Spiritual experience may be shaped by familiar previous articulations in Scripture, Quaker tradition, or other spiritual or religious literature. But to be credible among Friends, expressions of faith grow out of direct spiritual experience and are accompanied by spiritual fruit evident in love of God and of others. In his *An Apology for the True Christian Divinity*, Robert Barclay articulates the classic Quaker perspective:

> Not by strength of arguments or by a particular disquisition of each doctrine, and convincement of my understanding thereby, came [I] to receive and bear witness of the Truth, but by being secretly reached by [the] Life. For, when I came into the silent assemblies of God's people, I felt a secret power among them, which touched my heart; and as I gave way unto it I found the evil weakening in me and the good raised up; and so I became thus knit and united unto them, hungering more and more after the increase of this power and life whereby I might feel myself perfectly redeemed; and indeed this is the surest way to become a Christian; to whom afterwards the knowledge and understanding of principles will not be wanting, but will grow up so much as is needful as the natural fruit of this good root, and such a knowledge will not be barren nor unfruitful.[10]

Terminology tying friends of God or friends of Christ to faithful, spiritually worthy behavior is not unique to Quakers. Ancient voices of the first centuries of the Christian community also refer to the saints as "friends" of God, whose lives and virtues speak out Christian truth.[11] This traditional usage is particularly common in Eastern Orthodox Churches today, where formally recognized saints are typically named as friends of God.[12]

Who went to the Council of Nicaea? A small number of Council participants are formally identified as saints today. St. Alexander of Alexandria led the delegation from Alexandria to the Council of Nicaea and was an important contributor to the theological formulation. He is recognized as a canonized saint by the Oriental and Eastern Orthodox Churches and the Catholic Church. St. Athanasius was a deacon in service to Alexander at the Council. He was a major figure in the reception of the Nicaean theology over the subsequent decades.[13] Athanasius is recognized as a saint by the Oriental Orthodox Churches, the Eastern Orthodox Churches, the Assyrian Church of the East, the Catholic Church, Lutheranism, and the Anglican Communion. Constantine, the first Christian Roman Emperor, sponsored the Council. He is venerated as a saint by the Eastern Orthodox Churches. St. Paphnutius of Egypt, venerated by Eastern Orthodox Churches, the Oriental Orthodox Churches, and the Roman Catholic Church, is included in some ancient lists of participants at the Nicaean Council. Finally, some place St. Nicholas of Myra—that St. Nicholas—at Nicaea.

According to church tradition, 318 bishops, each with an entourage, went to Nicaea for the Council. The number 318 is a recognizable biblical reference. It is the number of Abraham's servants cited in Genesis 14:14. None of the written records of the Council of 318 Bishops, as the Council of Nicaea is sometimes called, specifically identifies all these bishops. Historians today do not ascribe much accuracy to this number. Bishops were invited from across the Roman Empire. Ancient churches, such as the Indian Thomas Christians and the nascent Ethiopian Christian community, from beyond the Roman Empire, were also represented, through the presence of the parent church bodies with which they were historically connected.

Today, reconstructions of the list of bishops in attendance identify 199 to 250 bishops. Most bishops were from the Greek-speaking Eastern Mediterranean area: Greece, Western Asia, and Northeastern Africa. Only a small number of bishops, or their representatives, from the Western Mediterranean were present. Pope Sylvester was represented by two Roman priests. However, it appears that Ossios of Cordoba (Spain) may have been the presider of the Council.[14]

Bishops were accompanied by theological advisors and other staff. In addition, Constantine's court personnel and support staff took care of the practical matters of the event. As many as two thousand people in total may have been involved in the meeting.

Bishops, and the bishop of Rome's two priest representatives, were the decision-makers. Similarly to Quaker decision-making today, decision-making was understood to be articulation of truth, rather than personal assessment or preferences. Although the Council process utilized voting, the process called for unity, not majority rule.[15] Two bishops, Secundus of Ptolemais and Theonas of Marmarica, did not accept the results of the Council's work and declined to sign. Each later agreed to the Nicaean formulation.[16]

It is hard to reconstruct much about the lives or thoughts of most participants separate from the Council. However, we know the personal investment of each participant in the Council was substantial. Each day involved participation in, or at least listening to, lengthy theological debate on calculating the date of Easter,[17] resolution of a schism,[18] and a widely contested theological proposal from an Alexandrian priest, Arius, on the relationship of Jesus to God the Father.[19] The Council began in May or perhaps June and continued through July 325. Traveling to and from Nicaea would have been arduous even with the transport provided by the emperor. The trip from Alexandria to Nicaea would have taken more than two weeks, from Edessa more than a month.[20] The written decisions of the Council produced the Creed,[21] twenty canons,[22] and a synodal epistle.[23] For those who attended, participation in the Council was itself a religious life event. We can today draw spiritual knowledge, wisdom, and insight from the participants' experience.

The practical realities of participating in the Nicaean Council required the attendees put substantial effort into meeting and mutual exchange with colleagues from very different cultural contexts. The language of the Creed shows that they were open to adding together conceptual insights from diverse voices, rather than insisting on a briefer articulation that might have been less widely accepted. They faced challenges and disagreements together.

These virtues are much needed today within the global Christian community at the local, national, and world councils of churches. They are needed across expressions of the same church family in the global North and in, or immigrant from, the global South, where churches may commonly utilize cultural elements unfamiliar to others. These virtues are needed in addressing climate challenges and urgent human needs. They are needed by Friends, other noncreedal Christian communities, and churches that ordinarily use the Nicaean-Constantinopolitan Creed, as we work together to bring peaceful problem-solving to strained and alienated societies.

Notes

1 John S. Mbiti, *Introduction to African Religion* (London: Heinemann Educational, 1975), 82.

2 Mbiti, 82.

3 George Fox, *Journal*, rev. ed. J.L. Nickalls (Cambridge: UP, 1952), 263.

4 Ann K. Riggs, "The Place of Creeds and Confessions among Friends (Quakers)" and "Response by Riggs," in Ted A. Campbell, Ann K. Riggs, Gilbert W. Stafford, eds., with assistance from Charles Hikaru Simpson, in *Ancient Faith and American-Born Churches: Dialogues Between Christian Traditions* (Mahwah, NJ: Paulist Press, 2006), 143-54, 166-71.

5 Simon Webb, *George Fox in Barbados: With the Complete Text of the Letter to the Governor of Barbados* (Durham, UK: Langley Press, 2013), Kindle ed., location 265-332 of 341.

6 Rufus Jones and James Wood, "Statement of Essential Truths," reprinted in *Discipline of Iowa Yearly Meeting of Friends* (Oska-

loosa, IA: Iowa Yearly Meeting of Friends [Friends United Meeting], 2016), pp. 1-3—1-5.

7 The Richmond Conference, 1887, "A Declaration of Faith," reprinted in *Discipline of Iowa Yearly Meeting of Friends* (Oskaloosa, IA: Iowa Yearly Meeting of Friends [Friends United Meeting], 2016), pp. 1-6—1-18.

8 Ibid., 1-12.

9 Ibid., 1-7.

10 Robert Barclay, *An Apology for the True Christian Divinity* (1678 rpt.; Farmington, ME: Quaker Heritage Press, 2002), prop. XI, sec. 7.

11 For example, see St. John Damascene, *"On Holy Images,"* trans. Mary H. Allies (London: Thomas Baker, 1898), II, 74.

12 "The Role of Saints in Orthodox Christianity: Friends, Intercessors, and Role Models," Orthodox Calendar Company (March 1, 2025), accessed April 10, 2025, https://www.livesofthesaints-calendar.com/blog/the-role-of-saints-in-orthodox-christianity-friends-intercessors-and-role-models.

13 Sara Purvis, "The Reception of Nicaea and *Homoousias* to 360," in *The Cambridge Companion to the Council of Nicaea*, ed. Young Richard Kim (New York: Cambridge University Press, 2021), 225-255.

14 Ian Mladjov, "The Signatories: The Bishops at Nicaea," in *The Cambridge Companion to the Council of Nicaea*, 368–375.

15 Michael J. Sheeran, *Beyond Majority Rule: Voteless Decisions in the Religious Society of Friends* (Philadelphia: Philadelphia Yearly Meeting of Religious Society of Friends,1983); and Barry Morley, *Beyond Consensus: Salvaging Sense of the Meeting* (Wallingford, PA: Pendle Hill, 1993), pamphlet 307.

16 David M. Gwynn, "Reconstructing the Council of Nicaea," in *The Cambridge Companion to the Council of Nicaea*, 90-110.

17 See Daniel P. McCarthy, "The Council of Nicaea and the Celebration of the Christian Pasch," in *The Cambridge Companion to the Council of Nicaea*, 177-201.

18 See "The Letter of the Synod in Nicaea to the Egyptians," trans. Norman P. Tanner, SJ, Papal Encyclicals Online, accessed April 11, 2025, https://www.papalencyclicals.net/councils/ecum01.htm.

19 See Rebecca Lyman, "Arius and Arianism: The Origins of the Alexandrian Controversy," in *The Cambridge Companion to the Council of Nicaea*, 177-201.

20 See The Stanford Geospatial Network Model of the Roman World, Orbis, website, accessed April 10, 2025, https://orbis.stanford.edu.

21 See Mark J. Edwards, "The Creed," in *The Cambridge Companion to the Council of Nicaea*, 135-157.

22 See Andreas Weckwerth, "The Twenty Canons of the Council of Nicaea," in *The Cambridge Companion to the Council of Nicaea*, 158-176.

23 See "Appendix 2: Letter of the Synod of Nicaea to the Egyptians," in *The Cambridge Companion to the Council of Nicaea*, 376-377.

4

The First Council at Nicaea: Revealing Lessons in Adaptive Leadership

Michael Reid Trice

"IT'S THE YEAR 325 and it's a pretty chill time to be a Christian," according to the 2021 board game, *Nicaea*, by Amabel Holland.[1] In the game, up to six players battle for ninety minutes over conflicting theological truths, amid a lack of Christian unity, in their effort to win the approval of the first Christian Roman Emperor. In an hour and a half, the winner with the most "power, unity, and truth," sets the future course for Christendom.

Games teach through whimsy and strategy. Historical review and leadership assessment reveal much as well, which are our tasks ahead. On the 1700th anniversary of the First Council of Nicaea, this chapter reviews the history and leadership of Nicaea's relationship to emerging Christian orthodoxy,[2] the unity of the Christian community, and the association of *both* to its political context. We follow this question throughout: *What does the Council of Nicaea (and the centuries leading up to it) teach us about best practices for leadership from the early Christian community that also assist us in addressing challenges today, especially the challenge of Christian nationalism?*

Nicaea: Adapting and Intervening

The First Council of Nicaea (325 CE) was an ambitious ecumenical council at a formative time for establishing Christian theological orthodoxy, Christian ecclesial unity, and the association (for good or ill) of both within the Roman Empire. The Council of Nicaea is responsible for the Nicene Creed, a first ever universally adopted and binding statement of Christian faith. Pre-Nicene creeds, such as the Apostles' Creed and predecessor creeds or statements of faith, were important albeit provincial teaching tools with specific aims, like instructing recent converts, or enduring successive persecutions.[3] The Nicene Creed, however, was the first creed to emerge from a universal, ecumenical council, always with the intent to articulate a standard of theological orthodoxy for the whole Christian church—both West *and* East.[4]

In the first two centuries CE, the young Christian religion spread across the Roman Empire. In the first generation of leadership, house churches flourished yet were often unremarkably distinguished and less exotic than the mystical religions buzzing around them. Over time and for reasons of organizational need, Christian leadership helped to sinew these disparate house communities to one another through a stream of letter writing (epistles), and to enculturate them to the Greco-Roman culture as they grew, adopting forms of self-governance in structures (dioceses) and leadership oversight increasingly organized and familiar to Roman life.[5]

From the earliest epistles, unity was *the* keystone Christian value.[6] The Greek word for unity is a feminine noun ἑνότης (henotēs), which means "oneness" that requires attention and diligence (Ephesians 4:3 and 13). Oikos is another Greek word that means "extended household," popularized by the apostle Paul in the early Christian house church movement. Unity is an organic, maturing, even mystical oneness requiring the labors of its members who are sinewed into one household and increasingly across households; unity is a keystone value, perhaps even better understood as the spiritual DNA of Christian identity, drawn from the earliest teachings of Jesus of Nazareth.

Over time, the Christian community grew in number as did the visibility of its leadership values and social ethos, which appeared extraordinarily odd and even suspect in the Roman worldview, in several ways: The Christian message introduced radical new norms whereby slave and free were equals, inverting class distinctions. Unhindered, basic egalitarianism allowed for quick mobility of resources to major projects, like the Church in Rome's year-on-year financial support of 1,500 poor and widows circa 250 CE. Christians professed love of neighbor but refused to pay homage to a neighbor's gods (an expected courtesy). Christians were devoted to local unity as three centuries of letter writing reveals, yet expressed a cosmopolitan faith that transcended local allegiances in favor of the whole Church, as these same letters also reveal. Skirting imperial obligations, Christians avoided perjuring their faith by taking state oaths, and yet Christians were increasingly administrators and thereby assisted the state in sending resources throughout the empire, such as to Africa and Cappadocia from the churches in Rome and Carthage in 254 and 256 CE.

Not to be underestimated, Christian leadership instructed their communities to avoid the public spectacle—"the madness of the circus, the immodesty of the theatre, the atrocities of the arena"[7]—and the madness of the crowds, within Roman life, to be reviled for the evil honored and defilements produced. At stake in the spectacle was the violence, idolatry, and immorality of this kind of entertainment, which proved toxic to the keystone value of unity and anathema to a life of service to one's neighbor.

For many Roman citizens laboring under high taxes, civic corruption, and eroded private trust, Christianity was an enigma, but by the fourth century CE, an increasingly attractive enigma at that: Here was a religious community offering equal enrichment and organic unity to a new spiritual lifeline using familiar stated norms in four centuries of love letters rooted to distant fidelities and the hope of its founders, assuring promises from a God who cherished the world, who provided the divine offering of a son without cost or high tariff for life's redemption. This was good news.

Three hundred years of Christian enculturation led to increasing societal and theological disagreements, gaining the attention of the Roman mperor, Constantine I, whose intervention prevailed in influencing the resolution of these conflicts and shaping the course of the Christian future. In fact, without Constantine's conversion to Christianity in 312 CE and his ultimate leadership intervention, social historians argue whether the Christian religion might have remained a continuously persecuted sect around the Mediterranean Sea, with additional modest expressions existent in northern Africa and India, rather than the culturally influential force which it would become.[8]

A difference of opinion in the second century between house churches grew in the fourth century into a theological flash point on the nature of Christ. A public and irrepressible dispute—the Arian Controversy—was excruciating for a religion grown up on unity and truth. The dispute was ignominiously named after Arius, who cut a strident patriarchal archetype as a tall, handsome, theologically unflappable, wholly earnest, and popular priest from Alexandria. Arius argued that Jesus Christ was a created being and not co-eternal with God the Father; his theological position included a substantial followership and presented a direct challenge to the young orthodox theology of the Church. Finally, in 325 CE, Emperor Constantine convened a council at Nicaea and summoned the bishops to address theological differences amid social and political unrest that was challenging greater unity.[9]

As a leadership decision, Constantine's timed intervention to convene a council at Nicaea gained a political advantage in the present *and* for the future. In the present, he positioned his leadership as a convener or arbiter for discerning Christian truth, bolstering his role as both the political head of the empire and as an expected divinely sanctioned spiritual leader. For the future, a unified Christian creedal affirmation would provide him with guiderails to potential controversies, rendering Nicaea a further asset to his empire's stability down the road. For the sake of present and future prospects, Constantine convened the Council with the aim of producing a creed that would unify a people in theological, communitarian, and political ways.

Constantine's intervention reveals a brilliant leadership stroke for acknowledging ecclesial differences while providing guides for pluralism within the limits of conciliar discernment. A swath of Christian leadership would determine a cohesive religious framework to unify disparate groups within the empire, incorporating regional and cultural differences where possible, and setting the limits of theological and ecclesiastical inclusion. Even today, ecumenical (and interreligious) dialogues reveal the imprint of conciliar discernment from this time. Constantine's leadership determination, his ability to observe, interpret, and to intervene at the right moments, was effective for unifying Christian leadership and setting a new paradigm for the next generation of Christian leaders.

Even so, the Nicene Creed was uniquely orchestrated out of political as much as theological and ecclesial necessity in a time of accelerated unification within the Roman Empire. Naturally, a coalescing empire also created ease of access in the areas of theology, church unity, and ecclesial leadership, which likewise meant simultaneous complexities within Christian enculturation wherever differences emerged.

After Nicaea: Overcoming and Excelling

If Christian leaders carried misgivings about the unifying capacity of the synods and councils of the first four centuries of the church, then the Council of Nicaea offered a new opportunity and model for seeking theological clarity that sustained the unity of the Christian community. These leaders learned in the intervening arc of fifty-six years to the first council of Constantinople in 381 CE that the labors of cultivating Christian unity and shaping theological doctrine were a continuous, deliberative process of creative theological nimbleness, courage of conviction, and an alloy of hope and faith. The keystone value of unity—of oneness and the household—was an organic, maturing, sinewed labor of love in the spiritual DNA of Jesus.

They modeled adaptability throughout, clear in the Nicene-Constantinopolitan creedal revisions of 381 CE. Revisions affirmed Christ is "of the same essence as the Father" in response to the Apollinarians who downplayed Christ's full humanity, while also acknowledging the co-equality of the Holy Spirit within the Trinity "who proceeds from the Father" in response to the Pneumatomachians, who denied the divinity of the Holy Spirit.[10]

The first four centuries leading to Nicaea reveal a unifying, multi-generational Christian leadership that was, in its stellar executive moments, an enculturating force connected to its apostolic roots and open to emerging forms of local self-governance. They proved able to overcome major divisions and to adapt to changing political and religious contexts, learning from new models including Constantine's capacity to observe, to interpret, and to intervene at critical junctures. They effectively orchestrated and maximized appropriate levels of discernment to the advantage of unity, truth, and civic influence. These leaders excelled through synods and ecumenical councils for an astounding seven hundred years, the last ecumenical council of its kind taking place in 787 CE, the Council of Nicaea II.

Above all, Nicaean and Post-Nicaean Christian leadership proved able to adapt to the conditions and challenges of their historical moment. Their leadership adaptability was a fundamental advantage during the Nicaean period and advanced both Christian unity and Christian truth, demonstrated whenever the Nicene-Constantinopolitan Creed is recited in Christian liturgies within local churches around the world today.

The Spectacle of Christian Nationalism: Learning from Nicaea

Early Christian leadership in the first four centuries up and through the Council of Nicaea was never unalloyed by human ugliness. It is important not to forget how, just prior to the Council's formal opening, Constantine ceremoniously and publicly burned the many (unopened) letters he received from bishops and priests seeking to denounce one another; yet open the Council he did on or around May 20, 325 CE.[11] Today, Christian executive leadership is still uniquely situated at the axis of responsibility in the areas of unity, truth, and civic engagement, as they must be. Thankfully, the leadership at Nicaea reveals much about the ethos of Christian identity then and now.

In the past forty years, the United States is witness to the rise of a powerful ideological movement—American Christian Nationalism—which treats rigid moral values and patriotism as an inseparable measurement of faithfulness. Leaders within the Christian nationalist movement are enjoined with a charismatic US President, Donald Trump, who is the first American fascist executive leader. A fascist leader is one who convinces the lower and middle classes to accept the efforts of the empowered upper classes in a temporary effort to secure expressed aims, even if the effort means undermining the tenets of the US Constitution and thus destabilizing the Republic.

Once in power, fascist leaders are a danger to American society because, whereas a liberal constitutional democracy includes checks and balances of power guided by the US Constitution, the current illiberal democracy within the US Republic involves a conflated executive branch, acquiescing judicial and legislative branches, and weakened protections for the Constitution. Fascist leadership and illiberal democracy are a distortion of the democratically minded executive leadership that is intended to be, however imperfect, structurally accountable within the liberal democratic process.

Many of the current self-purported architects of a Christian nationalist codebook titled *Project 2025* are powerful administrators within the Trump administration, led by a common commitment to allegiance and uniformity instead of national unity. Compared with Christian leadership in the legitimate legacy of Nicaea with its keystone value of unity, social egalitarianism, and an understanding of faith not reduced to an instrument of the power of the state, Christian nationalism will appear especially disturbing as a spectacle and a distortion.

Christian nationalism is the spectacle from which Christian leadership warned because, first, it colludes oaths of faith and patriotism, reducing religion to a political instrument and prioritizing national interest over a robust social ethic; and second, it distorts the language of faith through weaponizing its outcomes. Adherents will express faithful piety and national prudence to justify cruel actions against the weakest in society. A forthcoming faith-based discourse that separates families, reduces access to basic needs, and increases marginalization will displace unity inclusive of the neighbor for loyalty aligned to the national good. Early Christian leadership admonished the community from participating in the spectacle because doing so weakened one's moral center. Christian executive leadership might have seen this ideology coming in various historical influences, if we took a historical review.

Consider the multi-decade debate across every Christian communion in the United States over human sexuality, which revealed a rift within American moral, cultural, and religious life. The flashpoint of this debate is not unlike the Arian Controversy except rather than the nature of Christ, Christians have struggled with the nature of the human being, sexuality, and gender. Decisions on all sides contributed to a current irreconcilable moment with grave consequences for Christian unity, which is but one more stressor that coincides with a current tragic political threat to the American future. How far down the throat of power an aberration of faith like an ideology of American Christian nationalism will go, whether Christian leadership in the legacy of Nicaea can or will effectively respond, *and* what degrees of danger await in the years ahead, no one can fully forecast.

Conclusion

The historical lessons from the field of early Christian adaptive leadership are clear and include four features. These are: a keystone value of unity typified as oneness and the undivided house as nimble, organic, and following in the path of Jesus; a belief that the world and humanity are loved by God equally, individually, and collectively; a faith life simultaneously personal and also cosmopolitan; and a moral and creative practice that accesses power to assist the neighbor, while restricting access to the spectacle or toxicity of power that corrupts the moral and creative practice precisely in service to the neighbor and to the world.

The rise of Christian nationalism in the United States has global ramifications, as American Christianity heavily influences faith communities worldwide. Nicaea's leadership emphasized a universal, cosmopolitan vision of faith, uniting diverse Christian communities across the Roman Empire under a shared keystone value. The narrow America-first value of Christian nationalism damages the credibility of a Christian witness on the world stage. Christian leadership must work at home and abroad to adapt an inclusive approach that is rooted in unity and responds to shared challenges rather than succumbing to the imposition of divisive, nationalistic visions. The work ahead can learn from the adaptive capacities of Christian leaders of the Nicaean period, beginning with their keystone value of unity. Convening a council today would do well to begin with this adaptive model of Christian leadership forebears.

Notes

1 See Amabel Holland, "Nicaea," boardgame, Hollandspiele, website, accessed May 30, 2025, https://hollandspiele.com/products/nicaea.

2 The chapter refers to Christian Orthodoxy and Truth interchangeably, intending the beliefs, teachings, and practices discerned via consensus by the Church over the ages. For an exhaustive inclusion of the creeds, see John H. Leith, ed., *Creeds of the Churches*, 3rd ed. (Louisville, Kentucky: John Knox Press, 1982).

3 Early creedal affirmations include the Old Roman Creed, the Rule of Faith, and additional acknowledgments of faith.

4 Emperor Constantine I gained control over the western half of the Roman Empire in 312 CE in the defeat of Maxentius. By 324 CE his defeat of Licinius ended the historic division or Tetrarchy of the empire, rendering Constantine the sole emperor of a new, unified empire, and producing new complexities as the administrative, political, and spiritual head of government.

5 The narrative chronology in this section is wholly indebted to Leo Donald Davis, S.J., *The First Seven Ecumenical Councils (325-787): Their History and Theology* (Collegeville, MN: The Liturgical Press, 1990), 11-80; Francis Young, *The Making of the Creeds* 3rd ed. (Viborg, Denmark: SCM Press, 2010) 1-15; Kenneth Scott Latourette, *Christianity Through the Ages* (New York: Harper, 1965), 23-30; and Ernest Trice Thompson, *Through the Ages: A History of the Christian Church* 5th ed. (New York: The Macmillan Company, 1965), 20-89.

6 Peter Heather, *Christendom: The Triumph of Religion, AD 300-1300* (New York: Alfred A. Knopf, 2024), 27.

7 Tertullian, *Apology*, trans. T. R. Glover. Loeb Classical Library, vol. 250 (Cambridge, MA: Harvard University Press, 1949, ch. 38.

8 A year after his conversion (313 CE), Constantine I issued the *Edict of Milan*, granting Christianity legal status that ended its persecution throughout the Roman Empire.

9 Constantine's trusted ecclesiastical advisor, Osseous, Bishop of Cordoba, moderated the Council of Nicaea. Constantine participated, drawing upon his experience of the Donatist Schism. Unfortunately, no full record of proceedings exist of the Council of Nicaea, only notes later assembled from attendees and collated to provide as full a picture as possible.

10 *The Status of the Nicene Creed as Dogma of the Church, Theological Consultation between Representatives of the USA National Committee of the Lutheran World Federation and the Bishops' Commission for Ecumenical Affairs*, July 6-7, 1965, Baltimore, Maryland.

11 The leadership of this era were born to an age of controversy. A principal figure and Arius's main adversary, Athanasius, bishop of Alexandria, railed against his opponents for nearly fifty years, surviving three exiles until his death in 373 CE. See *Athanasius*, ed. William A. Clebsch (New York: Paulist Press, 1980).

5

The Importance of Nicaea Moving Forward

Don Thorsen

THE FORMULATION OF the Nicene Creed represents a turning point in the history of the Christian church. In the Roman Empire, during the fourth century, Emperor Constantine made it possible for Christians to assemble legally. He then initiated an ecumenical council in Nicaea in order for Christians to summarize their basic beliefs. This summarization process helped them to decide what came to be known as right beliefs or opinions (Lat., *orthodoxy*). Of course, from the outset of Christianity, there was not unanimity about what Christians believed. Even in Scripture, early Christians disagreed with one another. Paul disagreed with Peter (Galatians 2:11-19), and later Paul and Barnabas disagreed (Acts 15:36-41). However, the council in Nicaea helped Christians to begin thinking about what constituted their basic beliefs.

Over time, Christians emphasized that their actions were important alongside their beliefs, and they placed importance on praxis—the practical outworking of Christians' beliefs and values. Christians considered some religious practices more important than others, and they coined the phrase *orthopraxis* (Lat., right practice).[1] Orthopraxy most often dealt with righteous, just practices, though other times it referred to proper liturgy or ritual practices. Increasingly, Christians focused on the ethical effects of their religious practices, since Scripture emphasized the importance of acting justly as well as compassionately.

In my experience of Christianity, other aspects of Scripture have become more important. For example, the experience of God in my life deeply influenced me. It had to do with what I describe as a personal, spiritual relationship with God. I did not have a formal way to describe my relationship with God until I learned about John Wesley's emphasis on "heart religion."[2] Wesleyan scholars talk about this understanding of spirituality as *orthokardia* (Lat., right heart), referring to Christians having heartfelt trust in and intimacy with God.[3]

To these so-called "orthos," I could add others. One that I especially find helpful is the concept of *orthosocietas* (Lat., right society, right social relations).[4] I mention this concern for right Christian relations with others in society, since in Western churches, Christians too often think about loving their neighbors more in personal, isolated terms rather than in social, public terms. Yet, I think that Scripture clearly talks about the need for redemptively loving people socially and physically, and not just individually and spiritually.

Moving Forward

Although the Nicene Creed represents an invaluable historic starting point for talking about Christian beliefs (*doxa*), Christians and churches need to move forward in service to others by implementing their beliefs in action (*praxis*), in heartfelt (*kardia*) relationship with God, and in loving their neighbors collectively (*societas*) as well as individually. If Christians want the church to flourish—by the grace of God—then they need to focus on more than right beliefs. They also need to emphasize right actions, personally having a right heart with God, and having a right relationship with others in society, both collectively and individually.

Thinking about the celebration of Nicaea's 1,700th anniversary in 2025 reminds us that we need to reaffirm the importance of churches' solid doctrinal foundations. They need more, though, in order to flourish in the future. For this reason, I emphasize the following orthos: orthodoxy, orthopraxy, orthokardia, and orthosocietas.

Orthodoxy

When Christians think about what orthodoxy means, they often turn to the Nicene Creed. I think the same way. I like the conciseness as well as the content of the Nicene Creed in setting up a baseline of historic Christian beliefs, based on Scripture and ancient church tradition.

Huston Smith describes creeds as "the bedrock of Christian theology for being the earliest attempts by Christians to understand systematically the events that had changed their lives."[5]

Keep in mind that Christians understand the Nicene Creed differently. For example, Orthodox Churches rejected the Catholic addition of the *filioque* (Lat., and the son) clause, arguing that the Pope did not have the authority to modify historic, ecumenical, conciliar wording in the Nicene Creed. The disagreement contributed to the East-West Schism or Great Schism in 1054.

With regard to apostolic succession, Catholic and Orthodox Christians have a different view of apostolicity than do Protestants. The former think in terms of apostolic succession that dates back to the apostles by a continuous succession of bishops. Protestants think about apostolicity in terms of fidelity to the teachings of the apostles, particularly as found in Scripture.

The Nicene Creed does not serve as the standard of orthodoxy for all churches. However, it serves as the baseline of basic beliefs for the majority of Christians in the world, at least in its original wording. Thus, the Nicene Creed can serve as a useful theological foundation on which many churches may move forward in the future.

Orthopraxy

One could argue that Christians have always put their beliefs and values into practice. However, especially in Western civilization, great emphasis has been placed on rationality in philosophical and theological matters. As a result, Christians intellectually valued right beliefs and made their acceptance central in understanding biblical Christianity.

In the past century, Christians increasingly focused on praxis, which critically examined the outcomes of Christian actions along with their theological articulations. Praxis then became the focus of theology, emphasizing the importance of how Christian beliefs and values impact the world—maintaining it, reforming it, or radically transforming it.

For example, liberation theology places priority on praxis, both in its theoretical understanding and in its practical implementation. According to João Libânio, liberation theology "views historic and liberating praxis in relation to the oppression of the poor . . . in the pursuit of justice, solidarity, and charity."[6] Libânio talks about the relationship between orthodoxy and orthopraxy in the following way:

> Liberation theology stresses orthopraxis not to eliminate orthodoxy, which in the past had uncontested primacy in Christian life but oftentimes merely meant adherence to an obsolete tradition or a debatable interpretation. Rather, the intent is to achieve a balanced relationship between right belief and right action to the mutual nourishment of both (Gutiérrez).[7]

Thus, focusing on the advocative impact of Christians in the world complements, rather than replaces, the importance of their beliefs and values. Together, orthopraxy and orthodoxy give greater balance in living out the gospel of Jesus Christ.

One of the lessons I learned from liberation theology is that Christians ought to be concerned about more than ministering compassionately in response to the *effects* of injustice and impoverishment in the world. They also need to advocate against the *causes* of injustice and impoverishment. Through advocacy, Christians help to bring about greater care for the systemic needs of people, doing preventive care and not just curative care.

Orthodokardia

Christianity has a long history of "soul care," that is, caring for the relationship of individuals with God.[8] Some describe soul care as mysticism, sanctification, or spirituality. It primarily has to do with the discipling of Christians in their interior, spiritual lives. I. M. Lewis says that religion begins with experience: "belief, ritual, and spiritual experience, and the greatest of these is the last."[9] If churches do not care for the spiritual well-being of people, then holistically speaking, how can they expect to flourish in the future?

I first became mindful of the need for soul care in my reading of Gregory Clapper's book about *John Wesley on Religious Affections*. He says:

> Wesley's vision of Christianity contains an important place for both right belief and right action. But "orthodoxy" and "orthopraxis" do not exhaustively describe what was essential to his vision of Christianity. What is missing is what I term the ortho*kardia*—the right heart.[10]

What is meant by orthokardia? Clapper explains, "It was Wesley's ability to convey the truth of Christianity in the terminology of the heart that made his vision so compelling during his time, and it is this same characteristic which continues to make it relevant, even to our post-modern age."[11]

Wesley talked about the love, joy, and peace of holiness, which reflected his concern for heart religion. In my pursuit of Christian spirituality, I have learned from the centuries-old disciplines practiced for the sake of spiritual formation. Disciplines have long been practiced by Catholic and Orthodox Christians, though they have been revived recently by Protestants such as Richard Foster and Dallas Willard. For example, Willard gives helpful categories for talking about historic disciplines. He talks about disciplines of abstinence, including solitude, silence, fasting, frugality, chastity, secrecy, and sacrifice, and Willard also talks about disciplines of engagement, including study, worship, celebration, service, prayer, fellowship, confession, and submission.[12] God uses these spiritual disciplines as general means of grace by which Christians grow in their relationship with God and grow into greater Christ-likeness through the presence and power of the Holy Spirit.

If churches want to move forward in ministering to the world, then they cannot neglect the care of souls among their congregants, including their clergy and lay leaders. Churches cannot assume that Christians will automatically mature and flourish. Congregants need spiritual nourishment alongside aiding them in what they are taught (orthodoxy) and in how they live and minister (orthopraxy).

Orthosocietas

One could talk about many "ortho" ideas that would be helpful to Christians and churches. One that I find especially helpful is the concept of orthosocietas. I use it in correcting centuries of Western civilization's emphasis on individualism, which promotes independence, self-reliance, and freedom from discipling by others. For example, Western Christianity has appropriately been criticized for its overly individualistic understanding of Scripture and Christianity, focusing more on its relevance for individuals than on its relevance for people in society.

What does it mean to love our neighbor as ourselves? Do we love our neighbor individually, one-on-one? Is there relevance for how we ought to love our neighbors collectively, societally? Perhaps our earlier reference to orthopraxy answers these questions in part, since the emphasis on praxis cares for the impoverishment of people in society and for injustices perpetrated against them. Liberation theology advocates for the social, political, and economic liberation of societies, believing that spiritual liberation needs to occur alongside other needed liberations. Overall, I think that Christians and churches need to become more cognizant about how their beliefs and values can contribute constructively to social problems that plague humanity. After all, people become impoverished in numerous ways—financially, emotionally, relationally, and culturally as well as spiritually.

Regrettably, some Christians have gone to an extreme in trying to change society. Rather than promoting the common good, they emphasize dominion over society, even to the point of using violence. In the United States, for example, Christian nationalists seek to Christianize the country, forcibly if need be, partnering with politicians and political parties. They promise dominion over all aspects of society: family, religion, education, media, arts and entertainment, business, and government.[13] In countering this extremism, I contributed to a document entitled "The Dangers of Christian Nationalism in the United States," which was adopted as a policy statement by the National Council of the Churches of Christ in the USA.[14]

In order for Christians and churches to move forward in service to the world, they cannot neglect the need for ministering to others societally as well as individually. There are dangers, though, in overstepping their involvements. Social involvements should follow the role model of Jesus and of Scripture. They emphasize service and responsible public engagements for the common good, and not the Christianization of society through domination that excludes and that does violence toward others who do not fit into their narrow-minded views of acceptability.

Final Thoughts

Christians and churches need to develop balance in how they apply their beliefs and values in service to people inside their places of worship as well as outside in their communities, locally and beyond. They do not just need to develop and protect doctrines based on sound biblical interpretation. Churches and denominations also have to put their beliefs into practice; they have to care for the spiritual needs of the congregations; and they have to care for the social needs of people to whom they minister and not only care for their private needs. Certainly the necessity of balancing all of the priorities of Scripture is a challenge. However, thinking about church life in terms of orthodoxy, orthopraxy, orthokardia, and orthosocietas is one way of achieving greater balance in life and ministry and, by God's grace, greater flourishing.

Nicaea 2025 reminds us of basic building blocks of Christian faith, hope, and love. Sound teachings are a start, but they are not the end of biblical living and ministering. For the sake of moving on constructively in the future, Christians and churches do well to promote greater balance in how they proclaim the gospel of Jesus Christ in word, deed, heart, and society.

Notes

1 For example, see João B. Libânio, "Praxis/Orthopraxis," tr. Phillip Berryman, in *Dictionary of Third World Theologies*, eds. Virginia Fabella and R. S. Sugirtharajah (Maryknoll, NY: Orbis Books, 200), 172.

2 John Wesley often talks about "heart religion," for example, see "Prophets and Priests," §18, sermon 121, *The Works of John Wesley*

(Bicentennial ed.), vol. 4, ed. Albert C. Outler (Nashville: Abingdon Press, 187). Cf. Wesley's references to "religion of the heart" in The Way to the Kingdom," I.6, sermon 7, *The Works of John Wesley* (Bicentennial ed.), vol. 1, ed. Albert C. Outler (Nashville: Abingdon Press, 1984), 221.

3 For example, see Gregory S. Clapper, *John Wesley on Religious Affections: His Views on Experience and Emotion and Their Role in the Christian Life and Theology* (Metuchen, NJ: Scarecrow Press, 1989), 154.

4 See my discussion of "orthosocietas" in *Calvin vs Wesley: Bringing Belief in Line with Practice* (Nashville: Abingdon Press, 2013), xxii. Etymologically, it might be more appropriate to talk about ortho-politics (Greek, *politiká*); however, politics suggests specific political interaction rather than general social interaction, which I emphasize.

5 Huston Smith, *The World's Religions*, 50th anniversary edition (1991 rpt.; New York: HarperCollins, 2009), 340.

6 Libânio, 172.

7 Libânio, 172.

8 For example, see Gordon D. Pike, *Soul-Care: God's Path of Redemption and Restoration: Tracing the Path of Soul-care through the Bible, History and the Local Church*, eds. Keith R. Anderson and Herbert Hand (Scotts Valley, CA: CreateSpace, 2016), and Coleman M. Ford and Shawn J. Wilhite, *Ancient Wisdom for the Care of Souls: Learning the Art of Pastoral Ministry from the Church Fathers* (Wheaton, IL: Crossway, 2024).

9 I. M. Lewis, *Ecstatic Religion* (1971 rpt.; New York: Penguin, 1978), 11.

10 Clapper, 154.

11 Clapper, 155.

12 Dallas Willard, *The Spirit of the Disciplines: Understanding How God Changes Lives* (New York: HarperCollins, 1988), 158. Cf. Richard Foster, *Celebration of Discipline: The Path to Spiritual Growth* (New York: Harper & Row, 1978).

13 For example, see books published in support of the Seven Mountain Mandate: Johnny Enlow, *The Seven Mountain Mantle: Receiving the Joseph Anointing to Reform Nations* (Lake Mary, FL: Creation House, 2009); Robert Henderson, *Impacting the Seven Mountains from the Courts of Heaven: Kingdom Strategies for Revival in the Church and the Reformation of Culture* (Shippensburg, PA:

Destiny Image Publishers, 2023); and Deborah McClendon, *Mandate to Invade the 7 Mountains of God: A Candid Look at Christianity's Influence on the 7 Spheres of Culture* (Scotts Valley, CA: CreateSpace, 2018).

14 "The Dangers of Christian Nationalism in the United States: A Policy Statement of the National Council of Churches," adopted April 20, 2021, National Council of the Churches of Christ in the USA, website, accessed September 4, 2023, https://nationalcouncilofchurches.us/common-witness-ncc/the-dangers-of-christian-nationalism-in-the-united-states-a-policy-statement-of-the-national-council-of-churches/.

6

Nicea: Remembering the Past, Through the Present, For the Future

Philip J. Halikiás

Ὑπερδεδοξασμένος εἶ, Χριστὲ ὁ Θεὸς ἡμῶν, ὁ φωστῆρας ἐπὶ γῆς τοὺς Πατέρας ἡμῶν θεμελιώσας, καὶ δι' αὐτῶν πρὸς τὴν ἀληθινὴν πίστιν, πάντας ἡμᾶς ὁδηγήσας· πολυεύσπλαγχνε, δόξα σοι.

You are greatly glorified, O Christ our God, who established our Fathers as luminaries upon the earth, and through them led us all to the true Faith. O Most compassionate, glory to You.

THESE WORDS ARE known as an apolytikion in Greek, which translates as a dismissal hymn. The dismissal hymn for a feast day, or for a Sunday, is first sung the night before toward the end of Vespers. The Orthodox follow the tradition, still preserved in Orthodox monastic practice as well as *beyond* the liturgical life evident through monastic practice on Mt. Athos, that the new day begins at sundown. This was inherited from the Jewish tradition and enhanced by the twenty-four-hour cycle of the eight daily monastic offices. Traditionally, and in today's practice, most of these offices do not find their home in the Cathedral Rite, of which parishes inherited from Constantinopolitan practice.

The seventh Sunday after Pascha in the Greek Orthodox Church is dedicated to the Fathers of the First Ecumenical Council. While these Fathers were overwhelmingly from the East, widespread Christendom was represented in one way or another. What is the true faith spoken about by this dismissal hymn, and how was this preserved by the Fathers? Were there significant contributors, or spokespeople, to use a modern term, for what the unwavering truth is? What implications does this Council, 1,700 years removed from our current anthology, have on the Church, and Christianity, in 2025?

It is first essential to set the contextual scene for the First Ecumenical Council, and then to speak a bit about the critical piece of formulaic dogma memorialized in the Nicene-Constantinopolitan Creed. Ultimately, we will see ways in which this God-inspired, God-breathed, and God-led Council continues to shape the faith of all Trinitarian Christians.

In the first few centuries after Christ, division and dissension were experienced in both the East and the West. However, the Church, in its diversity, was overwhelmingly united as a body of Christ. Differences in cultural, liturgical, and linguistic practices were noticeable, but not the source of fragmentation. Heresy was the source of division, that is, teachings and beliefs that negated the faith passed down through the generations from Jesus's disciples. This very concept, known as Apostolic Succession,[1] or the succession of the bishop as being a link in the unbroken chain of the church stretching back to the disciples, is foundational for many communions, e.g., Eastern and Oriental Orthodox, Catholics, Anglicans/Episcopalians, and many Lutheran churches. Is Apostolic Succession essential for these churches? If so, why?

Without the continuity of this chain of succession, we lose a sense of belonging to the origin of our faith and a sense of stability because it is upon this faith that Jesus told St. Peter that he [Jesus] would build the church,[2] and it has been a safeguard in keeping the faith against occupation, invasion, religious persecution, and other human-caused atrocities. Additionally, after Christianity was legalized by the Edict of Milan in 313, there were not only significant changes to the previously persecuted Church at the hands of the Roman Empire, but actually became at times both a source of ecclesial and secular unity through the role of the bishops. I would be remiss if I didn't at least mention that this great responsibility was also used at times for the interest of the state, more than the Church.

Although it may sound foreign or absurd to the modern ear, it is important to understand that the emperor maintained great influence in the church's life. When addressing conciliarity in the life of the church, careful clarification is made: Conciliarity at the universal level, exercised in the ecumenical councils, implies an active role of the bishop of Rome as protos [first] of the bishops of the major sees, in the consensus of the assembled bishops.[3] Although the bishop of Rome did not convene the ecumenical councils of the early centuries and never personally presided over them, he nevertheless was closely involved in the decision-making process of the councils.[4]

So, what could this active role have been if the emperor had convened the ecumenical councils? We know the emperor was also able to weigh in on issues and bring the councils to a conclusion. The emperor was in close relationship, naturally, with the bishop of Rome, for Rome was the patriarchate of the original pentarchy (Rome, Constantinople, Alexandria, Jerusalem, and Antioch) tied with imperial rule. Even after the establishment of Constantinople, and its elevation as capital of the empire (330), the Western segment of the church remained close to Rome.

The First Ecumenical Council was largely called by (St.) Emperor Constantine because of the heresy being spread by Arius, the cleric, along with his constituency. The very topic at hand was the nature of Christ, being, he was said (by Arius) created by the Father, therefore, removing any possibility of being co-eternal with the Father, and an equal member of the Triune God.[5] Naturally, both East and West were deeply troubled by Arius's teaching and division. The Council, while it was composed of 318 church fathers, was primarily representative of the East. This did not, however, impede its acceptance by the West.

Additional topics were presented, e.g., canon law, constructing the first segment of the Creed, and the common date of Pascha/Easter, which we will return to later. For clarification, we recognize the ecumenical councils as truly being ecumenical over time. It is not as though the councils were convened with the invitation: "Save the date for the First Ecumenical Council to be held in Nicaea." While this may sound facetious, we often view the past through the lens of the present. These matters took time to spread and be accepted throughout the entirety of the church. Concerning the reception of the ecumenical councils, it has been said:

> The Church's understanding of the criteria for the reception of a council as ecumenical developed over the course of the first millennium. For example, prompted by historical circumstances, the Seventh Ecumenical Council (Nicaea II, 787) gave a detailed description of the criteria as then understood: the agreement (*symphonia*) of the heads of the churches, the cooperation (*synergeia*) of the bishop of Rome, and the agreement of the other patriarchs (*symphronountes*). An ecumenical council must have its own proper number in the sequence of ecumenical councils, and its teaching must accord with that of previous councils. Reception by the Church as a whole has always been the ultimate criterion for the ecumenicity of a council.[6]

Written in the first person plural, the first seven articles of faith currently found in the Nicene-Constantinopolitan Creed were composed in 325 in Nicaea. These articles first address our Heavenly Father, and then the remaining six elaborate on the relationship between the Father and the Son, as well as the emphasis on the dual natures of Christ, the primary theological topic, and key heresy, dispelled by Nicaea. Note the words of the Creed:

> We believe in one God. The Father Almighty. Maker of heaven and earth, and of all things visible and invisible. And in one Lord Jesus Christ, the Son of God, the only begotten, begotten of the Father before all ages. Light of Light; true God of true God; begotten not made; of one essence with the Father, by whom all things were made; who for us men and for our salvation came down from heaven, and was incarnate of the Holy Spirit and the Virgin Mary, and became man. And He was crucified for us under Pontius Pilate, and suffered, and was buried. And the third day He rose again according to the Scriptures; and ascended into heaven, and sits at the right hand of the Father; and he shall come again with glory to judge the living and the dead; whose Kingdom shall have no end.[7]

St. Nicholas of Myra in Lycia

It is important to address at least one of the key members of the First Ecumenical Council, and since he is both a universally beloved saint, and the patron of the community I'm blessed to serve, I want to highlight St. Nicholas of Myra of Lycia. St. Nicholas was one of the most prominent participants in the First Ecumenical Council in Nicaea.

He, in his unwavering faith, sought to pastorally correct Arius for his heresy. However, when Arius's arrogance led him to continue to deny the truth about Christ being fully God and fully human, St. Nicholas became outraged. He struck Arius, causing a great scandal for all in attendance.[8] In the Orthodox Church, to this day, it is uncanonical for a clergyman to physically strike someone. Several key hierarchs retired to their quarters that night and had simultaneous dreams of Christ and the *Theotokos* (God-bearer) indicating that St. Nicholas should not be deposed, for he, in his love for them and for defending the true faith, did what he did. Therefore, the following day, St. Nicholas was not deposed. This is one example of how he defended the faith and dogma of the Church during his life. There are many other beautiful stories of his interceding for those in need of financial support, the hungry, the meek, etc. Let us take a brief look at his dismissal hymn (Greek and English), for it offers an eloquent synopsis of his character and love of Christ. It says:

> Κανόνα πίστεως, καὶ εἰκόνα πραότητος, ἐγκρατείας διδάσκαλον, ἀνέδειξέ σε τῇ ποίμνῃ σου,ἡ τῶν πραγμάτων ἀλήθεια·διὰ τοῦτο ἐκτήσω τῇ ταπεινώσει τὰ ὑψηλά, τῇ πτωχείᾳ τὰ πλούσια. Πάτερ ἱεράρχα Νικόλαε, πρέσβευε Χριστῷ τῷ Θεῷ, σωθῆναι τὰς ψυχὰς ἡμῶν.

> A rule of faith and the icon of gentleness, the example of your life has shown you forth to your sheepfold to be a master of temperance. You obtained thus through being lowly, gifts from on high, and riches through poverty. Father and Hierarch Nicholas, intercede with Christ our God that He may save our souls. [9]

The dismissal hymn of St. Nicholas gives a glimpse into the profundity of his life and ministry. Being a rule of faith, St. Nicholas epitomized what we, as living icons made in the likeness of God, strive for. He was a man who left all the riches of life behind to help the poor. He maintained temperance in his thoughts and actions, giving way to his will being more easily aligned with God's. In striving to delve more deeply into humility, St. Nicholas attained the heights of spiritual gifts, including but not limited to wisdom, compassion, discernment, and love. He taught us that wealth comes in the form of blessings from God, from caring for the other, from shedding need for material that weighs us down. As our spiritual father, and as hierarch for his flock in Myra of Lycia, he did, does, and will always intercede on our behalf to the Lord almighty.

Centuries later at the Seventh Ecumenical Council, the continuation of the faith, dogmatized from the first Council of Nicaea, was proclaimed with great exuberance after the restoration of the icons after the period of iconoclasm (destruction of icons, altars, even churches, for they were seen as idolatrous, not as didactic or spiritual tools for prayer and connection). The following proclamation continues to be read by the priest in every Eastern Orthodox Church the first Sunday of Holy and Great Lent. It says:

> As the Prophets beheld, As the Apostles taught, As the Church received, As the Teachers dogmatized, As the Universe agreed, As Grace illumined, As the Truth revealed, As falsehood passed away, As Wisdom presented, As Christ awarded, Thus we declare, Thus we assert, Thus we proclaim Christ our true God and honor His saints, In words, In writings, In thoughts, In sacrifices, In churches, In holy icons. On the one hand, worshipping and reverencing Christ as God and Lord. And on the other hand, honoring and venerating His Saints as true servants of the same Lord.
>
> This is the Faith of the Apostles. This is the Faith of the Fathers. This is the Faith of the Orthodox. This is the Faith which has established the Universe. Amen![10]

This faith of ours is a precious gem, a pearl "of great value" (Matthew 13:46). We may take time to reread the aforementioned proclamation and think about the struggles and triumphs that our faith and Trinitarian dogma have weathered victoriously. This is precisely why our Lord did not remain on earth after his glorious resurrection. If he did, then the manifestation of faith, teaching, communion, and community formed within his bride, the Church, would not have been built upon faith, love, and relationship, but on necessity. Jesus did not stay on Earth because humankind would've felt mandated to believe and follow him. The whole premise of our faith is built on a willingness to believe, to follow, to serve, and to love the Lord our God with all our heart, mind, soul, and strength, because we choose to, not because we have to.

Where We Go from Here?

The lingering question that is probably on your mind or in your heart is: "Where do we go from here?" I'm glad you asked! For starters, we are called to reaffirm our baptismal vows and commitment to our faith and upholding the dogma of the Church. Second, we are to "avoid stupid controversies" (Titus 3:9) as St. Paul lovingly exhorts Titus, as well as you and me. We ought to strive for a permanently shared calculation for Pascha/Easter each and every year. The Fathers of the Council understood this importance for Christians to worship our Lord, in the diversity of our communities, but in unity, on the day of his glorious third-day resurrection. It just so happens that this 1700th anniversary coincides with the East and West celebrating together. Conferences in ecumenical, academic, and informal settings continue to take place, from the heads of church all the way down to local gatherings, for the purpose of hoping to find an agreeable way to reconcile two distinct and historical calendars (Julian and Gregorian).

We continue to pray for unity on these matters, and for our Triune God to bless all those who labor in the Lord's vineyard for peace, healing, and reconciliation among the various members of his body. Let us ask for the intercessions of the Holy Fathers of the First Ecumenical Council to guide and guard our Church, the clergy, the laity, and the catechumens, to defend the faith with the same conviction, passion, and efforts, as they did. Now and forever, and to the ages of ages. Amen.

Notes

1 Nicon Patrinacos, *A Dictionary of Greek Orthodoxy* (Minneapolis: Light and Life Publishing, 1984), "Apostolic Succession and Episcopacy."
2 Matthew 16:18: "And I tell you, you are Peter, and on this rock I will build my church, and the gates of Hades will not prevail against it."
3 Cf. Joint International Commission for the Theological Dialogue between the Roman Catholic Church and the Orthodox Church, "Ecclesiological and Canonical Consequences of the Sacramental Nature of the Church: Ecclesial Communion, Conciliarity and Authority," sec. 41, Dicastery for Promoting Christian Unity, website, October 13, 2007, http://www.christianunity.va/content/unitacristiani/en/dialoghi/sezione-orientale/chiese-ortodosse-di-tradizione-bizantina/commissione-mista-internazionale-per-il-dialogo-teologico-tra-la/documenti-di-dialogo/testo-in-inglese.html.
4 Ibid., sec. 42.
5 Patrinacos, *A Dictionary of Greek Orthodoxy*, "Arianism and Arius."
6 Joint International Commission for the Theological Dialogue between the Roman Catholic Church and the Orthodox Church, "Synodality and Primacy during the First Millennium: Towards a Common Understanding in Service to the Unity of the Church," sec. 18, Dicastery for Promoting Christian Unity, website, September 21, 2016, http://www.christianunity.va/content/unitacristiani/en/dialoghi/sezione-orientale/chiese-ortodosse-di-tradizione-bizantina/commissione-mista-internazionale-per-il-dialogo-teologico-tra-la/documenti-di-dialogo/testo-in-inglese.html.
7 From the Nicene Constantinopolitan Creed as translated for the Greek Orthodox Archdiocese of America and used throughout the Archdiocese in Divine Liturgy Texts, parish websites, and prayer books.
8 Nikolaj Velimirović, *The Prologue of Ohrid: Lives of Saints, Hymns, Reflections and Homilies for Every Day of the Year*, vol. 2 (July to

December), trans. Fr. T. Timothy Tepsić, ed. Fr. Janko Trbović (Alhambra, CA: Sebastian Press, Western American Diocese, 2008), 600.

9 "Nicholas the Wonderworker, Archbishop of Myra - Greek Orthodox Archdiocese of America - Orthodox Church," Greek Orthodox Archdiocese of America (English text adapted according to the author's parish usage), accessed January 6, 2025, https://www.goarch.org/chapel/saints?contentid=325&PCode=12LF&D=F&date=12%2F06%2F2024.

10 This is the universal declaration of faith proclaimed in every Orthodox Church around the world on the first Sunday in Great Lent, known as the Sunday of Orthodoxy. This Sunday commemorates the restoration of the icons after the period of Iconoclasm. The entire service can easily be found on the Greek Orthodox Archdiocese of America webpage, accessed January 6, 2025, https://www.goarch.org/-/commemoration-of-the-restoration-of-the-holy-icons.

7

Nicea: Recordando El Pasado, A Través Del Presente Y Para El Futuro

Philip J. Halikiás

Ὑπερδεδοξασμένος εἶ, Χριστὲ ὁ Θεὸς ἡμῶν, ὁ φωστῆρας ἐπὶ γῆς τοὺς Πατέρας ἡμῶν θεμελιώσας, καὶ δι' αὐτῶν πρὸς τὴν ἀληθινὴν πίστιν, πάντας ἡμᾶς ὁδηγήσας· πολυεύσπλαγχνε, δόξα σοι.

Oh, Cristo nuestro Dios, altamente glorificado, tú que estableciste a nuestros Padres como luminares en la tierra, y a través de ellos nos guiaste a todos hacia la verdadera Fe. ¡Oh, más compasivo, gloria a Ti!

ESTAS PALABRAS SE conocen como apolitikion en griego, que se traduce como un himno de despedida. El himno de despedida para una fiesta o para un domingo se canta por primera vez la noche anterior, hacia el final de las Vísperas. La Iglesia Ortodoxa sigue esta tradición, que aún se conserva en la práctica monástica ortodoxa, en los seminarios y en los hogares de las familias, donde el nuevo día comienza al atardecer. Esta práctica litúrgica se heredó de la tradición judía y se enriqueció con el ciclo de veinticuatro horas de los ocho oficios monásticos diarios de la Ortodoxia. Tradicionalmente, y también en la práctica actual, la mayoría de estos oficios no se celebran en el Rito de la Catedral, que es una práctica heredada del rito de Constantinopla.

El séptimo domingo después de Pascua está dedicado a los Padres del Primer Concilio Ecuménico, el Concilio de Nicea (325 d.C.), en la Iglesia Ortodoxa. Aunque la mayoría de los Padres provenían del Este, la Cristiandad universal estaba representada de una manera u otra. ¿Cuál es la verdadera fe de la que habla este himno de despedida, y cómo la preservaron los Padres? ¿Tenemos ejemplos de algún contribuidor significativo o portavoz (para usar un término moderno) que testifique sobre esta verdad y fe inquebrantables? A 1700 años de distancia de este evento, ¿qué implicaciones tiene el Concilio de Nicea para el Cristianismo en 2025?

Para responder a estas preguntas, es necesario considerar el contexto del Primer Concilio Ecuménico, incluyendo una revisión de la pieza crítica del dogma formulaico que está memorializada en el Credo Niceno-Constantinopolitano (381 d.C.). Finalmente, veremos cómo este Concilio, inspirado, soplado y guiado por Dios, sigue moldeando la fe de todos los cristianos trinitarios hoy en día.

En los primeros siglos después de Jesucristo, la división y la discordia fueron experimentadas en el Este y el Oeste. Sin embargo, la Iglesia del Imperio Romano en el Oeste y el surgimiento del Imperio Bizantino en el Este, con su diversidad, seguían siendo un cuerpo unido en Cristo. Las diferencias culturales, litúrgicas y lingüísticas no fueron una fuente de fragmentación. *La herejía* fue la causa de la división; es decir, enseñanzas y creencias que invalidaron la fe transmitida por los discípulos de una generación a la siguiente. Este concepto es conocido como Sucesión Apostólica[1], o la sucesión de un obispo dentro de una cadena ininterrumpida de liderazgo eclesiástico desde los discípulos hasta los obispos contemporáneos. Este es un fundamento de muchas comuniones, como la Iglesia Ortodoxa, la Iglesia Católica, las Iglesias Anglicanas/Episcopales y muchas Iglesias Luteranas. ¿Es la Sucesión Apostólica esencial para comunicar la fe verdadera en estas iglesias hoy en día? Si es así, ¿por qué?

Sin la continuidad de esta cadena de sucesión, la Iglesia pierde el sentido de pertenencia al origen de nuestra fe y la estabilidad, porque fue sobre esta línea de fe que Jesús le dijo a San Pedro que construiría su Iglesia[2]. A lo largo de los milenios, la sucesión apostólica ha salvaguardado la fe en tiempos de ocupación, invasión, persecución y otras atrocidades humanas. Además, después de que el Edicto de Milán (313 d.C.) legalizara el cristianismo, los cristianos experimentaron cambios significativos en la Iglesia, que previamente había sido perseguida bajo el Imperio Romano; el cuarto siglo mostró al cristianismo como una fuente de unidad tanto eclesiástica como secular a través del papel de los obispos. No puedo dejar de mencionar que esta gran emergencia de responsabilidad eclesial a veces fue utilizada para los intereses del estado más que para la verdad de la Iglesia. Sin embargo, aunque pueda sonar extraño o absurdo a los oídos modernos, es importante entender que los emperadores romanos (comenzando con Constantino) mantuvieron una gran influencia en la vida de la Iglesia.

A continuación, al comunicar la fe verdadera junto con la Sucesión Apostólica, debemos considerar el concepto de *conciliaridad* en la vida de la Iglesia. *La conciliaridad*, ejercida en los concilios ecuménicos, implica un papel activo y universal del Obispo de Roma como *protos* (o primero) entre los obispos de las principales sedes (del latín sedes, que significa "sede" o, en este caso, el "trono" de la diócesis), en el consenso de los obispos reunidos[3]. Aunque el Obispo de Roma no convocó los concilios ecuménicos de los primeros siglos ni los presidió personalmente, estuvo estrechamente involucrado en el proceso de toma de decisiones de dichos concilios[4].

Entonces, ¿cuál era este rol activo y universal del Obispo de Roma, especialmente si el emperador romano era el convocante principal, como sabemos que fue el caso del primer concilio ecuménico en Nicea? Entendemos que el emperador podía intervenir en los asuntos y concluir los concilios. El emperador mantenía una relación estrecha, naturalmente, con el Obispo de Roma, ya que Roma era un patriarcado de la *pentarquía* original o los cinco dominios del imperio – estos eran Roma, Constantinopla, Alejandría, Jerusalén y Antioquía – todos unidos por el gobierno imperial. Incluso después de la fundación de Constantinopla y su elevación como la capital del Imperio Romano (330 d.C.), el segmento occidental de la Iglesia permaneció cercano a Roma.

El Primer Concilio Ecuménico fue convocado en su mayoría por el (Santo) Emperador Constantino debido a la herejía propagada por Arius, el clérigo de Alejandría, junto con sus seguidores. El tema principal era la naturaleza de Cristo, a quien Arius creía que había sido *creado* por el Padre, dentro de la economía de la Trinidad. Sin embargo, la afirmación de Arius elimina cualquier posibilidad de que el Hijo fuera coeterno con el Padre y un miembro igual del Dios Triuno[5]. Naturalmente, tanto el Este como el Oeste se sintieron profundamente preocupados por la enseñanza de Arius y la división consecuente. Como se mencionó anteriormente, el concilio, compuesto por 318 padres de la Iglesia, estuvo principalmente representado por líderes eclesiales del Este, lo que no impidió que el Oeste aceptara los resultados del Concilio de Nicea.

Se presentaron temas adicionales relacionados con el derecho canónico, incluidos, pero no limitados a, el desarrollo de una fórmula para determinar la fecha de la Pascua cada año utilizando el calendario juliano. A lo largo del mundo cristiano, se usaban numerosos calendarios, con variaciones en las fechas de las fiestas fijas, como la Navidad y la Teofanía/ Epifanía. Este sigue siendo un tema prevalente que se aborda entre el Este y el Oeste, ya que el calendario gregoriano, desarrollado siglos después, es científicamente más avanzado y preciso. Para aclarar, los Concilios Ecuménicos fueron llamados "ecuménicos" de manera retroactiva. No es que los concilios fueron convocados con la invitación: "Reserva la fecha para el primer Concilio Ecuménico que se celebrará en Nicea, 325 d.C." Aunque esto pueda sonar irónico, a menudo vemos el pasado a través del lente del presente. Estos asuntos tomaron tiempo para difundirse y ser aceptados en toda la Iglesia. A medida que las noticias viajaban y los concilios eran adoptados, la Iglesia se refiere a esta actividad como la *recepción*, mediante la cual la Iglesia recibe sus enseñanzas. "Sobre la recepción de los Concilios Ecuménicos, la Iglesia creía que:"

> La comprensión de la Iglesia sobre los criterios para la recepción de un concilio como ecuménico se desarrolló a lo largo del primer milenio. Por ejemplo, impulsado por circunstancias históricas, el Séptimo Concilio Ecuménico

> (Nicea II, 787) dio una descripción detallada de los criterios tal como se entendían en ese momento: el acuerdo (symfonia) de los jefes de las iglesias, la cooperación (synergeia) del obispo de Roma y el acuerdo de los otros patriarcas (symfronountes). Un concilio ecuménico debe tener su propio número en la secuencia de concilios ecuménicos, y su enseñanza debe estar de acuerdo con la de concilios anteriores. La recepción por parte de la Iglesia en su conjunto siempre ha sido el criterio último para la ecuménicidad de un concilio.[6]

Escrito en primera persona plural, los primeros siete artículos de fe que actualmente se encuentran en el Credo Niceno fueron compuestos en 325 d.C. en Nicea. Sin embargo, los artículos restantes fueron añadidos 56 años después durante el segundo Concilio Ecuménico convocado en Constantinopla. Por lo tanto, el Credo es conocido, principalmente en contextos ortodoxos, como el Credo Niceno-Constantinopolitano.

Estos artículos de fe primero se dirigen a nuestro Padre celestial, y los seis restantes elaboran sobre la relación entre el Padre y el Hijo, así como el énfasis en las dos naturalezas de Cristo, el tema teológico principal y la herejía clave, que fue disipada en Nicea a través del Credo Niceno, como se expone a continuación:

> Creo en un solo Dios, Padre todopoderoso, Creador del cielo y de la tierra, de todo lo visible e invisible. Creo en un solo Señor, Jesucristo, Hijo único de Dios, engendrado del Padre antes de todos los siglos: Luz de Luz, Dios verdadero de Dios verdadero, engendrado, no creado, de la misma naturaleza del Padre, por quien todo fue hecho; que por nosotros los hombres y por nuestra salvación descendió del cielo, y por obra del Espíritu Santo se encarnó de María, la Virgen, y se hizo hombre; y por nuestra causa fue crucificado bajo el poder de Poncio Pilato; padeció, murió y fue sepultado; y al tercer día resucitó, según las Escrituras; y ascendió al cielo, y está sentado a la derecha del Padre; y de nuevo vendrá con gloria para juzgar a vivos y muertos, y su reino no tendrá fin.[7]

San Nicolás de Mira en Licia

Consideremos nuestra pregunta: ¿qué es la fe verdadera que fue hablada y preservada por los Padres?– Podemos ver esa fe en acción a través de uno de los participantes más destacados del Primer Concilio Ecuménico, San Nicolás de Myra en Licia, un santo venerado en todo el mundo y el patrón de la comunidad a la que tengo el privilegio de servir.

Con su fe inquebrantable, San Nicolás intentó corregir a Arius por su herejía de manera pastoral. Sin embargo, cuando la arrogancia de Arius lo llevó a seguir negando la verdad sobre Cristo como totalmente Dios y totalmente hombre, San Nicolás se indignó. Golpeó a Arius, lo que causó un gran escándalo entre todos los presentes[8]. Hasta el día de hoy, en la Iglesia Ortodoxa, es incanónico que un clérigo golpee a alguien físicamente. Varios obispos clave se retiraron a sus cuartos, profundamente conflictuados, esa noche. Tuvieron sueños simultáneos de Cristo y de la Madre de Dios, indicando que San Nicolás no debía ser removido ni depuesto, ya que él, en su amor por ellos y por defender la verdadera fe, hizo lo que hizo. Como resultado, San Nicolás no fue depuesto al día siguiente, lo que habría significado su despido inmediato de los procedimientos del concilio. Este es solo un ejemplo, entre muchos, de cómo San Nicolás defendió la fe y el dogma de la Iglesia durante su vida. Además, existen muchas hermosas historias sobre sus intercesiones por otros, como aquellos que necesitaban apoyo financiero, los hambrientos, los humildes, y más. Cuando tomamos un momento para entender el himno de despedida de San Nicolás (en griego y español), nos ofrece una elocuente sinopsis de su carácter y amor por Cristo. Dice:

> Κανόνα πίστεως, καὶ εἰκόνα πραότητος, ἐγκρατείας διδάσκαλον, ἀνέδειξέ σε τῇ ποίμνῃ σου,ἡ τῶν πραγμάτων ἀλήθεια·διὰ τοῦτο ἐκτήσω τῇ ταπεινώσει τὰ ὑψηλά, τῇ πτωχείᾳ τὰ πλούσια. Πάτερ ἱεράρχα Νικόλαε, πρέσβευε Χριστῷ τῷ Θεῷ, σωθῆναι τὰς ψυχὰς ἡμῶν.

> Regla de fe e imagen de mansedumbre, el ejemplo de tu vida te ha mostrado ante tu redil para ser maestro de templanza. Así obtuviste, siendo humilde, los dones de lo alto y riquezas

> a través de la pobreza. Padre y Jerarca Nicolás, intercede ante Cristo nuestro Dios para que salve nuestras almas.[9]

El himno de despedida de San Nicolás ofrece una visión profunda de su vida y su ministerio. Siendo un modelo de fe, San Nicolás personificó lo que buscamos como iconos vivientes hechos a imagen de Dios. Fue un hombre que dejó atrás todas las riquezas de la vida para ayudar a los pobres. Mantuvo la templanza en sus pensamientos y acciones, permitiendo que su voluntad se alineará más fácilmente con la de Dios. Al esforzarse por profundizar en la humildad, San Nicolás alcanzó las alturas de los dones espirituales, incluyendo, entre otros, la sabiduría, la compasión, el discernimiento y el amor. Nos enseñó que la verdadera riqueza viene en forma de bendiciones de Dios, del cuidado del prójimo y del desprendimiento de las necesidades materiales que nos pesan. Como nuestro padre espiritual y como jerarca de su rebaño en Mira de Licia, él hizo, hace y siempre intercederá por nosotros ante el Señor Todopoderoso.

Siglos más tarde, en el séptimo Concilio Ecuménico (787 d.C.), la continuación de la fe, dogmatizada desde el primer Concilio de Nicea, fue proclamada con gran exuberancia durante la restauración de los iconos, tras el período de iconoclasmo. La siguiente proclamación continúa siendo leída por el sacerdote en todas las iglesias ortodoxas el primer domingo de la Gran Cuaresma. Dice:

> Como los Profetas vieron, como los Apóstoles enseñaron, cómo la Iglesia recibió, como los Maestros dogmatizaron, como el Universo acordó, como la Gracia iluminó, como la Verdad reveló, como la falsedad pasó, como la Sabiduría presentó, como Cristo concedió, así declaramos, así afirmamos, así proclamamos a Cristo nuestro verdadero Dios y honramos a Sus santos, en palabras, en escritos, en pensamientos, en sacrificios, en iglesias, en iconos sagrados. Por un lado, adorando y reverenciando a Cristo como Dios y Señor. Y por otro lado, honrando y venerando a Sus Santos como verdaderos siervos del mismo Señor. Esta es la Fe de los Apóstoles. Esta es la Fe de los Padres. Esta es la Fe de los Ortodoxos. Esta es la Fe que ha establecido el Universo. ¡Amén![10]

La verdadera fe mencionada en el apolitikion de arriba, junto con una reflexión sobre la vida y el ejemplo de San Nicolás, nos enseña cómo esta fe nuestra es una joya preciosa, una perla 'de gran valor' (Mateo 13:46). Podemos tomarnos un tiempo para releer la proclamación de arriba y reflexionar sobre las luchas y triunfos que nuestra fe y dogma trinitario han superado victoriosamente.

¿Adónde vamos desde aquí?

Una pregunta que probablemente está en su mente o en su corazón es: '¿Adónde vamos desde aquí?' ¡Me alegra que la haya hecho! Para empezar, los cristianos en todas partes estamos llamados a reafirmar nuestros votos bautismales y nuestro compromiso con la fe, así como a mantener el dogma de la Iglesia. En segundo lugar, debemos 'evitar las controversias necias' (Tito 3:9 NRSVUE), como San Pablo exhorta cariñosamente a Tito, lo cual sigue siendo cierto hoy para usted y para mí. Debemos esforzarnos por alcanzar una fórmula compartida para la fecha de la Pascua cada año. Los Padres del Concilio comprendieron la importancia de que los cristianos adoráramos a nuestro Señor en la diversidad de nuestras comunidades y en la unidad del día de Su gloriosa resurrección al tercer día. Justo en este 1700° aniversario, en el año 2025 d.C., coincide con que el Este y el Oeste celebren la Pascua juntos. Siguen realizándose conferencias en contextos ecuménicos, académicos e informales, desde los líderes de la Iglesia hasta los encuentros locales, con la esperanza de encontrar una manera aceptable para reconciliar los dos calendarios históricos (Juliano y Gregoriano).

Seguimos orando por la unidad en estos asuntos y para que nuestro Dios Trino bendiga a todos aquellos que trabajan en la viña del Señor, buscando la paz, la sanación y la reconciliación entre los diversos miembros de Su Cuerpo. Pidamos las intercesiones de los Santos Padres del Primer Concilio Ecuménico para que guíen y protejan nuestra Iglesia, al clero, los laicos y los catecúmenos, a fin de defender la fe con la misma convicción, pasión y esfuerzo con que ellos lo hicieron. Ahora y siempre, y por los siglos de los siglos. Amén.

Notes

1 Patrinacos, Nicon. *A Dictionary of Greek Orthodoxy*. Minneapolis, MN: Light and Life Publishing Co., 1984. Cf. Apostolic Succession and Episcopacy.

2 Matthew 16:18: "And I tell you, you are Peter, and on this rock I will build my church, and the gates of Hades will not prevail against it."

3 Cf Joint International Commission for the Theological Dialogue between the Roman Catholic Church and the Orthodox Church. "Ecclesiological and Canonical Consequences of the Sacramental Nature of the Church: Ecclesial Communion, Conciliarity and Authority." www.Christianunity.va October 13, 2007. Section 41 http://www.christianunity.va/content/unitacristiani/en/dialoghi/sezione-orientale/chiese-ortodosse-di-tradizione-bizantina/commissione-mista-internazionale-per-il-dialogo-teologico-tra-la/documenti-di-dialogo/testo-in-inglese.html. Accessed December 6, 2024.

4 Ibid. Section 42.

5 Patrinacos, Nicon. *A Dictionary of Greek Orthodoxy,* Cf. Arianism and Arius

6 Joint International Commission for the Theological Dialogue between the Roman Catholic Church and the Orthodox Church. "Synodality and Primacy During the First Millennium: Towards a Common Understanding in Service to the Unity of the Church." www.Christianunity.va September 21, 2016. Section 18 http://www.christianunity.va/content/unitacristiani/en/dialoghi/sezione-orientale/chiese-ortodosse-di-tradizione-bizantina/commissione-mista-internazionale-per-il-dialogo-teologico-tra-la/documenti-di-dialogo/testo-in-inglese.html. Accessed December 12, 2024

7 From the Nicene Constantinopolitan Creed as translated for the Greek Orthodox Archdiocese of America and used throughout the Archdiocese in Divine Liturgy Texts, parish websites, and prayer books.

8 Velimirović, Nikolaj. *The prologue of ohrid: Lives of saints, hymns, reflections and homilies for every day of the year*. vol. 2 July to December by St. Nikolai Velimirovic. transl. from the Serbian by Fr. T. Timothy Tepsić. Ed. by Fr. Janko Trbović, the st. herman of Alaska serbian orthodox monastery, and the st. paisius serbian

orthodox monastery. Alhambra, Calif: Sebastian Press, Western American Diocese, 2008, 600.

9 "Nicholas the Wonderworker, Archbishop of Myra - Greek Orthodox Archdiocese of America - Orthodox Church." Greek Orthodox Archdiocese of America. (English text adapted according to the author's parish usage), https://www.goarch.org/chapel/saints?contentid=325&PCode=12LF&D=F&date=-12%2F06%2F2024. Accessed January 6, 2025.

10 This is the universal declaration of faith proclaimed in every Orthodox Church around the world on the first Sunday in Great Lent, known as the Sunday of Orthodoxy. This Sunday commemorates the restoration of the icons after the period of Iconoclasm. The entire service can easily be found on the Greek Orthodox Archdiocese of America webpage here: https://www.goarch.org/-/commemoration-of-the-restoration-of-the-holy-icons. Accessed January 6, 2025.

PART 2

Creedal Theology: Incarnation, Spirit, and the Mystery of God

8

Nicaea's Incarnational Theology: Its Crucial Role in Christian Unity

Douglas A. Foster

> The glory that you have given me I have given them, so that they may be one, as we are one, I in them and you in me, that they may become completely one, so that the world may know that you have sent me and have loved them even as you have loved me (John 17:22-23).

THE 1700TH ANNIVERSARY of the Council of Nicaea and of the Nicene Creed in 2025 provides an opportunity to reexamine the historical and theological richness of this pivotal moment in Christianity. This essay examines consequences of the Creed's statement on the nature of Jesus Christ for the unity of the church, especially in light of Jesus's prayer recorded in John 17:20-23. There he names two reciprocal sets of incarnations as the basis for the unity of his disciples throughout time.

The first incarnation is the doctrine of the fullness of the deity enfleshed in Jesus Christ, stated forcefully in the Nicene Creed, which he pairs inseparably with his being in the Father. This perfect unity is the model for the unity he now prays for. Just as he and the Father were one, Jesus fervently prays that his followers—then and in the future—would also be one "in us."[1]

Christ immediately moves to the second incarnational discussion. He starts by saying that the glory the Father had given him, he now gives to his disciples! Jesus's glory—his full reception of, and perfect unity with, the fullness of deity, is somehow reflected in a second incarnation in which Christ is incarnate in his followers—that in some powerful, spiritual, and mysterious way Jesus Christ comes into us, into our very bodies and being. This "second incarnation" of Christ in us serves as the key to his disciples' unity: "*I in them* and you in me, that they may be completely one" (John 17:23, emphasis mine). Having just affirmed his own incarnation—the fullness of deity dwelling in the human Jesus—he now describes his incarnation in his followers, a reality he links inseparably to their complete oneness.[2]

This "second incarnation" is certainly Christ in every individual disciple. Yet it is a mistake to understand this profound truth exclusively in individualistic terms. Jesus's prayer always uses the plural—"that *they* be one as we are one, I in *them* and you in me." Jesus was praying that he be incarnated in or united with his disciples collectively, all who make up Christ's body on earth, the church, of which he is the head.[3]

Another caution is that though Christ is in us, and we are the body of Christ on earth, we are not identical to Christ—we are not *new Christs*. We do not share the fullness of the deity. We are human beings and remain very much subject to sin. The breathtaking promise is that Christ is in each of us *and* all of us as the church, expressed in other Scriptures as God's Holy Spirit in us (1 Corinthians 6:19; Romans 8:9). As a result of this incarnation, in the words of 2 Corinthians 3:17-18, followers of Christ are being transformed "from one degree of glory to another" into the image of Christ, "for this comes from the Lord, the Spirit." This transformation doesn't happen instantaneously or evenly. It could be seen like a stock market chart with ups and downs, advances and reversals. Or perhaps like a weather forecast that calls for cloudy days followed by sun, then rain, then mixed. Yet God's Spirit continues the process of increasingly shaping us to be like Jesus Christ until we die.

In *The Holy Longing: The Search for a Christian Spirituality*, spiritual writer Ronald Rolheiser explains that the second incarnation is not an obscure metaphysical mystery with no relevance to the daily lives of Christ's disciples. Rather, the second incarnation is profoundly practical and delivers consequences for how the church—Christ's human body in the world—continues Christ's ministry in all of life.[4] When Christians pray through Christ for God's action in some matter, they are not simply praying for some detached action from God. As the body of Christ or the Church, when Christians pray for something in Christ's name, we are also addressing ourselves and our own moral responsibility in the world. We are responsible for doing whatever we can to bring about what we asked for in that prayer. The same is true with the mission Christ gave Christians to take the good news of the unlimited love of God and Christ's salvation of the world to everyone. Incarnational mission does not primarily mean starting religious broadcast networks or flooding a city with religious tracts and literature. It means, again in Rolheiser's words, "to radiate the compassion and love of God, as manifest in Jesus, in our faces and our actions. That is how we live our incarnation."[5] We must "put flesh on" our petitions.

Most important for our discussion, an inevitable consequence of the second incarnation for Christians is Christ's supplication for the visible unity of his Church for the sake of the world. That is, Christ's impassioned prayer for the unity of his followers means that the whole Church, and each of us as his body, shares responsibility for doing everything we can to make evident the ontological unity of Christ's body. That is, to show that by its very nature, in its very being, Christ's body is one—it cannot be anything else. ("There *is* one body," Ephesians 4:4, emphasis mine.) God empowers Christians to do this work through our growth in understanding of the profound truth of Christ's incarnation *in us*, rooted in our contemplation and acceptance of the fullness of divinity in Christ. The apostle Paul says, "In him the whole fullness of deity dwells bodily, and you have come to fullness in him, who is the head of every ruler and authority" (Colossians 2:9-10).

The crucial action of the Nicene Council was to make normative the doctrine that many Christians already held, that Jesus Christ and the Father completely shared the divine nature. The Nicene-Constantinopolitan Creed brings together the Scriptures and the theological wrestling that, in light of the story of

Christ's redemption of humanity, define the nature of Christ.[6] The Creed says:

> And [we believe] in one Lord, Jesus Christ,[7]
> the only begotten Son of God,
> begotten from the Father before all ages,
> light from light,
> true God from true God,
> begotten not made,
> of one substance with the Father,
> through Whom all things came into existence,
> Who because of us [humans] and because of our salvation came down from the heavens,
> and was incarnate from the Holy Spirit and the Virgin Mary and became [hu]man,
> and was crucified for us under Pontius Pilate,
> and suffered and was buried,
> and rose again on the third day according to the Scriptures
> and ascended to heaven, and sits on the right hand of the Father,
> and will come again with glory to judge living and dead,
> of Whose kingdom there will be no end.[8]

The crucial Greek words ὁμοούσιον τῷ Πατρί (*homoousion to patri*) appear in English as "of one substance" with the Father. This was a hotly disputed point that led to the Council of Nicaea. To the theologians and church leaders who held unswervingly to the necessity of Christ's full divinity, the concept of sharing the identical essence or substance was uncompromisable. For those who stood against teachings that Christ was a created being, anything less than full divinity would mean that Jesus Christ was incarnated by and is a subordinate created being, insufficient for the work of salvation. If Christ was a mere created being, the Church, the body of Christ on earth, would also be incarnated by a lesser entity—a created being. The implications were unacceptable.

Athanasius of Alexandria (296-373) was one of the most articulate and aggressive champions of the Nicene view. In his classic *The Incarnation of the Word*, Athanasius explained that humanity could only be saved from corruption by the Word's (that is, by the divine Christ's) death, but that was impossible because of Christ's immortality and deity. The Word, therefore, inhabited a human body that could die, making that body incorruptible and "worthy to die in the place of all"; through this death and "the grace of the resurrection," the Word ended human corruptibility.[9]

Athanasius argued that for God "to renew his image in humanity"—the image that was lost in the Fall of humankind—it would take the very image of God. That full image of God came in our Lord Jesus Christ. No creature—no human or angelic being—could achieve the task. According to Athanasius, "Therefore the Word of God came in person, so that, being the image of the Father, he would be able to recreate humanity afresh in that image."[10]

The issue was salvation. Salvation would not have been possible had the Word been (as Arius taught) a creature—even a highly exalted one. Athanasius explained that Christ had to be God to save and deify humankind. He said we could not have been delivered from sin and the curse, unless it had been by nature human flesh, which the Word put on (for we should have had nothing in common with what was foreign). So also, the man could not have been deified, unless the Word who became flesh had been by nature from the Father and true and proper to him. For therefore the union was of this kind, that he might unite what is human by nature to him who is in the nature of the Godhead, and his salvation and deification might be sure.[11]

Cyril of Alexandria (375-444), in dealing with division in the church of his day, wrote a commentary on the Gospel of John, partly to affirm the definition of Christ in the Nicene Creed. The unity of Christ's disciples is not identical to the unity of the Father and the Son! It can't be because the divine Father does not have a physical body and is not human. Yet, because full divinity, that is, *all* of the divine nature, *and all* of human nature, are perfectly joined in Christ, and all disciples of Christ have Christ in them, Christians are blended with one another. When Christians are added to the body of Christ, they are united with each other. Cyril said:

> [B]eing at the same time God and Man, in order that, uniting as it were in Himself things widely opposed by nature, and

> averse to fusion with each other, He might enable [humans] to share and partake of the Nature of God. For even unto us has reached the fellowship and abiding Presence of the Spirit, which originated through Christ and in Christ first.[12]

Christians are one with each other *physically* because of Jesus's humanity, his flesh—which is part of his nature.[13] We are one *spiritually* through Christ and God's Holy Spirit. Cyril continued: "the power of His holy Flesh maketh those in whom It exists to be of the same Body, so likewise also the indivisible Spirit of God That abideth in all, being one, bindeth all together in spiritual unity."[14]

As mentioned, Cyril's motivation for writing the commentary on John was partly to defend the Nicene definition of Christ. After the Council of Constantinople of 381, the Creed included an expanded article on the Holy Spirit, who figures prominently in Cyril's description of the nature of the unity of the body, which is identical with the Church. Cyril hoped that the Nicene-Constantinopolitan definition of the Trinity would bring consensus, peace, and unity among the churches of his time.[15]

The decrees of the Council of Nicaea stated that Jesus Christ shared the exact same divine nature or substance with God the Father. In other words, Jesus Christ was fully divine. The full deity of Christ was indispensable for Christ to do the work of saving humanity. Still, the establishment of Christ's full deity had consequences for understanding the Trinity, Christ's humanity, the nature of salvation, and—in light of Christ's prayer in John 17 and Paul's proclamation in Ephesians 4:4—the ontological reality of the unity of the Church, Christ's body on earth.

Opposition to the validity of Nicaea's theological decrees centered on Constantine's heavy association in calling, presiding over, and enforcing the Council's decisions. The free church tradition generally views Constantine's involvement as a corrupting precedent of using coercive government power to endorse, propagate, and enforce one theological position over another.[16] The Council of Nicaea for some in the free church tradition marks the "fall" or apostasy of the church predicted in 2 Thessalonians 2:3-4. (The lawless one would exalt himself above every god and object of worship, declaring himself to be

God. Some understand this to be Constantine, but more see the Pope as the enemy.) By his actions, Constantine brought church and state under the emperor and gave the church governmental sanction to judge and persecute all who disagreed with an officially state-sanctioned theological position. Furthermore, the Nicene definition failed to usher in unanimity among the followers of Christ. For instance, Arianism still flourished in southeast and central Europe among the Goths, Visigoths, and Vandals, and Emperor Constantius II (337-361) tried to unite the Empire under Arian Christianity.[17]

Despite serious concerns by some, the decrees of Nicaea regarding the divinity of Christ were not simply the result of who had the most power to enforce their theological preferences. Christian theologians did make the case that the consequences of a savior who was less than fully divine were fatal to the core of Christian belief and that the full divinity (and humanity, defined at the Council of Chalcedon in 451) of Christ was crucial for the ontological reality of the unity of Christ's body, the Church. Today, the Nicene Creed exists as a central tenet of the Christian faith, accepted explicitly or implicitly by the vast majority of Christians around the world.[18]

Through a tumultuous period of conflict and disagreement in the first centuries of the church regarding the nature of Christ and all the consequences of it, wise and dedicated church leaders concluded that Christ was of one substance with the Father. That teaching, along with the statements of John 17 that God is in Christ, and Christ is in us, become the solid foundation for understanding the united nature of Christ's body on earth—the Church.

Notes

1 The term *perichoresis* came to be used by the late patristic period for the "interpenetration" and full sharing of the divine nature by the three persons of the Trinity, yet each maintaining their personhood—Father. Son, Holy Spirit. It was also used to describe the relation between Christ's human and divine natures and Christ's indwelling in the Christian. See Charles C. Twombly, *Perichoresis and Personhood: God, Christ, and Salvation in John of Damascus,* Princeton Theological Monograph Series, no. 216 (Eugene, OR: Wipf and Stock Publishers, 2015).

2 These relationships are also described in Colossians 2, where Paul states in verses 9 and 10 that Christians have come to fullness in Christ in whom the fullness of deity dwells bodily.

3 See Colossians 1:18-20: "He is the head of the body, the church . . . in him all the fullness of God was pleased to dwell," and Ephesians 1:22-23: "And he has put all things under his feet and has made him the head over all things for the church, which is his body, the fullness of him who fills all in all."

4 There is a long history of thinking along these lines, often centered on the interpretation of 1 Corinthians 12:27 and following concerning spiritual gifts distributed among members of the body—"Now you are the body of Christ and individually members of it." See for example John Chrysostom's Homily 32 on 1 Corinthians (see https://www.newadvent.org/fathers/220132.htm); cf. Martin Luther's "The Freedom of the Christian," where he insists that Christian freedom in Christ means being the servant of all others (see https://courses.washington.edu/hist112/Freedom%20of%20Xtian%20text.htm#:~:text=Since%2C%20then%2C%20works%20justify%20no,work%2C%20no%20law%2C%20for%20his).

5 Ronald Rolheiser, *The Holy Longing: The Search for a Christian Spirituality* (New York: Image, 1999), 82-102.

6 According to tradition, the Council of Constantinople in 381 reaffirmed the Nicene Creed but revised or expanded parts of it, especially the original clause from 325 that simply mentioned the Holy Spirit. See J. N. D. Kelly, *Early Christian Creeds* (London: Longmans, Green and Co. 1950), 305, 307, 322–331.

7 Note that while the Latin form of the creed used *credo*, "I believe," the Greek version used *pisteuomen*, "we believe." See Gerald L. Bray, ed., *We Believe in One God*, vol. 1, Ancient Christian Doctrine Series (Lisle, IL: IVP Academic, 2009), viii.

8 "The Nicene Creed—Agreed at the Council of Constantinople 381," Early Church Texts, website, accessed April 11, 2025, https://earlychurchtexts.com/public/nicene_creed.htm.

9 Athanasius, *The Incarnation of the Word*, ch. 2, sec. 9, Christian Classics Ethereal Library, website, accessed April 11, 2025, https://ccel.org/ccel/athanasius/incarnation/incarnation.iii.html.

10 Athanasius, *The Incarnation of the Word*, ch. 3, sec. 13, Christian Classics Ethereal Library, accessed April 11, 2025, https://ccel.org/ccel/athanasius/incarnation/incarnation.iv.html.

11 Athanasius, *Second Discourse Against the Arians*, section 9, Orthodox Life, website, accessed April 11, 2025, https://orthodoxy.life/2017/07/19/deification-in-the-works-of-st-athanasius-of-alexandria/#:~:text=For%20man%20had%20not%20been,had%20put%20on%20the%20body.

12 Cyril of Alexandria, *Commentary on the Gospel of John*, ch. 11, par. 4, in The Tertullian Project, website, accessed April 11, 2025, https://www.tertullian.org/fathers/cyril_on_john_11_book11.htm.

13 For Cyril, disciples contact the body especially through the Eucharist.

14 Cyril, *John*, ch. 11, par. 4.

15 Cyril would state many of the same convictions in his *Tomes Against Nestorius*, 3.1, 5, in The Tertullian Project, website, accessed April 11, 2025, https://www.tertullian.org/fathers/cyril_against_nestorius_03_book3.htm.

16 The "Free Church" tradition emerged during the era of the Protestant Reformation in the sixteenth century. The name means free from state control. Groups include Anabaptists and others rejecting the concept of a state church and any form of government control.

17 For example, see Nigel Goring Wright, *Disavowing Constantine: Mission, Church, and the Social Order in the Theologies of John Howard Yoder and Jurgen Moltmann* (Milton Keyes, UK: Paternoster, 2000), and J. David Ray, "Nicea and its Aftermath: A Historical Survey of the First Ecumenical Counsel and the Ensuing Conflicts," *Ashland Theological Journal* 39 (2007): 19-32.

18 See John Courtney Murray, "The Status of the Nicene Creed as Dogma," *Chicago Studies: An Archdiocesan Review* 5 (Spring 1966): 65-80.

9

Incarnate of the Virgin Mary . . . Crucified . . . under Pontius Pilate: The Hidden Presence of the Oppressed

David N. Field

DESPITE THE ECUMENICAL status of the Nicene Creed, James Cone challenged the easy affirmation of the universal normativity of its Christology, arguing that the "question about the Son's status in relation to the Father did not arise in the historical context of the slave codes and slave drivers."[1] Cone writes that, if the Christological question had been proposed by a Black slave, then it might have been "about the status of the Son in relation to slaveholders."[2] Nicene Christology, for all its profound depth, does not address the liberation of the oppressed, which is for Cone the center of the Gospel. Despite this omission, the Council could not fully suppress the subversive reality of claiming that Jesus, a person born under dubious circumstances on the periphery of the empire, who in the power of the Spirit proclaimed justice for the oppressed, was truly God.

The challenge to Nicaea is not merely that the Council was not posing the questions of the oppressed; Nicaea is also problematic due to the central role played by Roman Emperor

Constantine in the organization of, and discussions within, the Council.[3] The issue here is not the interference of the political in the realm of the theological as would be posited by modern concepts of the separation of church and state. In the Roman Empire, religion and politics were often deeply intertwined with various forms of religion, playing a significant role in the legitimation of the imperial state.[4] Christianity was persecuted not because it was apolitical but because its theological message was rightly perceived to be subversive to the interests of the Roman Empire. Whatever the intentions and questions of the bishops, the final outcome of the Nicene Creed was shaped by imperial interests and priorities. Constantine's primary interest was not the relationship of the Father to the Son but the unity of a domesticated church that would strengthen the unity of the empire. Hence, at the conclusion of the Council, he enforced its decisions by exiling Arian bishops and ordering the burning of Arian literature. His later lifting of the exile and his baptism by an Arian bishop suggest that theological orthodoxy was not his priority. It could be argued that an Arian theology would have been equally useful if it had won broad acceptance insofar as neither Arianism nor Nicene orthodoxy as theologies subverted his rule.

The Nicene Creed refers to the Son becoming incarnate but does not refer to Jesus's identification with the poor, the rejected, and the oppressed. The Creed confesses that the purpose of the Incarnation was "our salvation," but it does not refer to the message of God's reign of love and justice that was proclaimed and enacted by Jesus. The Creed refers to the incarnate Son suffering in oblique terms, but it does not refer explicitly to his death by crucifixion on the orders of the Roman governor. The Nicene Creed of 325 CE is not the text used in liturgies of the church. Churches today use a longer text correctly attributed as the Nicene-Constantinopolitan Creed.

As its name indicates, this longer Creed has been traditionally ascribed to the work of the Creed of the Council of Constantinople in 381 CE, held a full fifty-six years after the Council of Nicaea. While the Nicene-Constantinopolitan Creed was affirmed by the Council of Chalcedon in 451 CE, there are significant questions related to the role played by the Council of Constantinople in its formulation. We know very little about the discussions at the Council in 381 CE, and the records we have do not refer to the actual writing or editing of a creed. In addition, the exact relationship between the shorter and the longer Creed of 381 CE is not easy to determine as it both adds and omits parts of the earlier text. In terms of additions, some of these deal with the continuing controversy about the nature of the Trinity. There are two additions that do not address the nature of the Trinity but which are found in earlier catechetical creeds. These additions affirm that the Son became "incarnate . . . of the Virgin Mary" and that "he [the Son] was crucified for us under Pontius Pilate." Why these two human actors are introduced is not certain given the lack of information about the drafting of the Creed (whether or not this was done by the Council of Constantinople). However, the presence of the two additions does provide an alternative way of reading the text that was probably not envisaged by its formulators. This alternative reading subverts the political interests of the Roman Empire and others who wish to maintain oppressive political systems by focusing on the victims of oppressive political power. Together they pose a challenge to what it means for the way the dominant Church understands who God is and what God does; the challenge begins with the earthly life of the Son and the pregnant Virgin Mary and ends on a Roman cross at the order of Pilate the representative of the Roman Empire. We can clarify through scriptural readings rooted in the Gospels of Matthew and Luke, which exemplify the challenge seated within these conciliar additions, as a next step.

Matthew's Gospel situates the announcement to Joseph of the coming birth of "God with us" to the young woman [Mary] he was betrothed to in the context of a genealogy located in the Hebrew Scriptures. The genealogy confirms Joseph's descent from David but unusually includes a reference to four women. The first woman mentioned is Tamar, a widow, who gave birth to two sons after pretending to be a prostitute to seduce her father-in-law Judah after he had refused to allow her to marry the brother of her husband. In the end, Judah declares her to be more righteous than he was (Genesis 38:26). The second woman is Rahab, the Canaanite sex worker who protected Israelite spies, helping them to escape from Jericho. The third woman is Ruth, a Moabite. Moabites and their descendants were excluded from Israel, according to Deuteronomy 23:3-6. Despite exclusion, Ruth is a model of faithfulness to her Israelite mother-in-law and takes the initiative in arranging a marriage with Boaz. The fourth woman is Bathsheba, who is identified in Matthew as the "wife of Uriah," emphasizing the scandal of David's adulterous coercion of her into having sex with him and then arranging her husband's death. The genealogy is followed by the account of the annunciation to Joseph who is planning to quietly divorce Mary whose pregnancy is a humiliating disgrace to him.

The exact significance of these four women in Matthew's genealogy is debated and cannot be reduced to one feature. These features include: some women who are non-Israelites, including Ruth, who is forbidden to become an Israelite; some are victims of abusive patriarchy; some had engaged in scandalous activities; and some asserted their agency in unconventional ways in the face of cultural restrictions. In all cases we witness women subjected to an oppressive culture. This is important. While later Christian traditions associated the virgin conception of Jesus with ideas of purity and sexual restraint, Matthew locates virginity in the context of marginalized, excluded, and abused women who express faithfulness and righteousness in unusual if not scandalous ways.

Matthew states that Mary's pregnancy was the work of the Spirit in fulfillment of a prophecy from the book of Isaiah. At various significant places in Jesus's ministry, Matthew connects his mission and ministry to prophecies from Isaiah. One significant prophetic inclusion is Matthew 12:15-21, which quotes Isaiah 42 to emphasize that the ministry of Jesus is to bring justice to the nations in a way that is directed toward the weak and the vulnerable. This recurring theme reveals how the one born in dubious circumstances is empowered and equipped by the Holy Spirit to bring justice to the nations as he embodies and teaches a lifestyle that contrasts with that of the rich and powerful.

Next, in Luke's Gospel, the announcement of the coming birth of Jesus—the one to be called the "Son of the Most High"—occurs in a context filled with references and allusions to Israel's prophetic hope of God's eschatological intervention to establish the divine reign, renew the people of God, liberate the oppressed, bring justice to the nations, and heal creation. For Luke, the agency of the Spirit of God is central to the inbreaking of the reign of God. The angel announces that Mary, a young virgin, will conceive the Messiah through the power of the Spirit. The definitive inbreaking of the divine reign of God occurs in Nazareth in the backwaters of the empire. Unlike the announcement of John the Baptist's birth, Jesus is born in the home of a peasant, far from the sacral space of the Jerusalem temple. The glory of God is displayed through the disgrace of the pregnancy of an unmarried teenager. Mary later sings of how the reign of God will turn the social world upside down through the agency of one who is lowly to bring down the rich and mighty in favor of the lowly, the poor, and hungry. Later Jesus announces that the same Spirit who brought about his birth from a virgin has anointed him to announce good news to the poor and liberation to the oppressed.

In the Gospels of Matthew and Luke, each testify to the virgin conception of Jesus—God with us and the Son of the Most High—as the Spirit of God seizing the initiative to destabilize patriarchal hierarchies, to favor the poor and the marginalized, to reject the imperial power structures, to scandalously work through the shameful, to enable the agency of the disempowered, to welcome the excluded and rejected, and to bring justice and liberation to the nations. In Matthew and Luke, the virgin birth stands opposed to the authoritarian and abusive hierarchies of power that characterized Roman imperial rule even under Roman Emperors who confessed to be Christians.

In the Gospels the narratives of the virgin birth, with their subversive potential, introduce accounts of the ministry and message of Jesus, which is ignored by the formulators of the Nicene and the revised Nicene-Constantinopolitan Creed. This message and ministry unfold the subversive implications of the narratives of Jesus's birth and bring him into increasing confrontation with the religious and political authorities culminating in his arrest and execution. When the Creed is revised in 381, Jesus's death is affirmed with the statement that the Son "was crucified for us under Pontius Pilate." This fact, like the affirmation of the virgin birth, is disruptive in important ways. We may ask, of all the inclusions possible in a creedal statement, we see only two people named. It is understandable that

Mary as the mother of Jesus be included, but why should Pilate be the only other human being mentioned? Surely it would have made sense to include some of the apostles. Why bring the representative of Roman imperial authority into the core confession of the Christian faith? It is noteworthy that Pilate is named as responsible for the Crucifixion amid an emerging tendency, even located within the Christian Scriptures, to blame the Crucifixion on the Jews. That being true, why is Pilate prominent in a creed and not the Jewish leaders?

As in the case of all empires, the Roman Empire needed ways of assuring that those it exploited and oppressed did not engage in resistance, subversion, and rebellion. One way to secure assurances was through the application of terrifying punishments to all who subverted the social and political order. Crucifixion was a terrorizing form of punishment reserved for rebels, slaves, and the socially undesirable. It was an orchestrated and ritualized display of imperial power through the public humiliation, torture, and execution of those who resisted Roman domination. The victim was humiliated by being stripped naked (without strategically placed loin cloths that are common in depictions of Jesus's crucifixion), scourged by ripping flesh of the person's body, nailed or tied to a plank of wood, which was then hauled up and affixed to a vertical post. The person was left to die in agony. Once they died, it was common to leave the body hanging on the cross as a reminder to all passers-by what happened to those who resisted the empire. To confess that Jesus was crucified in the Creed is to affirm that he was ritually degraded, tortured, and executed as a disruptor of the Roman imperial order.

Whatever the idealized picture of peace and prosperity portrayed in imperial propaganda, the reality was that that the Roman Empire was a system of oppression structured to maintain the wealth, power, and glory of Rome and its citizens. The main beneficiaries of the system were the elites in Italy and in the provinces. The poor of Rome benefited from the regime of bread and circuses designed to keep them subservient to the system. The army ensured that there was little dissent. The system was maintained by the taxation and exploitation of the colonized peoples and lands. The emperor claimed to be appointed by God to maintain and expand this system by whatever means necessary. Order and peace had to be maintained in the conquered areas to ensure the flow of tax money, goods, food, and luxury goods to Rome. Roman governors, such as Pilate, played a key role in supporting the system. In Rome, much of the actual work of government was carried out by local elites. They were responsible to the governors for ensuring the system of exploitation functioned. The governors as representatives of the imperial government controlled the tax system, developed and maintained relationships with the local elite, administered law and order, commanded the armed forces, and suppressed resistance and rebellion.

Crucifixion was the ultimate punishment that ensured that the system continued to work. Whatever the intentions of the formulators of the Creed and their imperial patrons, to confess that Jesus was crucified under Pontius Pilate is to confess that he was one of the thousands of victims of Roman imperial power, and it is to affirm that in his death he is identified with them and not with the emperor and his representatives. The legacy of the confession for humanity on the margins of power is profound to Christians who recite the Nicene-Constantinopolitan Creed each week.

A consequence (whether intended or not) of the expansion of the original Nicene Creed to include the affirmations that the Son became incarnate of the Virgin Mary and was crucified under Pontius Pilate fundamentally reshapes the accepted theology of the Creed for millions upon millions of human beings. The profound statements about the relationship of the Father and the Son, and thus of the nature of the divine, must now be essentially understood in relation to the Son's identification with the marginalized, the poor, the oppressed, and the victims of society who become the agents empowered by the Spirit to embody and bear witness to God's reign in the world. The God in whom Christians confess their faith in the words of the Creed is the God whose nature is defined by justice and compassion, by entering into the realities of the poor, the oppressed, the exploited and excluded. From these margins we witness the inauguration not of authoritarian power but of the divine reign of love and justice through the active presence of the divine Spirit.

To faithfully confess the Nicene-Constantinopolitan Creed requires that those who profess allegiance to the God who "became incarnate through the Virgin Mary and suffered under Pontius Pilate" take their place where God has located Godself on the side of justice, and from there to live and proclaim the divine reign that turns the world upside down.

Notes

1 James H. Cone, *God of the Oppressed* (Minneapolis: Seabury, 1975), 14.

2 Cone, 14.

3 See J. N. D. Kelly, *The Early Christian Creeds* (London: Continuum, 2006), 296-331.

4 See James B. Rives, *Religion in the Roman Empire* (Malden, MA: Blackwell, 2007), 132-157.

10

Nicaean Christology's Impact on the Integrative Methodology

Kirsten Sonkyo Oh

THE COUNCIL OF NICAEA (325 CE) significantly contributed to the development of Christian theology, particularly in the field of Christology. This historical council prominently addressed and asserted a clear Christology that integrated both the divine and human natures of Christ, identifying a core tenet of theological orthodoxy against the Arian heresy.

The Arian heresy centered around Arius, a Cyrenaic ascetic, and his followers, who purported a polytheistic understanding of God through the worship of creation, Jesus. To Arius and his followers, Jesus was a created being rather than someone divine, since Christ cannot at once be a created being and a creator. By denying the nature of Christ as one who shares the very substance with the creator God, Arius's assertion effectively stripped Christ's redemptive and salvific work.[1]

After much dispute between Arius, Athanasius of Alexandria, and others, the controversy was settled at the Council of Nicaea. The Council declared Arius's Christology as a heresy and issued the resultant Creed that affirmed the dual nature of

Christ. Jesus was indeed divine (one being or substance with the Father or *homoousios*) and truly human:

> [E]ternally begotten of the Father,
> God from God, Light from Light,
> true God from true God,
> begotten, not made,
> of one Being with the Father;
> through him all things were made.
> For us and for our salvation
> he came down from heaven,
> was incarnate of the Holy Spirit and the Virgin Mary
> and became truly human.[2]

In the Nicene Creed, we find a Christology that integrates the dual natures of Jesus Christ within the Trinitarian formula for which Athanasius, the Patriarch of Alexandria, unequivocally affirmed as the proper theological orthodoxy.[3] As such, John of Damascus affirms the Creed the with these words:

> The one who was born of her was God made flesh, not merely a divinely inspired human. He was not a prophet anointed with power, but the full presence of the anointer. Therefore, the anointer became the anointed, not by a change of nature, but by the hypostatic union.[4]

This Christology articulated at Nicaea opens a path to a methodology for integrating diverse perspectives, disciplines, or cultural contexts into a coherent whole. This chapter explores how the Nicene Christological principle can inform an integrative methodology with insights from an Asian American philosophy.

An Integrative Approach

The integrated dual natures of Christ as both fully human and fully God makes understandable the integration of two seemingly divergent natures like sacred and secular, faith and science, and other interdisciplinary work. Christology has also been used in the work of racial integration; the multiple racial identities present within one person can be reconciled through the theological understanding of Christ.[5] In essence the Nicene Christology gives us these core principles of integration: Affirming distinctions without division; resolving paradox through tension, not elimination; and allowing cultural or intellectual traditions to contribute to the conversation.

Affirming Distinctions Without Division

The Nicene Christology maintains a critical balance: While affirming the unity of Christ's divinity and humanity, it does not conflate the two. Each nature retains its integrity, such that the uniqueness of the two or more divergent natures are not erased in the integration process.

Deborah van Deusen Hunsinger's integrative work between psychology and theology demonstrates such by likening the integration in a bilingual sense.[6] In this bilingual approach, van Deusen Hunsinger's model purports a code-switching mechanism from one to the other discipline, rather than a melting pot approach where two separate disciplines become melded into another so that neither of the disciplines retains its own distinctiveness. Such distinctives can hold paradoxes in tension rather than elimination.

Resolving Paradox through Tension, Not Elimination

Nicene Christology embraces paradox: Christ is fully divine and fully human, a mystery that defies simplistic categorization. The integrative approach for both personal and dialogical work not only permits tension and ambiguity in its process, but demonstrates the inevitable, and perhaps the necessary, requirement for tensions and ambiguities to not only exist but also to remain without prematurely resolving them. In other words, paradoxes do not mandate an elimination of one in order to retain a false homeostasis or stability. Rather, the two (or more) categories in tension require dialogical relationships that may seek a balance.

Gustavo Gutiérrez gives us what this balance looks like between the sacred and profane:

> There are not two histories, one profane and one sacred, "juxtaposed" or "closely linked." Rather, there is only one

> human history, irreversibly assumed by Christ, the Lord of history. His redemptive work embraces all the dimensions of existence and brings them to their fullness. The history of salvation is the very heart of human history.[7]

Paradoxes that seek balancing invite conversations with other cultural or intellectual traditions to contribute to the concept with meaningful, time-honed understanding of harmony.

Allowing Cultural or Intellectual Traditions to Contribute to the Conversation

Integration from the Nicene Christology recognizes the physical, human nature of embodiment. As such, one's race, gender, sexual orientation, and ethnicity as well as disciplinary expertise contribute to the integrative conversation. As an Asian American, my social location seeks the understanding of "harmony" or "balance" when paradoxes emerge for a fuller and more robust integration.

Similar to the divine and human Christological distinctives in the Nicene Creed, Asian American perspective holds harmony and balance retain two distinct connotations. The concept of harmony is the keeping in tension of two opposing things, while balance is juggling in tandem multiple worthwhile or good things. They are shaped by a cultural framework of "both-and." This nonlinear, holistic, and dynamic Eastern philosophy is derived from the Tao as reflected in the South Korean flag's four trigrams surrounding the red and blue circle. The Tao relays the necessity that multiple things must be held in tension rather than compartmentalized into separate spheres. The result is an integrative model espoused by a dialectic Yin-Yang worldview in which the opposing elements are set in tension as complementary, rather than conflicting sides.

My Asian heritage recognizes and embraces paradoxes as inevitable, persistent, and even desirable with the following three key tenets of dialectical thinking:

1) The principle of change indicating that reality is a dynamic, a perpetually changing process;

2) The principle of contradiction suggesting that opposites exist in everything and are mutually complementary; and
3) The principle of relationship and holism suggesting that nothing is isolated and independent.[8]

These three tenets of dialectical thinking contribute to the integrative methodology to recognize the various natures and disciplines must retain their particularity and distinctiveness. In so doing, they often present paradoxes that are neither easily nor immediately resolvable. Instead, they require an active and dynamic interplay to find balance and harmony.

An Example of Integration

An example of the integration outlined above is the first-generation immigrant who is navigating a new reality of the new environment and the culture thereof while retaining the culture of their previous environment. (Here, culture refers to language, social customs, mannerisms, attitudes, practices, and conventions.) The integration model of the incarnate Jesus, the Son, who possesses the same divine substance as God the Father in the Nicene formula explains the ways in which the immigrant navigates the new world. Jesus comes in fully human form while he retains his divine nature.

The stark environmental shift is at once shocking and welcomed as the immigrant left the other environment for the new one for various reasons. Although the environmental and cultural shifts are mostly anticipated, the ever-present nature of the new culture necessitates the integrative processes outlined above. The immigrant is at once at home in the new land and on the margins of this new land.

In particular, the Asian American immigrant, and other immigrants from countries where one presents distinct appearances due to phenotypes such as physiological, behavior, and cognitive characteristics, must navigate the integration with greater intention to combat the harmful trope of being a perpetual foreigner. The imperative to affirm both Asian and American through the integrative model is desired while assimilation is neither possible nor even desired.

The distinctions to be both Asian and American stand in paradox: between the Western and Eastern cultural mores as discussed more in detail elsewhere.[9] Accordingly, these cultural paradoxes are not resolved by elimination. Rather, they are held in a constant tension between them. For instance, immigrants code switch between their native language to the new language that have paradoxical grammatical patterns, culturally laden expressions, philosophical differences, and more.

The level of the integration is always dynamic, depending on a variety of factors such as the relational, special, cultural interplay. Such tension breeds complex forms of hybridity so that the immigrant cannot be essentialized either this or that person. The cultural borrowing that integration allows for the tenets of dialectical thinking in play so that while in paradox, at once similarities between them are assessed and differences are bridged through this integrative mode.

Conclusion

The Christology of the Council of Nicaea offers a rich and robust framework for integration. By emphasizing unity without erasure, holding tensions productively, and grounding integration in embodied practice from diverse social locations, it provides a methodology that is both nuanced and nimble. Whether applied to theology, philosophy, or broader interdisciplinary efforts, this approach ensures that integration is coherent, faithful to its core, and responsive to the complexities of the world.

Notes

1 See Bengt Hägglund, *History of Theology*, trans. Gene J. Lund (St. Louis: Concordia Publishing House, 1968), 79-88.

2 *The United Methodist Hymnal: Book of United Methodist Worship* (Nashville: The United Methodist Publishing House, 1989; Forty-first Printing, 2003), 880.

3 The Trinitary formula came down from Clement and Origen who asserted that "the Logos emanated from the Deity and is, therefore, of the same substance as the Father. According to Tertullian, Father, Son, and Spirit are of the same substance." Hägglund, *History of Theology*, 73.

4 John of Damascus, *On the Orthodox Faith* 4.14, quoted by Justo L. González. *Luke: A Theological Commentary on the Bible* (Louisville, Westminster John Knox Press, 2010).
5 See Brian Bantum, *Redeeming Mulatto: A Theology of Race and Christian Hybridity* (Waco, TX.: Baylor University Press, 2010).
6 See Deborah van Deusen Hunsinger, *Theology and Pastoral Counseling: A New Interdisciplinary Approach* (Grand Rapids: Eerdmans Publishing, 1995).
7 Gustavo Gutiérrez, *A Theology of Liberation: History, Politics, and Salvation*, trans. and ed. Sister Caridad Inda and John Eagleson (Maryknoll, NY: Orbis, 1973), 153.
8 See Kaiping Peng and Richard Nisbett, "Culture, Dialectics, and Reasoning About Contradiction." *American Psychologist* 54, no. 9 (1999): 741-754.
9 See Kirsten S. Oh, "What's Love Got to Do with It? Sex and the Korean American College Student and Young Adult," in *Pastoral Care in a Korean American Context*, ed. Angella Son. Cham (Switzerland: Palgrave Macmillan, 2021), 99-115.

11

When the Brown One Came to Nicaea

Loida I. Martell

IN MATTHEW 16:13-15, Jesus asks his disciples two important questions: The first is, "Who do *people* say that the Son of Man is?" and second "Who do *you* say that I am?" (emphasis added to both). As I have noted elsewhere, this second question becomes *una pregunta vigente*, a critical [lifegiving] question, not only for the disciples who surrounded Jesus but for the Christian community throughout the ages.[1] Each generation must face this question and answer it according to their context and the critical life questions (*preguntas vigentes*) they face.

The Council of Nicaea, an ecumenical gathering of bishops convened by Emperor Constantine in 325 CE, wrestled precisely with this critical "Who do you say that I am?" question. For those bishops, the question was not whether Jesus was indeed human (which they assumed, although that issue was to arise later in the fifth century at Chalcedon), but rather who Jesus is in relation to God. It was a *pregunta vigente* for fourth-century Christians because, if the answer to "Who do you say that I am?" was not "the divine Son of God," then Jesus could not be salvific in the way that the Church understood salvation. One could argue that the *pregunta vigente* being debated at Nicaea was not who was *God* (i.e., the divine ontological essence as distributed in three *personae*) but rather that it was a critical Christological debate with soteriological implications for the Church. Here, I will focus on this incarnational aspect of soteriology—that it was a particular human person that Nicaea declared to be "divine" and therefore "saving." In debates over the meaning of *ousia* and *hypostasis*, Nicaea became associated with "Trinitarian controversies" rather than with its biblical underpinnings—the statements that affirm the importance of Jesus's incarnation, and thus of God's presence in the world then and today.[2]

Jesus, the True *Sōtēr*

One of the key differences between those in the biblical world and fourth-century Christians was the latter's understanding of salvation. In the Bible, salvation was expressed in concrete ways. It was a corporate event rather than an individualized event. God saves God's people from distress, oppression, or danger. In the First Testament, the defining moment is the Exodus.[3] From that and other subsequent experiences, the people of Israel learn that the Divine One is a God who rescues (*nasal*, *yāša'*), restores (*šûb*), forgives (*sālah*), and redeems (*gā'al*). God heals, feeds, speaks, and provides the means for repentance and renewal (*kŏper*). God is the Living One who is present in our midst to bring life in places of death. False gods/idols are not the living God because they cannot speak, see, or breathe, and therefore cannot give life (Psalm 34:15–18). By contrast, idols are often death-dealing.

In the Second Testament, salvation continues to have this corporate meaning of God redeeming God's people, but is now proclaimed through Jesus Christ as the coming of God's *basileia*, God's reign—an eschatological (that is, an anticipated) reality that is yet to be fulfilled but is already coming to fruition through Jesus's ministry, praxis, and presence. Jesus proclaims *euangelion* (good news) in particular to the poor, release to the imprisoned, recovery of sight to the blind, and freedom to the oppressed (Luke 4:18-19). Jesus's death is a crisis moment, leading the Church to ask a *pregunta vigente*: "Are you the one who is to come, or are we to wait for another?" (Matthew 11:3). Was it in vain that they followed this poor, brown Galilean and placed themselves at risk in a colonized space surrounded by the emperor's Roman soldiers? The Resurrection enables the Church to renew its claim but now in a different way: Jesus, this one who walked in our midst to proclaim the *basileia* of God, brought God's salvation to the people through his life, ministry, death, resurrection, and ascension.

Yet, if the fourth-century Church is to respond to the *pregunta vigente*, "Who do you say that I am?" by claiming Jesus as *sŏtĕr* (savior)—a wonderfully subversive claim since the emperors of Rome had declared themselves to be the *sŏtĕrs* of the world—then what is Jesus's relationship to God? By the fourth century, the Church was defining salvation less in communal-sociological terms (danger, disasters, and oppression) and more in ontological terms, that is to say, in terms of existence of being. The Church conceptualized salvation as *theosis* or divinization—as human participation in the divine that transformed them existentially, from corruptible to incorruptible, from mortal to immortal, living beings.[4] In the well-known words of Irenaeus, "[Jesus] would become the Son of man for this purpose, that man also might become the son of God."[5]

Influenced by Platonism and Neoplatonism, among other prevalent trends of thought, post-biblical Christians eventually conceived of God as the immutable, omnipotent, omniscient Other, the incorruptible and immortal One who could never be in touch directly with created materiality, which through sin was corrupted and mortal. Thus patristic Christian theologians faced a quandary: How could this human being, Jesus, also be the divine Son of God? If he was not divine, could he be *sŏtĕr* (savior)? From the second through the fourth centuries, different configurations of thought tackled the issue. One of the responses came from Arius, who conceived of Jesus as a created being, albeit superior and unique among all creation, having been created before the world and all its inhabitants. Jesus served in this capacity as a "mediator" between God and humanity. However, Arius emphatically insisted that God was not always "Father," and there "was a time in which [Jesus] was not."[6] Bishop Alexander of Alexandria and later Athanasius opposed Arius's position, and eventually the Eastern Church was divided into pro-Arian and anti-Arian camps.

Jesus the Galilean Is the "Son of God"

Emperor Constantine convened the bishops from the Western and Eastern Church in an ecumenical council at Nicaea in 325 CE to resolve what came to be known as the Arian Controversy, a controversy that was engulfing and endangering Constantine's vast empire, among some other issues that had arisen within the Church. This Council produced a statement of belief—or creed, that we know as the Nicene Creed—that I believe has three key implications for the Church's belief and doctrine. First, in refraining from using "Logos" or similar Christologically abstract language then in vogue, instead preferring "Jesus Christ," the Council's statement intentionally linked a human being, the Galilean Jesus of Scripture, to the divine Son of God. For the Council, the answer to the question, "Who am I?" was that the poor brown man of Nazareth, born of Mary, the One who walked and ministered among the marginalized, the poor, the suffering, the oppressed, the broken and brokenhearted, was indeed "Immanu-el," the Incarnate God in human history who is "God from God, Light from Light." In this methodological turn to Scripture, Nicaea affirmed that Jesus's incarnation, and therefore his humanity, was as essential to salvation as his divinity. Consequently, they rejected theologies that disembody Jesus (e.g., Docetism and Gnosticism) and empty him of his social location and context. It is part of the message of salvation that God chose to pitch his tent (John 1:14) precisely in the margins. This Jesus "smells of the stables," residing and ministering in the everyday spaces (*lo cotidiano*) of the suffering poor and rejected.[7] He understood the pain, the suffering, the hunger, and the needs of the peoples of Galilee and surrounding areas. It is equally significant that this brown man died a horrific death "outside the gates" of justice, among the refuse and the rejected at the hand of Empire, and from there still "beckons us" to join him.[8] Thus the locus of salvation lies not in the centers of power but in the margins where the suffering are to be found. It is this brown Galilean whom the Council of Nicaea recognized as Savior and Lord, "God from God, Light from Light." It is ironic, then, that we in the modern Western Church, who claim to believe in the Incarnation, have so spiritualized Jesus that we have ignored the cries of the suffering, broken, and exploited bodies of the oppressed, the forgotten, the marginalized, the trafficked, the migrants and the displaced, those we consider of little value, those whom we have pushed outside the gates of justice, grace, and mercy.

The second critical implication of the Nicene Creed is that it is the Triune *God* who saves. Now if it is indeed the Creator God (God the Parent) who saves through Jesus the Christ in the power of the Spirit, then the first important consequence of this is that creation, redemption, and eschatology are not three separate moments but rather one salvific movement. Salvation begins with creation and is fulfilled at the completion of what we refer to as the "end times" or what the Bible refers to as the fulfillment of the *basileia* (the reign) of God. God's salvific vision entails a divine intimate relationality of God with all of creation, humankind in communion among itself, and humanity in communion with creation.[9] Sin is the rupture of these communal *vínculos* intended from "the beginning" and embodied in the Incarnation, the very nature of Jesus, the saving brown one declared to be divine.[10] It is precisely this Jesus who came and comes to call into communion those who have been turned away by sinful "powers and principalities." Jesus does not come to appease a wrathful God, as so many atonement soteriologies have articulated. The Nicene Creed calls us to accountability, to remember the embodied Jesus Christ of the Gospels, the One whom God called to save the lost sheep, the lost coins, and others that society have given up as of "no value" (*sobrajas* or leftovers). Jesus is the One who the Spirit has empowered to initiate and embody the agenda of the *basileia* as articulated in Luke 4:18-19. Jesus is the Second Person, the very human who has come to humanize those whom the dehumanizing, death-dealing structures depersonalize. In and of itself, that God sent the Son precisely as a marginalized and poor brown one who "smells of the stables" is a profound soteriological statement. The Council at Nicaea acknowledged this.

Nicene Creed: The "Outside Gates" Beckon

The *pregunta vigente*: "Who do you say that I am?" continues to echo throughout the ages, despite repeated attempts to spiritualize Jesus and dislocate him to centers of power. During the Enlightenment, he became more a reflection of the European bourgeoisie than of Scripture.[11] Over time, Western sensibilities erased his brownness, perfumed his stable smell, all but eradicated his gritty humanity, and transformed his death into a cipher for an internalized and privatized piety (claiming that "Jesus Christ is 'for me'").[12] Thus unmoored from life and ministry, this white Jesus became the sordid justification for African enslavement, Indigenous genocide, and European expansionism under the guise of "Manifest Destiny." In the twenty-first century, a new version of Manifest Destiny called white Christian nationalism is roiling the churches and the nation. White Christian nationalism is an ideology wrapped in religious language that has distorted Christian truths in service of partisan political and nativist aims to ensure the hegemony of a select portion of our population defined in the most narrow of ways.[13] Christian nationalists' hyper-spiritualized Christ is a fully Aryan, MAGA-hat-wearing deity who in the United States empowered the violent acts of insurrectionists on January 6, 2021, and who blesses the nativist, xenophobic, homophobic/transphobic, patriarchal, and ultra-right leaning tendencies of a select group of people who have declared themselves to be "true Americans."

It is indeed a *kairos* moment in which we now find ourselves celebrating the 1700th anniversary of the Council of Nicaea. Let our celebration be a stark contrast and reminder to those who would forget that it is the embodied, incarnated, brown One who is present in Scripture and who was and is confessed in Nicaea and in its Creed. Nicaea confessed this Jesus, the One who spent his life among the suffering poor, healing, espousing the forgotten, to form *vínculos de amor* (loving community) between God and creation, among humankind, and between humankind and creation, *that none would be lost,* to be Son of God, "God from God, Light from Light." The Council of Constantinople (381 CE) and the Council of Chalcedon (425 CE) later reaffirmed the prophetic insights of Nicaea. Indeed, in light of the repeated attempts to "dehumanize" Jesus, Chalcedon in no uncertain terms declared that Jesus was *fully human* and *fully divine*. For this, the Church is thankful and says, "Amen."

Notes

1 Loida I. Martell-Otero, "Encuentro con el Jesús Sato*:* An Evangélica Soter-ology," in *Jesus in the Hispanic Community*, eds. Harold Recinos and Hugo Magallanes (Louisville, KY: Westminster John Knox Press, 2010), 74.

2 Susan Durber, "Celebrating Nicaea: Convincing Sceptical Protestants Including Myself," *The Ecumenical Review* 75, no. 3 (April 2023): 210.

3 I refer to what has traditionally been called the Old Testament or Hebrew Bible as the First Testament and to what traditionally has been called the New Testament as the Second Testament.

4 See Vladimr Kharlamov, *Theosis: Deification in Christian Theology*, Vol. II (Eugene, OR: Pickwick Publications, 2011), 9.

5 St. Irenaeus, *Against Heresies*, in *The Ante-Nicene Fathers: The Writings of the Fathers Down to A.D. 325*, Vol. 1, eds. Alexander Roberts and James Donaldson (Peabody, MA: Hendrikson Publishers, 1994), III.10.2.

6 Benjamin Mogoİ, "Arius, Alexander, and Athanasius: The Essential Role They Played in the Development of Christology at the First Ecumenical Council of Nicaea and Its Immediate Context," *Jurnal teologic* 22 (2023): 90.

7 Gustavo Gutiérrez, *The God of Life*, trans. Matthew J. O'Connell (Maryknoll, NY: Orbis Books, 1991), 85.

8 Orlando E. Costas, *Christ Outside the Gate: Mission Beyond Christendom* (Maryknoll, NY: Orbis Books, 1982), 188-194.

9 Karl Barth, *Church Dogmatics*, Vol. IV.1, *The Doctrine of Reconciliation*, ed. G. W. Bromiley and T. F. Torrance, trans. G. W. Bromiley (Edinburgh: T&T Clark, 1956), 27, 36.

10 *Vínculos* can be translated as "intimate ties that bind."

11 Albert Schweitzer, *The Quest for the Historical Jesus: A Critical Study of its Progress from Reimarus to Wrede* (Baltimore: John Hopkins University Press, 1998), 4.

12 Martin Luther, *Luther's Works*, vol. 27, *Galatians (1535)*, ed. Jaroslav Pelikan (St. Louis: Concordia, 1964), 177.

13 It is beyond the scope of this essay to survey the rich literature on this topic, so I refer the reader to the National Council of Churches' recent publication, *Confronting Racism and White Supremacy in the US: Twenty-First-Century Theological Perspectives*, ed. Michael R. Fisher, Jr. (Wnycote, PA: Friendship Press, 2024).

12

Cuando el Moreno Llegó a Nicea

Loida I. Martell
Translated by: Jessica Lugo

EN MATEO 16:13-15 (NVI), Jesús plantea dos preguntas importantes a sus discípulos. La primera es: "¿Quién dice la *gente* que es el Hijo del hombre?"; y la segunda: "Y *ustedes*, ¿quién dicen que soy yo?" Como he señalado en otras ocasiones, esta segunda pregunta se convierte en una *pregunta vigente*, es decir, una pregunta crítica [y vivificadora] no solo para los discípulos que rodeaban a Jesús, sino para toda la comunidad cristiana a lo largo de los tiempos.[1] Cada generación debe enfrentar esta pregunta y responderla según su contexto y según las preguntas críticas (o vigentes) que confrontan.

El Concilio de Nicea, una asamblea ecuménica de obispos convocada por el emperador Constantino en el año 325 E.C., luchó precisamente con esta pregunta crítica: "¿Quién dicen ustedes que soy yo?". Para aquellos obispos, la cuestión no era si Jesús era verdaderamente humano (lo cual asumían, aunque esta cuestión surgiría posteriormente en el siglo V en Calcedonia), sino quién era Jesús en relación con Dios. Era una *pregunta vigente* para los cristianos del siglo IV porque, si la respuesta a la pregunta ¿Quién dicen ustedes que yo soy? no era que Jesús era "el Hijo divino de Dios", entonces Jesús no podría ser salvador según la comprensión que la Iglesia tenía de la salvación. Uno puede argumentar que la *pregunta vigente* debatida en Nicea no era sobre quién era *Dios* (es decir, la esencia ontológica divina distribuida en tres personas), sino un debate Cristológico crucial con implicaciones soteriológicas para la Iglesia. Aquí, me enfocaré en este aspecto encarnacional de la soteriología—que fue una persona humana particular la que Nicea declaró como "divina" y, por tanto, "salvadora". En las disputas sobre el significado de *ousía* e *hipóstasis*, Nicea se asoció más con las "controversias Trinitarias" que con sus bases bíblicas—las afirmaciones que subrayan la importancia de la encarnación de Jesús y, por consiguiente, de la presencia de Dios en el mundo entonces y ahora.[2]

Jesús, el Verdadero *Sōtēr*

Una de las diferencias clave entre aquellos en el mundo bíblico y los cristianos del siglo IV fue la comprensión que estos últimos tenían de la salvación. En la Biblia, la salvación se expresa de maneras concretas. Era un acontecimiento communitario más que un evento individualizado. Dios salva al pueblo de Dios del sufrimiento, la opresión, o el peligro. En el Primer Testamento, el momento definitivo es el Éxodo.[3] A partir de esa experiencia, y de otras posteriores, el pueblo de Israel aprende que el Ser Divino es un Dios que rescata (*nāsal, yāša'*), restaura (*šûb*), perdona (*sālah*) y redime (*gā'al*). Dios sana, alimenta, habla, y provee los medios para el arrepentimiento y la renovación (*kŏper*). Dios es el Viviente que está presente en medio de nosotros para dar vida en lugares de muerte. Los falsos dioses/ídolos no son el Dios viviente porque no pueden hablar, ver, ni respirar, y por consiguiente no pueden dar vida (Salmo 134:15-18). En contraste, los ídolos son a menudo portadores de muerte.

En el Segundo Testamento, la salvación continúa con este significado comunitario de que Dios redime a su pueblo, pero ahora se proclama a través de Jesucristo como la venida de la *basileia* de Dios, el Reino de Dios—una realidad escatológica (es decir, anticipada) que aún está por cumplirse pero que ya comienza a manifestarse mediante el ministerio, praxis, y presencia de Jesús. Jesús proclama el *euangelion* (buenas nuevas), en particular a los pobres, da libertad a los cautivos, vista a los ciegos, y liberación a los oprimidos (Lucas 4:18-19). La muerte de Jesús representa un momento de crisis, que lleva a la Iglesia a plantearse una *pregunta vigente*: "¿Eres tú el que ha de venir, o debemos esperar a otro?" (Mateo 11:3). ¿Acaso fue en vano que siguieran a este pobre galileo moreno, poniéndose en riesgo en un espacio colonizado, rodeados de soldados romanos del emperador? La resurrección permite que la Iglesia renueva su confesión, pero ahora de una manera distinta: Jesús, aquel que caminó entre nosotros proclamando la *basileia* de Dios, trajo la salvación de Dios al pueblo mediante su vida, ministerio, muerte, resurrección y ascensión.

No obstante, si la Iglesia del siglo IV ha de responder a la *pregunta vigente* "¿Quién dicen ustedes que soy yo?" afirmando que Jesús es *sŏtĕr* (salvador)—una afirmación maravillosamente subversiva, ya que los emperadores romanos se autoproclamaban *sŏtĕres* del mundo—entonces, ¿cuál es la relación de Jesús con Dios? Para el siglo IV, la iglesia había comenzado a definir la salvación no tanto en términos sociológicos-comunitarios (peligro, desastres y opresión), sino en términos más ontológicos; es decir, relativos al ser y la existencia. La iglesia conceptualizó la salvación como *theosis* o divinización—como la participación humana en lo divino que les transforma existencialmente en seres vivientes, pasando de lo corruptible a lo incorruptible, de lo mortal a lo inmortal.[4] En las conocidas palabras de Ireneo: "[Jesús] se hizo Hijo del hombre con este propósito: para que el ser humano pudiera llegar a ser hijo de Dios."[5]

Influenciados por el Platonismo y el Neoplatonismo, entre otras corrientes predominantes del pensamiento, los cristianos post-bíblicos llegaron a concebir a Dios como el Otro inmutable, omnipotente, omnisciente, e incorruptible, el Uno inmortal que no podía tener contacto directo con la materialidad creada, la cual, a causa del pecado, era corrupta y mortal. Así, los teólogos cristianos patrísticos se enfrentaron a un dilema: ¿Cómo podía este ser humano, Jesús, ser también el Hijo divino de Dios? Si no era divino, ¿podía entonces ser *sŏtĕr* (salvador)? Desde el segundo hasta el cuarto siglo, diversas configuraciones teológicas abordaron esta situación. Una de las respuestas provino de Arrio, quien concebía a Jesús como un ser creado, aunque superior y único entre toda la creación, habiendo sido creado antes del mundo y de todos sus habitantes. Jesús desempeñaba así el papel de "mediador" entre Dios y la humanidad. Sin embargo, Arrio insistía enfáticamente en que Dios no había sido siempre "Padre", y que "hubo un tiempo en el que [Jesús] no existía".[6] El obispo Alejandro de Alejandría y más tarde Atanasio se opusieron firmemente a la postura de Arrio, y eventualmente la Iglesia Oriental se dividió en bandos pro-arrianos y anti-arrianos.

Jesús el Galileo Es el "Hijo de Dios"

El emperador Constantino convocó a los obispos de las iglesias occidental y oriental a un concilio ecuménico en Nicea en el año 325 E.C., con el fin de resolver lo que llegaría a conocerse como la controversia arriana, una disputa que amenazaba con desestabilizar el vasto imperio de Constantino, junto con otras cuestiones que se habían levantado dentro de la Iglesia. Este Concilio produjo una declaración de fe—o credo, que hoy conocemos como el Credo Niceno—y que entiendo conlleva tres implicaciones claves para la creencia y doctrina de la Iglesia. Primero, al abstenerse de utilizar términos como *Logos* u otros lenguajes cristológicos abstractos de boga en la época, prefiriendo en cambio "Jesucristo", la declaración del Concilio vinculó intencionalmente a un ser humano histórico, el Jesús galileo de las Escrituras, con el Hijo divino de Dios. Para el Concilio, la respuesta a la pregunta "¿Quién soy yo?" era que el hombre pobre y moreno de Nazaret, nacido de María, Aquel que caminó y ministró entre los marginados, los pobres, los que sufren, los oprimidos, los quebrantados y los de corazón roto, era de hecho "Emmanu-el," el Dios Encarnado en la historia humana quien es "Dios de Dios, Luz de Luz." En este giro metodológico hacia las Escrituras, Nicea afirmó que la encarnación de Jesús, y por ende su humanidad, era tan esencial para la salvación como su divinidad. En consecuencia, rechazaron las teologías que despojan a Jesús de su corporeidad (como el docetismo y el gnosticismo) y que lo vacían de su ubicación social y contexto histórico. Es parte del mensaje salvífico que Dios haya elegido plantar su tienda (Juan 1:14) precisamente en los márgenes. Este Jesús "huele a establo," vive y ministra en los espacios de lo cotidiano, entre los pobres y rechazados que sufren.[7] Conocía el dolor, el sufrimiento, el hambre y las necesidades de los pueblos de Galilea y sus alrededores. Igualmente significativo es que este hombre moreno murió una muerte atroz "fuera de la puerta" de la justicia, entre los desechos y los rechazados, a manos del Imperio, y desde allí aún "nos llama" a unirnos a él.[8] Así, el *locus* de la salvación no reside en los centros de poder, sino en los márgenes donde habita el sufrimiento. Es a este galileo moreno a quien el Concilio de Nicea reconoció como Salvador y Señor, "Dios de Dios, Luz de Luz". Resulta irónico, entonces, que nosotros, en la Iglesia occidental moderna, que decimos creer en la Encarnación, hayamos espiritualizado tanto a Jesús que hemos ignorado los clamores de los cuerpos sufrientes, quebrantados y explotados de los oprimidos, los olvidados, los marginados, los traficados, los migrantes y desplazados, aquellos a quienes consideramos sin valor, los que hemos empujado fuera de las puertas de la justicia, la gracia, y la misericordia.

La segunda implicación crítica del Credo Niceno es que es el *Dios* trino quien salva. Ahora bien, si es en efecto el Dios Creador (*God the Parent*) quien salva a través de Jesucristo en el poder del Espíritu, entonces la primera consecuencia importante de esto es que la creación, la redención, y la escatología no son tres momentos separados, sino un único movimiento salvífico. La salvación comienza con la creación y se consuma en la culminación de lo que llamamos "los últimos tiempos," o lo que la Biblia denomina la plenitud de la *basileia* (reino) de Dios. La visión salvífica de Dios conlleva una relacionalidad divina e íntima con toda la creación, entre la humanidad en comunión consigo misma, y con la humanidad en comunión con la creación.[9] El pecado representa la ruptura de estos *vínculos* comunitarios intencionalmente dispuestos "desde el principio" y hecho cuerpo en la Encarnación, en la propia naturaleza de Jesús, el salvador moreno declarado divino.[10] Es precisamente este Jesús quien vino y viene a llamar a la comunión a quienes han sido excluidos por los "poderes y principados" del pecado. Jesús no viene a apaciguar a un Dios iracundo, como han articulado tantas soteriologías de expiación. El Credo Niceno nos llama a la rendición de cuentas, a recordar al Jesús encarnado de los evangelios, Aquel a quien Dios envió a salvar a las ovejas perdidas, a las monedas perdidas y a todos aquellos quienes la sociedad han descartado "sin valor"—como sobrajas. Jesús es Aquel a quien el Espíritu ha habilitado para iniciar y encarnar la agenda de la *basileia* tal como se articula en Lucas 4:18-19. Jesús es la Segunda Persona, tal cual humano que ha venido a humanizar a quienes las estructuras deshumanizantes y mortíferas han despersonalizado. El solo hecho de que Dios haya enviado al Hijo precisamente como un marginado pobre y moreno que "huele a establo" es una profunda declaración soteriológica. El Concilio de Nicea así lo reconoció.

Credo Niceno: Los "portones exteriores" Llaman

La *pregunta vigente*: "¿Quién dicen ustedes que soy yo?" continúa resonando a través de los años, a pesar de los repetidos intentos por espiritualizar a Jesús y desplazarlo hacia los centros de poder. Durante la era de la Ilustración, se convirtió más en un reflejo de la burguesía europea que de las Escrituras.[11] Con el tiempo, las sensibilidades occidentales borraron su morenidad, perfumaron su olor a establo, casi erradicaron su áspera humanidad, y transformaron su muerte en un símbolo de piedad privada e interiorizada (afirmando que "Jesucristo es 'para mí'").[12] Desarraigado así de su vida y ministerio, este Jesús blanco se convirtió en una justificación sórdida para la esclavitud africana, el genocidio indígena, y el expansionismo europeo bajo el disfraz del "Destino Manifiesto." En el siglo XXI, una nueva versión del Destino Manifiesto, denominada nacionalismo cristiano blanco, agita las iglesias y la nación. El nacionalismo cristiano blanco es una ideología envuelta en lenguaje religioso que ha distorsionado las verdades cristianas al servicio de fines políticos partidistas y nativistas, buscando asegurar la hegemonía de un sector selecto de la población, definido de las maneras más estrechas posible.[13] El Cristo hiperespiritualizado de los nacionalistas cristianos es una deidad completamente aria, con gorra de MAGA, que en los Estados Unidos legitimó los actos violentos de los insurrectos del 6 de enero de 2021, y que bendice las tendencias nativistas, xenofóbicas, homofóbicas/transfóbicas, patriarcales, y de extrema derecha de un grupo autoproclamado como los "verdaderos americanos."

Nos encontramos, sin duda, en un momento *kairós*, celebrando el 1700º aniversario del Concilio de Nicea. Que nuestra celebración sea un contraste radical y un recordatorio para aquellos que olvidan que es El histórico, encarnado, y moreno el que está presente en las Escrituras y quien fue y es confesado en Nicea y en su credo. Nicea confesó a este Jesús, Aquel que vivió entre los pobres que sufrían, sanando, vinculándose con los olvidados, para formar *vínculos de amor* entre Dios y la creación, entre los seres humanos entre sí, y entre la humanidad y la creación, para *que nadie se pierda*, como el Hijo de Dios, "Dios de Dios, Luz de Luz." El Concilio de Constantinopla (381 E.C.) y el Concilio de Calcedonia (425 E.C.) reafirmaron posteriormente las intuiciones proféticas de Nicea. De hecho, ante los repetidos intentos de "deshumanizar" a Jesús, Calcedonia declaró de manera inequívoca que Jesús era *completamente humano y completamente divino*. Por ello, la Iglesia da gracias y dice: "Amén".

Notes

1 Loida I. Martell-Otero, "Encuentro con el Jesús Sato: An Evangélica Soter-ology," en *Jesus in the Hispanic Community*, eds. Harold Recinos y Hugo Magallanes (Louisville, KY: Westminster John Knox Press, 2010), 74.

2 Susan Durber, "Celebrating Nicaea: Convincing Sceptical Protestants Including Myself," *The Ecumenical Review* 75, no. 3 (Abril 2023): 210.

3 Me refiero al Primer Testamento a lo que tradicionalmente se ha denominado el Antiguo Testamento o la Biblia Hebrea, y me refiero al Segundo Testamento a lo que tradicionalmente se llama el Nuevo Testamento.

4 Veáse Vladimr Kharlamov, *Theosis: Deification in Christian Theology*, Vol. II (Eugene, OR: Pickwick Publications, 2011), 9.

5 St. Irenaeus, *Against Heresies*, in *The Ante-Nicene Fathers: The Writings of the Fathers Down to A.D. 325*, Vol. 1, eds. Alexander Roberts and James Donaldson (Peabody, MA: Hendrikson Publishers, 1994), III.10.2.

6 Benjamin Mogoİ, "Arius, Alexander, and Athanasius: The Essential Role They Played in the Development of Christology at the First Ecumenical Council of Nicaea and Its Immediate Context," *Jurnal teologic* 22 (2023): 90.

7 Gustavo Gutiérrez, *The God of Life*, trans. Matthew J. O'Connell (Maryknoll, NY: Orbis Books, 1991), 85.

8 Orlando E. Costas, *Christ Outside the Gate: Mission Beyond Christendom* (Maryknoll, NY: Orbis Books, 1982), 188-194.

9 Karl Barth, *Church Dogmatics*, Vol. IV.1, *The Doctrine of Reconciliation*, ed. G. W. Bromiley and T. F. Torrance, trans. G. W. Bromiley (Edinburgh: T&T Clark, 1956), 27, 36.

10 Entiendo *vínculos* significar "lazos intimos que nos atan."

11 Albert Schweitzer, *The Quest for the Historical Jesus: A Critical Study of its Progress from Reimarus to Wrede* (Baltimore: John Hopkins University Press, 1998), 4.

12 Martin Luther, *Luther's Works*, vol. 27, *Galatians (1535)*, ed. Jaroslav Pelikan (St. Louis: Concordia, 1964), 177.

13 Va más allá del alcance de este ensayo abarcar toda la literatura abundante sobre este tema. Por lo tanto, refiero al lector a la publicación reciente del Consejo Nacional de Iglesias, *Confronting Racism and White Supremacy in the US: Twenty-First-Century Theological Perspectives*, ed. Michael R. Fisher, Jr. (Wnycote, PA: Friendship Press, 2024).

13

The Spacious God: Practicing Nicaea in a Time of Closing Borders

Anthony J. Chvala-Smith

> They're poisoning the blood of our country. . . . They're coming into our country from Africa, from Asia, from all over the world.[1]

> The love of God is broad like beach and meadow, wide as the wind, and an eternal home.[2]

THESE TWO QUOTATIONS voice starkly opposing visions of twenty-first-century life. We live amid a global conflict about the search for space—safe space for human flourishing, and moreover for simple survival. Refugees fleeing torture, violence, environmental degradation, and genocide regularly meet with nativist suspicion, malevolent populist rhetoric, restrictive immigration policies, separation of families, and denial of the very idea of their refugee status. Victims of massive economic, social, and ecological upheavals, their very existence has been turned to tinder by political opportunists who seek to set ablaze the same furnaces of nationalism that proved so deadly in the nineteenth and twentieth centuries. Across the globe, the recent past has witnessed elections "dominated . . . by nationalists emphasizing border control, national identity and the need to abandon international commitments."[3] Kaan's hymn deepens the agony of this situation: a longing for freedom, for "space and scope for dreaming," now met by walls and fences,[4] built expressly to bar the entry of the those deemed "other."

In brief, the Church now sojourns through a time of closing borders. Christian communities, embedded as they are in distinct times and places, perennially live from two necessary demands of their vocation. These are to be faithful to the God of the Jesus Story and to be morally and intellectually credible to the world in which they live. "Context" is never simply the concern of theologians and scholars; in their weekly life, congregations themselves must also attend to the social and political complexities of their own settings. Embodiedness in the particular is how the good news always makes its way through history. And so, the Church cannot avoid its current milieu, even when it wants to.

Churches widely acknowledge that they exist to serve the mission of God in the world. But in a social-political setting of borders barred and shut, refugees expelled, and immigrants deported, not to mention the racism—expressed or implied—that underwrites many of these policies, how do we articulate God's mission? And indeed, what will we affirm about the God who gives us this mission? What is our theological task in this moment? More precisely as related to this chapter, what would it mean to commemorate the 1700th anniversary of the "first draft" of the Nicene Creed,[5] an ancient text seemingly remote from the cruel, hate-filled, nationalistic landscapes of the present?

It is this contemporary setting, I maintain, that gifts us with a new lens by which to explore Nicaea and its Creed. In what follows I will insist that the Nicene understanding of God can give the Church today a renewed *theo*-logical foundation for confronting the ideology behind the rhetoric and action of closing borders.

The Council of Nicaea, 325 CE

The First Council of Nicaea met to confront a theological crisis. As theology can never be severed from politics and culture, it is to be noted that this council gathered under the aegis of an empire that once sought the Church's destruction. However, reductionism is the enemy of nuanced thought, and therefore relegating the meaning of Nicaea solely to imperial interference is unconstructive, missing the splendor of the forest for the sake of one tree. There was far more at stake for the Church at Nicaea than playing nice with Constantine.

What did Christians mean when they said "God"? In 325, as now, "God" could be a convenient cipher for nearly any human project, including those that sought to turn deity into a mascot for ends utterly inimical to the Jesus Story. The main questions Nicaea addressed were twofold. First, who is the God who "in Christ was reconciling the world to himself" (2 Corinthians 5:19)? And second, in what way is God *in* Christ?" These questions were not new: as Christianity increasingly became a notable religious phenomenon in the third century, the relationship of Christ as Son to God as ultimate source preoccupied theologians, leading to unsatisfactory answers, such as those of Paul of Samosata and Sabellius.[6]

In the decades leading up to Nicaea, those questions persisted, and it was an Alexandrian priest named Arius who proffered a new and controversial response. Following third-century precursors, Arius and his supporters sought to secure the one God's absolute transcendence by erecting a *cordon sanitaire* to wall off the ineffable Father from all that was less than God.[7] Arius's idea of God was a remix of the remote "One" of late Hellenistic philosophy, only now this One at some point prior to the creation of the world made the Word/Logos/Son as an exalted creature. Hence the Arians quipped, "There was when he [the Word/Son] was not." If Christ was divine for Arius, it was only as a lesser, derived, and purely contingent divinity. In effect, this theological move, which ostensibly wanted to preserve an absolute monotheism, ended up evacuating God from the world and appropriating to the Word the business of acting on the creaturely side of this wall. Arius's God turned out to be distant from creatures, an aloof monad dwelling in a philosophically compulsory quarantine from the creation. But many in the Church saw that this deity could hardly be the God who so loves the world and is love (1 John 4:16), and thus who reaches out to and welcomes creatures. As theologian Arthur

McGill concisely expressed it, "Arius was convinced that divinity . . . *cannot be communicated*. . . . Wholly by itself and within itself it is completely *absolute*."[8] Between the divine "Other" and all finite beings, Arius imagined an uncrossable border.

Nicaea rejected Arius's remix. Only God can make Godself known, and thus the Word / Son in whom this has decisively happened is not a "less than." The Word / Son is not some kind of middleman or broker, a demigod managing affairs on the creaturely side of Arius's wall. Rather, in the words of the Creed, Christ is: "God from God, light from light, true God from true God . . . consubstantial [*homoousion*] with the Father, through whom all things came to be."[9] The God of the Christian proclamation—even as infinite mystery—is not other than or removed from the one who welcomed sinners and ate with them (Luke 15:2). In light of Nicaea, to say "God," to confess faith in "God," and to worship "God" invites the Church to a way of life in which making room at the table is the binding ethos of Christian community. The infinite God is not other than what is revealed in Jesus Christ.

Athanasius's Generous God

In the aftermath of the Council of Nicaea, no figure towered over the ecclesial landscape more than Athanasius of Alexandria (296-373). This was true no less for his resolute defense of the Nicene doctrine of God, as for his endurance of multiple exiles for his uncompromising stance. As a deacon, he was present at Nicaea, serving as his bishop Alexander's secretary, but what other role he played there—if any—is unknown.[10] But after 325, few thinkers grasped more fully than he what was in the balance theologically when it came to articulating the relation of the Second to the First Person of the Trinity. Athanasius only commented directly on the Creed's contested term *homoousios* much later,[11] but his teaching and writing saw in Nicene theology neither an alien philosophical overlay nor a spiritual dead-end. Rather, he saw that the Creed voiced—as much as words can—the living center of the Church's faith, that "It is the only Son, himself God, who is close to the Father's heart, who has made [God] known" (John 1:18).

Athanasius grasped something of the profound implications of the Church's faith that God is eternally Christ-shaped. His invaluable treatise *On the Incarnation of the Word*, written around 335-336,[12] is profoundly relevant to our current context, reflecting as it does on Nicaea's claim that the Word who became flesh in Jesus of Nazareth is fully divine. As the Christian doctrines of creation and redemption overlap and mutually interpret each other, early in his treatise Athanasius reflects on the creation of the universe and the nature of its Creator. He says, "[T]hrough the Word God brought the universe into being from non-existence."[13] This act, he maintains, arises not out of necessity but from divine goodness, for, he writes, "the good has no envy for anything."[14] Then Athanasius makes the following quite remarkable statement: "Thus, because [God] envies nothing its existence, he made everything from nothing through the Word, our Lord Jesus Christ."[15] Through the Nicene lens, Athanasius sees that the very existence of that which is other than God is itself a gift of unfathomable generosity. Through the divine Word, God has ungrudgingly, graciously, liberally made a place for creatures.

Centuries later other theologians will develop this idea. The Swiss theologian Emil Brunner (1889-1966) writes, "A world that is not God exists alongside of Him [sic]. This, however, means that God does not wish to occupy the whole of Space Himself, but that he wills to make room for other forms of existence."[16] The self-emptying that comes to a climax in the death of Christ, Brunner goes on to say, "began with the creation of the world."[17] Similarly, Jürgen Moltmann (1926-2024), referencing the Jewish mystic Isaac Luria (1534-1572), argues that "in order to create a world 'outside' himself, the infinite God must have made room beforehand for a finitude in himself."[18] God creates in self-limiting love, Moltmann maintains, "by letting-be, by making room, and by withdrawing himself.[19]

The Spacious God

Nicaea envisions God's being in terms of an unfathomably outgoing generosity and an inner relationality. The doctrine of the Trinity never was a numbers game. "The issue between Arius and Athanasius," McGill writes, "has nothing to do with whether God is one or two or three. It has to do with what quality makes God divine. . . . Love and not transcendence, giving and not being superior, are the qualities that mark God's divinity."[20] This is true not only in the doctrine of creation, but also in the inner life of God. Much later the tradition will come to use the term *perichŏrĕsis* for the interrelationality or reciprocity of the three persons of the Trinity. In William Placher's words, that term indicates that "the three persons make room for each other."[21]

In brief, the Nicene Creed of 325 attempted to express that the God made known in Jesus Christ, adored in worship, re-presented in sacraments, attested in spoken word and liberative actions, and encountered in prayer, is the *spacious* God. God has acted freely in accord with the divine being and character—boundless Love, table-opening Word, life-freeing Spirit. God's nature is to unstintingly make room for finite creatures, who, created in the *imago trinitatis*, "long for freedom where our truest being is given hope and courage to unfold."[22]

It is quite one thing to commemorate the 1700th anniversary of the Council of Nicaea, and even to recite the later Nicene-Constantinopolitan Creed in worship. But in a world in which many nations are racing to close borders, turn away refugees, foster fear of the other, and marshal the nationalist rhetoric of protecting "ethnic purity," would it not be more faithful and responsive to the gospel if the churches *practiced* Nicaea? What would it mean if, in the spirit of Nicaea, we took deeply to heart the charge from Ephesians 5:1-2a, "be initiators of God, as beloved children, and walk in love, as Christ loved us"? What can Nicaea mean in our context, when political figures promise to create new *cordons sanitaires* to keep out those deemed less than, and when even churchgoing persons applaud a politics of exclusion and deportation that demonizes immigrants and ends their children's hope for a new future? Nicene Orthodoxy knew of divine spaciousness. But as the anniversary of the venerable First Ecumenical Council comes and goes, what must abide is a new, creative commitment to Nicene orthopraxy. To practice Nicaea will mean, among other things, to live, work, pray, and advocate in the light of the one whom the ancient Creed reveals to us as the space-making God.

Notes

1 Ginger Gibson, "Trump Says Immigrants Are 'Poisoning' the Blood of Our Country," NBC News, website, December 17, 2023, https://www.nbcnews.com/politics/2024-election/trump-says-immigrants-are-poisoning-blood-country-biden-campaign-liken-rcna130141.

2 Fred Kaan, "The Love of God," stanza 1in *Community of Christ Sings* (Independence, MO: Herald Publishing House, 2013), hymn 210.

3 Ben Anseti, "History Has Never Ended, but Are We at a Crossroads Again?" Nationalism vs. Liberalism: Is History at a Crossroads Again? NPR (December 20, 2024).

4 Kaan, "Love of God," stanza 2, in *Community of Christ Sings*, hymn 210.

5 The creed of 325 CE was revised at the Council of Constantinople in 381; whether in Eastern or Western churches, it is the 381 creed (the Nicene-Constantinopolitan Creed) that is commonly identified as the "Nicene Creed."

6 Paul of Samosata taught that Jesus was an inspired man, the terms Son and Word being merely names given to him; Sabellius taught that the terms Father, Son, and Spirit refer to successive appearances of the one God. See J. N. D. Kelly, *Early Chrisian Doctrines*, 5th ed. (London: Continuum, 2000), 117 and 121-123.

7 See Rowan Williams, "Athanasius and the Arian Crisis," in *The First Christian Theologians: An Introduction to Theology in the Early Church*, ed. by G. R. Evans (Malden, MA: Blackwell, 2004), 157-167.

8 Arthur C. McGill, *Suffering: A Test of Theological Method*, foreword by Paul Ramsey and William F. May (Philadelphia: Westminster, 1968/1982), 70.

9 "The Creed of Nicaea," in *Creeds and Confessions of Faith in the Christian Tradition, vol. I, Early, Eastern and Medieval*, ed. Jaroslav Pelikan and Valerie Hotchkiss (New Haven: Yale, 2003), 159.

10 Thomas G. Weinandy, *Athanasius: A Theological Introduction*, Great Theologians Series, ed. John Webster, et al. (Aldershot, England: Ashgate, 2007), 2.

11 See R. P. C. Hanson, *The Search for the Christian Doctrine of God: The Arian Controversy, 318-381* (Grand Rapids: Baker, 2005), 436-445.

12 Hanson, *The Search for the Christian Doctrine of God*, 418.

13 Athanasius, *Contra Gentes* and *De Incarnatione*, ed. and trans. Robert W. Thompson (Oxford: Clarendon, 1975), 3.5-7; p. 141.
14 Athanasius, *Contra Gentes* and *De Incarnatione*, 3:13-14.
15 Athanasius, *Contra Gentes* and *De Incarnatione*, 3:14-16.
16 Emil Brunner, *The Christian Doctrine of Creatin and Redemption, Dogmatics: Volume II*, trans. Olive Wyon (Philadelphia: Westminster, 1952), 20.
17 Brunner, *The Christian Doctrine of Creation and Redemption, Dogmatics*, 20.
18 Jürgen Moltmann, *God in Creation: A New Theology of Creation and the Spirit of God, the Gifford Lectures, 1984-85,* trans. Margaret Kohl (San Francisco: HarperCollins, 1991), 86.
19 Moltmann, *God in Creation*, 88.
20 McGill, *Suffering: A Test of Theological Method, 78.*
21 William C. Placher, *The Triune God: An Essay in Postliberal Theology* (Louisville: Westminster John Knox, 2007), 155.
22 Kaan, "The Love of God," stanza 2, in *Community of Christ Sings*, hymn 210.

14

Nicaea in a Time of Ceasefire

Paul A. McAllister

AS CHRISTIANS COMMEMORATE the 1700th anniversary of Nicaea, during which the First Ecumenical Council inaugurated a new era in the history of Christianity regarding both the faith and order of the Church, it does so in the context of a world that grapples with a parade of wars and conflicts influenced by ideology, nationalism, and economic interests. From ongoing strife in the Middle East to tensions in Eastern Europe and the Asia-Pacific region, each conflict not only engenders suffering but also complicates the Christian witness in society.

In this climate, the Church is confronted by many questions on aggression and the pretense of war as stalwart obstacles to peace and justice in the world. From a New Testament perspective, the call to peace (Matthew 5:9) is also an acknowledgment of the reality of conflict (James 4:1). The duality of this teaching suggests that Christians are compelled to grapple with the moral implications of conflict that exists among the nations as they learn under the influence of the Church to "beat their swords into plowshares and their spears into pruning hooks" (Isaiah 2:4). By taking such an active role in peacebuilding, the quest for Christian unity is recognized and realized by Jesus's high priestly prayer for his followers (John 17:21). Consequently, both the identity and the prayerful aspirations of Jesus, also represented in Nicaea, serve as the foundation for the modern Church's peacebuilding efforts. Divided denominations often project a fractious image, undermining the Church's credibility in advocating peace and reconciliation and abandoning disharmonious conflict in international relations, which may lead to war.

As the common heritage of all Christian denominations, the Nicene Creed may be interpreted to suggest the need for the Church to seek alternatives to the vengeful malice of war. "Through him all things were made" (see John 1:3, NIV; Colossians 1:16) emphasizes the positive, creative aspect of the divine nature, which humanity, also made in the image of God, richly shares. "For us and our salvation, he came down and was incarnate" attests to the strength to love of a caring Supreme Being who, despite the morally diminished condition of humankind and their incapacity to ascend toward God, performs the infinite act of descension to redeem and restore creation; to become "despised and rejected, a Man of sorrows, acquainted with grief," and familiar with human suffering (see Isaiah 53:3). "He will come again to judge the living and the dead" is a constant reminder of human accountability. The resolution of disputes ends with the divine and is not left to "the last one standing," in an apparent mal-attempt at self-vindication, versus those who, being faithful and loving despite evil, choose to be light on behalf of God toward others. Is not peacemaking the antithesis of war-making, and are not those who share communion with Christ also called to abhor conditions that make room for hostility? If so, it may be argued that the Nicene Creed, as the symbol of the faith "once and for all delivered to the saints," may be thought of as a charge to proactively contest the unvirtuousness of war in its various forms and call for a ceasefire among all nations.

In recent times, we have seen how the courage of many Christian denominations and individual leaders from various traditions has led them to sound the alarm of ceasefire and warn political officials and governments to "Depart from evil and do good; seek peace, and pursue it" (Psalm 34:14). Since 2010, conflicts in Asia, the Democratic Republic of the Congo, the Central African Republic, Israel-Palestine, Lebanon, Myanmar, Syria, Sudan, Ukraine, Russia, and Yemen have all occasioned calls for ceasefire from Christian churches and denominations around the world. Each call has emphasized the moral and ethical imperatives of peace and reconciliation, as well as humanitarian assistance rooted in Christian teachings. Among the many church bodies that have issued clear and compelling statements that demand a ceasefire are:

- World Council of Churches (WCC)
- Catholic Church under Pope Francis
- National Council of the Churches of Christ in the USA (NCC)
- Archbishop of Canterbury and the House of Bishops of the Church of England
- United Methodist Church
- Baptist World Alliance
- United Church of Christ
- Lutheran World Federation
- Federation of Asian Bishops' Conferences (FABC)
- Christian Churches in the Democratic Republic of the Congo (DRC)
- National Association of Evangelicals
- World Communion of Reformed Churches
- Anglican Communion
- Greek and Roman Orthodox Churches
- South African Council of Churches (SACC)

The United Nations Office for the Coordination of Humanitarian Affairs (OCHA) has also led faith-based initiatives for humanitarian responses that often include calls for ceasefires and peace efforts in war zones worldwide. Notwithstanding this list, Christians have not always been united in their theological views on the need for a truce. Denominationalism has not responded to the prayer of Jesus, aptly expressed in the words of one hymn writer:

> Christians all should dwell together in the bonds of peace,
> All the clashing of opinions, all the strife should cease,
> Let divisions be forsaken, all the holy join in one,
> And the will of God in all be done.[1]

Nicaea has been an impetus for the unity of thought and understanding in matters of Christian faith. It laid a firm foundation for what would later be established in the present ecumenical movement. Nonetheless, while peace, reconciliation, and the value of human life are resonant themes within the global Christian community, which has had numerous opportunities to extend the significance of Nicaea into the realm of statecraft vis-a-vis political theology, it does not exhibit unanimity on how to arrive at nonviolence and ceasefire. Such missed opportunities stem from churches having different theological interpretations of the Bible, political contexts, cultural backgrounds, and varying attitudes toward conflict, which often splinter and divide the Christian community. For example, concerning how the Bible must be read, one clergyman posted the following comment on social media:

> Notice how it's always "the Bible must be taken literally!" until it says, "When a foreigner resides among you in your land, do not mistreat them. The foreigner residing among you must be treated as your native-born. Love them as yourself" (Leviticus 19:33-34).[2]

The tragedy of indifference toward people is expressed in the following statement issued on February 14, 2025, by the Patriarchs and Heads of the Churches in Jerusalem. It captures the essence of what the message of the Church should be in a time of ceasefire:

> *A Humanitarian Plea from the Churches of Jerusalem: Defending the Dignity and Presence of the People of Gaza*
>
> As custodians of the Christian faith and conscience in this sacred land, we raise our voices in sorrow and steadfast resolve in the face of the ongoing suffering in Gaza. The devastation that has unfolded before the eyes of the world is a profound moral and humanitarian tragedy. Thousands of innocent lives have been lost, and entire communities stand in ruin, with the most vulnerable—children, the elderly, and the sick—enduring unimaginable hardship.
>
> Amid this anguish, we are compelled to speak against the grave threat of mass displacement, an injustice that

strikes at the very heart of human dignity. The people of Gaza, families who have lived for generations in the land of their ancestors, must not be forced into exile, stripped of whatever is left of their homes, their heritage, and their right to remain in the land that forms the essence of their identity. As Christians, we cannot be indifferent to such suffering, for the Gospel commands us to uphold the dignity of every human being. The words of our Lord remind us: "Woe to those who make unjust laws, to those who issue oppressive decrees, to deprive the poor of their rights and withhold justice from the oppressed" (Isaiah 10:1-2[NIV]).

In this critical moment, we acknowledge and support the position of His Majesty King Abdullah II of Jordan, President El-Sisi of Egypt, and others, whose firm and principled stance has remained clear and unwavering in rejecting any attempt to uproot the people of Gaza from their land. Their relentless efforts to provide humanitarian aid, appeal to the world's conscience, and insist on the protection of civilians exemplify leadership at its highest level of responsibility.

In this same spirit, we also call for the release of all captives from both sides so that they can be safely reunited with their families. We also appeal to all people of faith, to governments, and to the international community to act swiftly and decisively to halt this catastrophe. Let there be no justification for the uprooting of a people who have already suffered beyond measure. Let the sanctity of human life and the moral obligation to protect the defenseless outweigh the forces of destruction and despair. We call for immediate, unfettered humanitarian access to those in desperate need. To abandon them now would be to abandon our shared humanity.

As we lift our prayers for those in mourning, for the wounded, and for those who remain steadfast in the land of their forefathers, we remember the promise of Scripture: "The LORD upholds all who fall and lifts all who are bowed down" (Psalm 145:14). May the God of mercy strengthen the afflicted, soften the hearts of those who hold power, and bring forth a peace that upholds justice, preserves human dignity, and safeguards the presence of all people in the land to which they belong.[3]

Indeed, this statement confronts the fundamental question of human dignity. It also approaches the uneasy subjects of mass displacement, i.e., ethnic cleansing and the undeniable violence of unjust decision-making by political leaders. Like other tragic situations where unimaginable human suffering, disease, death, and destruction have occurred, Gaza has provided an opportunity for the Church to embrace a renewed Faith and Order statement about the life of Christ through whom God entered the world to reconcile humanity to God. Furthermore, the timing of Gaza (during the 1700th anniversary of Nicaea) should beckon the Church to consider how it interfaces with persons engaged in statecraft, as Jesus himself did, regardless of the type of government that is involved. A Church that "render(s) unto Caesar that which is Caesar's, and unto God the things that are God's" (see Matthew 22:21; cf. Mark 12:17) fulfills its duty to live faithfully in the world while not seeking to function in the same manner as the world. However, in the context of nonviolence, the legitimacy of the Church that lives and abides in Christ depends upon its willingness to not only "render unto Caesar" but mount strong arguments against his wrongdoing. In this vein, if the Church ever becomes mute in the face of legalistic and doctrinaire expressions of faith that justify wars grounded in militarism, materialism, and racism—three evils of society as branded by Martin Luther King, Jr.—it will cease to have relevance. Consequently, one of the significant aspects of Nicaea today is that it is celebrated at a time when there is consensus among the Church that looks into the shell-shocked eyes of Gaza and is willing to offer more than casual gestures of concern. Nicaea today means a Church committed to and empowered by its revolutionary leader to "do justice and to love kindness / and to walk humbly with your God" (Micah 6:8).

Consequently, one of the significant considerations for the Church is how its unity and witness become strengthened through its message of ceasefire, as it also remembers the ideas on violence and war of various theologians and philosophers. Among this group are St. Augustine and St. Thomas Aquinas (*Summa Theologiae*), whose contributions within the Christian tradition on the theory of just war became the foundation of later moral and philosophical frameworks on nonviolence and war that are more broadly applicable.[4] These include Immanuel Kant's deontological beliefs, where peace is a categorical imperative, where war is an untrusted means to achieving peaceful ends; Hannah Arendt's teaching of nature of power, violence, and ethical action; and John Rawls's exploration of a "just society" that involves peace, fairness and the moral responsibility of nations. Kant's arguments seem to resonate most with the contemporary human rights agenda, where despite inherent tensions of human nature, individuals and states are viewed as having sovereign rights that should be protected, and states should assemble to resolve grievances that can lead to war. St. Augustine's theory of just war, which contemporary philosopher Michael Walzer most closely follows, does not address the problem of war itself. On the contrary, their philosophical frameworks are limited to understanding the moral justification, military conduct, and the conduct of war. Nonetheless, a brief comparison of their views is essential as they have a tremendous bearing upon the unity of the Church that seeks to "do justice and to love kindness and to walk humbly."

When Augustine developed his theory of Just War within the framework of Christian theology during the decline of the Roman Empire, he sought to address the theodicy question: How can a just God permit violence and war? Aquinas would further his argument, war that can be justified only when the following conditions have been met: a) the cause itself, such as self-defense or protecting the innocent from those who would perpetrate evil, is just; a legitimate authority has declared war; righteous intent to restore peace and seek reconciliation supersedes all other intentions; and military action taken is proportional to the actual circumstances of war such that the benefits of military action outweigh the harm likely to occur.

The perspective of Augustine was grounded in Christian theology and emphasized divine justice and moral order. He also underscored the authority of legitimate government in declaring war, aligning with his understanding of divine order. While he touched on the ethical conduct of soldiers during warfare, he did not delve into critical issues that have since become important in the twenty-first century, such as rules of military engagement, the treatment of enemies, or innocent civilians in combat, as did later theorists such as Walzer.[5] His work is inherently prescriptive and linked to the moral obligations of rulers.

Published in 1977, Walzer's *Just and Unjust Wars* is viewed as an essential treatise that applies ethical reasoning to real-world warfare, drawing from historical, political, and philosophical analysis. Unlike Augustine, Walzer's theory embodies a secular ethics approach focused on collective human judgment regarding justice in warfare, reflecting a pluralistic moral landscape. Walzer also recognizes the role of state authority but opens the conversation to non-state actors, reflecting modern geopolitical realities. While supporting Augustine's four moral criteria for war, he assessed topics such as equal moral standing (the principles of conduct apply equally to all sides in a conflict, regardless of the war's legitimacy) and boundaries of moral unacceptability even in just wars. He sought to distinguish the difference between combatants and noncombatants and proportionality in using force.

While it is true that Christian unity depends upon the orthodoxy of faith—the correct belief or doctrine based on Scripture—it also needs to draw strength through orthopraxy, the proper practice or implementation of truth in life, rooted in the appropriate understanding, and the ability to comprehend and interpret information accurately. As a peacemaking community, the Church must continue its calls for a ceasefire while not becoming like a bystander to the realities of war. It can draw from the lessons of Nicaea and seize upon the opportunity to contend with the moral and theological considerations surrounding war and do so within an Augustinian construct, which laid the groundwork for the divine imperative in opposition to war. To do so would not only enhance the persuasiveness of the Church in its salvific mission but assure its bonds of unity across traditions and cultures, denominations, and geographies, which are not diminished in the presence of raging ideological tensions and political struggles throughout the world.

Notes

1 Charles W. Baylor and Andrew L. Byers, "The Reformation Glory," stanza 4, *Worship the Lord: Hymnal of the Church of God* (Anderson, IN: Warner Press, 1989), 311.

2 Benjamin Cremer, Facebook, April 9, 2025, https://www.facebook.com/share/p/1TL9iRMUP7/?mibextid=wwXIfr.

3 "Statement by the Patriarchs and Heads of Churches in Jerusalem," Patriarchate of Jerusalem, website, April 14, 2025, https://en.jerusalem-patriarchate.info/announcements/79743/.

4 "Just War Theory," Internet Encyclopedia of Philosophy, accessed April 14, 2025, https://iep.utm.edu/justwar/.

5 See Michael Walzer, *Just and Unjust Wars: A Moral Argument with Historical Illustrations* (New York: Basic Books, 1992).

15

More than a Bird: Pentecostal Reflections on the Creed and the Deity of the Holy Spirit

Robby Waddell

REFLECTING ON THE third article of the Nicene-Constantinopolitan Creed, this chapter provides an extended meditation on the doctrine of the Holy Spirit. The essay contributes to contemporary theological discourse by placing ecumenical doctrines and select passages of Scripture into dialogue with Pentecostal spirituality.[1] Underscoring the doxological shape of Trinitarian theology, the logic of the essay advocates for an approach that prioritizes worship over doctrinal formulations. From this doxological perspective, observations are offered about the life of the Holy Spirit within the interiority of the Trinity followed by a discussion concerning the mission of the Spirit in the life of Jesus Christ, his Church, and the world.

Pentecostals do not typically recite a creed in their worship services. In fact, many early Pentecostals were anti-creedal, believing that the creeds lacked the capacity to articulate or safeguard sound doctrine because they were not divinely inspired.[2] This early resistance to formal dogma notwithstanding, Pentecostal pneumatology is congruent with the ecumenical creeds, particularly the beliefs that the Spirit is divine and worthy of worship and that the Spirit has (and does) inspire prophetic speech. While it is true that some Pentecostals, though certainly not all, have imagined that they possess the Spirit in an exclusive way, making them superior to other Christians who lack their experience, that is not the view promoted here. Rather, I concur with the words of the ecumenist and Dominican theologian Yves Congar, "The Holy Spirit is the principle of catholicity."[3] The following reflections are offered in that spirit of ecumenism.

How (Not) to Speak of the Holy Spirit

Attempting to depict in word or image the nature and activity of the Spirit of God is a nearly impossible task because all comparisons ultimately fail to define the indescribable God. The Church's best thinkers have taught us that theology, at its truest, gestures toward but does not grasp the unfathomable mystery that is the divine. Irenaeus describes the Son and the Spirit as the two hands of the Father, working in the world to create and to restore, deifying creation and bringing it into union with the Father (*Against Heresies* 1.22.1).[4] Augustine utilizes the biblical metaphor of love, speaking of the Father as the Lover, the Son as the Beloved, and the Spirit as the Bond of Love between them (*On the Trinity* 15.5).[5] While helpful in certain ways, the latter metaphor was and sometimes still is taken to mean the Spirit is less personal. The Spirit is not an abstract power or energy, however. The Spirit is fully personal, which of course Augustine affirms in his Trinitarian theology. The Spirit interacts, communicates, and relates to and through the humanity of the incarnate Christ, and so to and through the Church, and to and through nature as well.

Iconography, which has often aided Christians in the contemplation of God, also has its carefully discerned and honored limits. For example, God the Father is frequently depicted as an old man, Jesus as a young man, and the Spirit as a dove. As Sandra Schneiders famously quipped, "God is more than two men and a bird."[6] Appealing to more diverse metaphors from Scripture that portray God in less human or masculine terms is helpful, though in the end, icons like words always fall short. It is said that "concepts create idols; only wonder comprehends,"[7] which is why Trinitarian theology ought to take a doxological form. In this way, the end goal is not to describe God but rather to worship, orienting the gaze of the Church and in turn the world toward the beauty and mystery of the triune God.

Worship of the ineffable God is best expressed apophatically (i.e., in silence beyond words, emotions, or images); and yet, this neither inhibits knowledge nor impoverishes intellectual reflection. As Paul writes, "I pray that you may have the power to comprehend, with all the saints, what is the breadth and length and height and depth and to know the love of Christ that surpasses knowledge" (Ephesians 3:18-19). The doxological character of this endeavor also carries profound ecumenical ramifications. Christian communities may articulate their faith in diverse ways, but such theological formulations are inherently partial and should be held loosely in light of the deeper unity they point toward. It is a travesty and betrayal of grace that Christians fail to welcome one another to the eucharistic table in the worship of the one God in whom they all confess. To paraphrase Paul, albeit maintaining the timbre of his verse: "For in the one Spirit we were all baptized into one body—Jews or Greeks, slaves or free [Catholic, Orthodox, Protestant, or Pentecostal]—and we were all made to drink of one Spirit" (1 Corinthians 12:13). Building unity through a shared devotion to the apostles' teaching, fellowship, breaking of bread, and the prayers constitutes the mission of the Spirit of Pentecost (Acts 2:42).

It is not uncommon in such discussions for theologians to differentiate between the immanent and the economic Trinity. This terminology is often associated with noted theologian, Karl Rahner and his well-known "rule": "the economic Trinity is the immanent Trinity and vice versa."[8] The *economic* Trinity, on the one hand, is shorthand for the self-revelation of God through history in the act of creation, the incarnation of the Son, and the gift of the Spirit. The *immanent* Trinity, on the other hand, is shorthand for speaking of God's aseity, beyond history and time—the blessedness and unity of the one God, or what could be characterized as the eternal, interior processions which are independent of any exterior creative action. The distinction between the immanent and the economic can be beneficial, though it poses potential problems. For example, from the perspective of the first half of Rahner's rule, Hans Urs von Balthasar theologized about God's infinite freedom, "because the economic Trinity is grounded in and made possible by the immanent. But to reverse the axiom too simplistically runs the risk of mythologizing the Trinity by subjecting God to the vicissitudes of history."[9] In other words, God is truly revealed in history, but historical revelation does not exhaust or place fixed limits on God. Notwithstanding Balthasar's nuanced caveat, it is the incarnation of the Son—the central economic act of divine self-communication—that most clearly and fully reveals God to humanity (Hebrews 1:1-4). This is why the trifold structure of the creeds orbit around the second article because Jesus is the center, the one in whom all things are held together.

Thus, and this is key, whatever can be said about the Spirit must always be understood in relation to Jesus Christ and to the Father and never independently. Furthermore, a theology of the Spirit must include reflections on the mission of God in the world, including the Spirit's role in the life and ministry of Jesus Christ and the Spirit's activity in the life of the Church and in the world at large. The remainder of this essay offers a modest contemplation on the pneumatology of the Nicene-Constantinopolitan Creed, using the rubrics of procession and mission, framed respectively as the Holy Spirit in the life of God and the Holy Spirit in the life of the world.

The Holy Spirit in the Life of God

In this section I want to highlight two comments in the Creed: (1) the Spirit is "Lord" and (2) the Spirit "proceeds from the Father." By confessing the Spirit as the "Lord and Giver of Life," Christians profess a belief that the Spirit is divine—on par with the Father and the Son. In other words, the Holy Spirit is not a creature, lesser than or subservient to the Father and the Son, but is truly and fully God, contrary to the belief of some Christians in the early Church, the so-called Macedonians. In the fifth century, the Church would unequivocally embrace the full divinity of the Trinity. The first stanza of the Athanasian Creed reads: "We worship one God in trinity and the trinity in unity, neither blending their persons nor dividing their essence. . . . But the divinity of the Father, Son, and Holy Spirit is one, their glory equal, their majesty coeternal."

The reticence within the Nicene-Constantinopolitan Creed to explicitly declare the divinity of the Spirit may stem in part from the ambiguity in the biblical narrative. Since the earliest days of the Church, theologians have acknowledged the presence of the Holy Spirit throughout the canon, from the Creation stories in Genesis and the anointing of the Hebrew prophets to the life of Jesus and his first followers. The practice of appealing to the Bible as a source for Christian beliefs is not problematic, though it would be anachronistic, however, to imagine that the Hebrew Bible speaks unequivocally about the deity of God's Spirit in the same manner that the Christian creeds would eventually profess.[10] For this reason, the creators of the modern English translation, the New Revised Standard Version Updated Edition (NRSVue), consistently translate the Hebrew word *ruach* as wind, breath, or spirit with a lower case "s," including in phrases such as "spirit of the LORD" and "holy spirit." Be that as it may, what can be traced over the centuries is the emergence of a distinct theology of the Spirit that emphasizes the unity of the one God and the triunity of the Father, the Son, and the Holy Spirit. On the one hand, the Jewish *Shema* remains an uncompromising mantra for Christians: "the LORD our God is one." On the other hand, there are texts that would contribute to an understanding that this one God is triune, such as the salutation of Peter's first epistle: "To the exiles of the dispersion . . . who have been chosen and destined by God the Father and sanctified by the Spirit to be obedient to Jesus Christ" (1:1-2). This text is just one example among many that would shape the Trinitarian theology of the early Church.

The clause "who proceeds from the Father [and the Son]," served as a catalyst for one of the most notorious theological disputes in the history of the Church: the *filioque* controversy. Absent from the ecumenical creeds, the phrase "and the Son" (*filioque* in Latin) was added later by churches in the West. Being noncreedal in their liturgies and relative newcomers on the ecclesial landscape, most Pentecostals have little investment in this debate.[11] The issue is complex, historically and theologically, and a full assessment is beyond the scope of this essay, though its centrality to the pneumatology of the Church makes it too important to leave unaddressed.

The Eastern Church protested the addition of *filioque* on multiple grounds. First, it was inserted unilaterally without ecumenical consent; second, it disrupted the balance of how the Trinitarian internal relations were conceptualized. Eastern theologians claim that the Spirit's being sent forth from the Father alone maintains the "monarchy" of the Father as the source of the Trinity and provides a necessary rationale for the distinctiveness of the triune Persons in regard to their relations of origin. Inserting the additional phrase problematizes this distinction and suggests a possible subordination of the Spirit.[12] In contrast, some Western theologians contend that the *filioque* clause underscores the unity and consubstantiality of the Father and the Son and acknowledges the missional interrelationship of the Son and the Spirit. The question remains whether the insertion of the phrase has the capacity to communicate such nuances or simply muddles the issue more than clarifying it. Despite the important concerns raised in the dispute, the reality is that the doctrines in the East and the West are essentially the same regarding the Trinity. As Bishop Robert Barron suggests, the Orthodox and Catholic traditions agree on the simplicity and "unity of God, the co-equality of the Trinitarian persons, and the unoriginated primacy of the Father."[13]

Notwithstanding the political objections, a possible unifying perspective may be found in the Cappadocian father, Gregory of Nyssa, who described the divine relationship as the Spirit proceeding *from* the Father and *through* the Son.[14] This statement has the advantage of occupying a space between the Eastern and Western articulations of the Creed. It maintains the uniqueness of the Father's economy while acknowledging the role of the Son in the mission of the Spirit. The interconnection between the Spirit, Jesus, and the Father is supported by the biblical narrative. As previously mentioned, the Spirit incarnates Jesus within the Virgin Mary. John the Baptist announces Jesus's ministry as the Spirit baptizer. At Jesus's baptism, the Spirit descends onto him, and he hears the epiphanic whisper, "You are my Son, the Beloved." At the end of Gospel, Jesus attests, "I am sending upon you what my Father promised" (Luke 24:49). In Acts, the gift of the Father that is administrated by Jesus Christ, the Son, turns out to be the Spirit of Pentecost. Rather than seeing the resurrection of Jesus as the culminating point of his vocation, Pentecostal theologian Frank Macchia argues that Spirit Baptism occupies this position. According to Macchia, "Jesus' impartation of his risen life—and not merely the risen life per se [most clearly indicates] his essential unity with the Father and with the leading of the Spirit in fulfilling the Father's cause in the world."[15]

The Holy Spirit in the Life of the World

The Holy Spirit's life in the world correlates to three affirmations in the Creed, namely the Spirit as the giver of life, the Spirit as the one who is worshipped and glorified along with the Father and the Son, and the Spirit's inspiration of prophetic speech. Affirming the Spirit as the giver of life equates the work of the Spirit with the original act of creation. This can be seen somewhat clearer in the original Greek in which the word used to describe the Spirit forms a cognate with the words used to define the Father's creative activity. The Father is called the *maker* (*poieten*) of heaven and earth, and the Spirit is described as "the life-*maker*" (*zoopoion*). Identifying the Holy Spirit in the biblical narrative as an actor in creation (Genesis 1:2) and in the ongoing work of its renewal (Psalm 104:30) may be anachronistic from a modern scholarly perspective, though this did not prevent theologians in the early Church from readily making such claims, perhaps bolstered by the logic found in *First Clement* that the Scriptures "are the true sayings of the Holy Spirit" (45:2). Less debatable are the numerous places throughout the New Testament that attest to the Spirit's role in salvation and sanctification, affecting not only the human followers of Jesus but the whole cosmic order (Romans 8:9-24).

The Creed's declaration that the Spirit is worshipped and glorified together with the Father and the Son certainly outdistances the teaching of the New Testament. Biblical characters typically worship and pray *to* the Father *in* the name of Jesus and *with* the power of the Spirit. For that matter, worship of Jesus in the biblical texts is relatively rare, and there are no instances of the Spirit being worshipped with one possible exception. In the book of Revelation, the Lamb is described as having seven horns and seven eyes, which are the seven spirits of God. John witnesses the worship of the One on the throne *and* the seven-horned, seven-eyed Lamb, presumably the Father and Jesus Christ. If the symbol of the seven spirits is a trope for the Spirit of God, as I have argued elsewhere, then this text contains the sole, albeit veiled, reference to the worship of the Spirit.[16] This speculative hypothesis notwithstanding, the lack of prayers to the Spirit in Scripture is matched by a paucity of prayers to the Spirit in the Church. Prayers are directed to the Father and/or Son to *send down* the Spirit, however. Most eucharist liturgies contain a version of the *epiclesis*, an invocation to the Father for the Spirit to descend and consecrate the elements of communion. A notable exception of a prayer to the Holy Spirit is the Trisagion Prayers of the Orthodox Church: "O Heavenly King, Comforter, Spirit of Truth, Who art … the Lord and Giver of life: Come and dwell in us, and cleanse us of all impurity, and save our souls." Although prayers to the Spirit remain scarce, Trinitarian dogmatics clearly justify the practice.[17]

The Creed's final comment about the Spirit's mission involves the inspiration of prophetic speech. The Church has understood this work to stretch from the Hebrew prophets through the ministry of Jesus and into the early Church. Luke's account of the Day of Pentecost records the commencement of the outpouring of the Holy Spirit. The modern Pentecostal Movement takes its name from this story. Like all other Christians, Pentecostals pray and worship in the Spirit. Similar to some, but different than others, Pentecostals anticipate the presence of charismatic gifts during worship, including healings, exorcisms, and most notably speaking and interpreting tongues and prophecy. Although these manifestations occur in communal worship, much of the focus in Pentecostal teaching is on an individual experience of being baptized in the Spirit. Pentecostal theologian Simon Chan counterbalances this emphasis stating, "the primary locus of the work of the Spirit is not in the individual Christian but in the church."[18] For metaphorical support, Chan appeals to the baptism of Jesus, noting that the Spirit descended upon his body, i.e., the Church. This line of reasoning parallels the thinking of Paul in his first letter to the Corinthians where he writes that individual human bodies are members of the body of Christ. What is lost in translation is that Paul continues by adding that it is the singular body (of Christ) and not their individual bodies that now serves as the one-and-only temple of the Holy Spirit (1 Corinthians 6:15-19).

Postscript: An Ecumenical Appeal for Unity in the Spirit

The occasion for this essay is the 1700th anniversary of the Council of Nicaea. My goal has not been to forge new theological ground but to invite my readers to ponder the Holy Spirit in the light of Scripture and theology. In a spirit of ecumenism, I have attempted to equitably represent various Christian perspectives, including my own Pentecostal tradition. Hopefully this has been accomplished in a way that is truthful and hospitable. Others will have to judge whether this has been achieved. My primary point—which I wish to underscore before closing—is that meditations on the Holy Spirit require a Trinitarian and doxological shape from the beginning to end. As a mystery, the Trinity is better contemplated than explained. The subsequent sections of the essay are simply attempts to reflect on the Spirit in the life of God and on the Spirit's mission in the life of the world. To be clear, this mission is to deify the world through Jesus Christ, bringing the world into an eternal loving relationship with the Father, the source of everything. Once again echoing the words of Paul, I offer this benediction: "[May] the grace of the Lord Jesus Christ, the love of God, and the communion of the Holy Spirit be with all of you" (2 Corinthians 13:13).[19]

Notes

1 Most, but not all, Pentecostals are Trinitarian in their beliefs. This essay is written from that perspective. A branch of the tradition known as Oneness Pentecostalism, as represented in the United Pentecostal Church, stands on the following two doctrinal affirmations: "(1) There is one God with no distinction of persons; (2) Jesus Christ is the fullness of the Godhead incarnate," see David Bernard et al., *Meet the United Pentecostal Church International* (Hazelwood, MO: Word Aflame, 1989), 56. For a discussion

of Oneness beliefs vis-à-vis the early church, see David Bernard, *Oneness and Trinity, A.D. 100-300: The Doctrine of God in Ancient Christian Writings* (Hazelwood, MO: Word Aflame, 1989).

2 Cecil M. Robeck, "A Pentecostal Perspective on Apostolicity," paper presented to Faith and Order, National Council of Churches, Consultation on American Born Churches, March 1992 (unpublished), 2-3.

3 Yves Congar, *I Believe in the Holy Spirit*, trans. David Smith, three volumes in one (New York: Crossroad, 1997), 2:24. For a critique of an exclusivist pneumatology within Pentecostalism, see Chris E. W. Green, "The Spirit that Makes Us (Number) One: Racism, Tongues, and the Evidences of Spirit Baptism," *Pneuma* 41, no. 3-4 (2019): 397-420, (esp. 416-417). For a Pentecostal articulation of catholicity, see Veli-Matti Kärkkäinen, "Catholicity, Full Gospel, and Fullness of the Spirit: A Pentecostal Perspective on the Third Mark of the Church 1," *Asian Journal of Pentecostal Studies* 23, no. 1 (2020): 5-14.

4 Irenaeus, "Against Heresies," in *The Ante-Nicene Fathers*, eds. Alexander Roberts and James Donaldson, vol. 1 (Peabody, MA: Hendrickson, 1994), 347.

5 Augustine, *The Trinity*, trans. Edmund Hill (Brooklyn: New York City Press, 1991), 418-426. For a theological critique of the analogy of love, see Vladimir Lossky, *The Mystical Theology of the Eastern Church* (Crestwood, NY: St. Vladimir's Seminary Press, 1976), 81.

6 Sandra Schneiders, "God Is More than Two Men and a Bird," *U.S. Catholic*, May 1, 1990.

7 Jürgen Moltmann, like many others, mistakenly attributes the statement to Gregory of Nyssa, whose theology nonetheless concurs with the sentiment of the phrase. Moltmann will, however, correctly advocate for the doxological form of Trinitarian theology; see Jürgen Moltmann, *The Spirit of Life: A Universal Affirmation* (Minneapolis: Fortress Press, 1992), 73.

8 Karl Rahner, "Oneness and Threefoldness of God in Discussion with Islam," in *Theological Investigations*, vol.18, trans. E. Quinn (New York: Crossroad, 1983), 105-121 (esp. 114).

9 Christopher Hadley, "The All-Embracing Frame: Distance in the Trinitarian Theology of Hans Urs von Balthasar" (PhD diss., Marquette University, 2015), 165.

10 For example, Jack Levison makes a strong case that the dichotomy between a human soul and the Spirit of God is not a con-

cept that would have been shared by the ancient Israelites; and therefore, their Scriptures do not attest to such a view. In the Hebrew Bible, the spirit of life that animates all living things is indistinguishable from the spirit or breath of God that empowers and enables wonderous outcomes. See John R. Levison, *Filled with the Spirit* (Grand Rapids: Eerdmans, 2009), 3-13.

11 A notable exception is the work of Pentecostal theologian, Amos Yong. Early in his career, as he developed a pneumatological theology of religions, Yong exhibited sympathy with the Eastern protest to the *filioque*. The absence of the phrase offered him an assist in delaying the Christological impasse when attempting to find common ground between Christianity and the other religions of the world. Later as he developed a theological hermeneutic, Yong found value in the Western articulation as a valid Trinitarian model for understanding salvation history, though he does not simply adopt it uncritically but places it into conversation with other models informed by various global contexts. See Amos Yong, *Discerning the Spirit(s): A Pentecostal-Charismatic Contribution to Christian Theology of Religions*, JPTSup 20 (Sheffield: Sheffield Academic Press, 2000), 64-70. Cf. Amos Yong, *Spirit-Word-Community: Theological Hermeneutics in Trinitarian Perspective* (Burlington: Ashgate, 2002), 59-72, and *The Spirit Poured Out on All Flesh: Pentecostalism and the Possibility of Global Theology* (Grand Rapids: Baker Academic, 2005), 224-227.

12 For example note the comment by Augustine, whose influence over the Church—especially in the West—can hardly be overstated: "We must confess that the Father and the Son are the origin of the Holy Spirit; not two origins, but just as Father and Son are one God, and with reference to creation one creator and one lord, so with reference to the Holy Spirit they are one origin" (*On the Trinity* 5.3.15). See Augustine, *The Trinity*, trans. Edmund Hill (Brooklyn: New York City Press, 1991), 199.

13 Robert Barron, *Light from Light: A Theological Reflection on the Nicene Creed* (Park Ridge, IL: Word on Fire Academic, 2021), 141.

14 Gregory of Nyssa, "On the Holy Spirit," in *A Select Library of the Nicene and Post-Nicene Fathers*, vol. 5, eds. Philip Schaff and H. Wade (Grand Rapids: Eerdmans, 1973), 317. Carrying Gregory's thinking to its logical conclusion, Thomas Smail writes, "we also have to say that if the historical relationships point to the eternal relationships, then the Son comes *from* the Father *through*

the Spirit" (emphasis added). See Thomas Smail, "The Holy Spirit in the Holy Trinity," in *Nicene Christianity: The Future for a New Ecumenism*, ed. Christopher R. Seitz (Grand Rapids: Brazos Press, 2001), 149-164, (esp. 159).

15 Frank D. Macchia, *Jesus the Spirit Baptizer: Christology in Light of Pentecost* (Grand Rapids: Eerdmans, 2018), ix.

16 Melissa L. Archer and Robby Waddell, "The Spirit in John's Apocalypse: Vision, Prophecy, Discernment," *Pneuma* 43, no. 3-4 (2021): 553-566, (esp. 555-559).

17 Sergius Bulgakov, *The Comforter*, trans. Boris Jakim (Grand Rapids: Eerdmans, 2004), 386-390.

18 Simon Chan, "Mother Church: Toward a Pentecostal Ecclesiology," *Pneuma* 22, no. 2 (2000): 177-208, (esp. 180).

19 I would like to thank my fellow members of the Faith and Order Commission of the National Council of Churches for their enlightening dialogue and questions that contributed to the formation of this chapter and special thanks to my colleagues Chris Green and Jeremy Sims, who gave valuable feedback on an earlier draft.

PART 3

Creed and Community: Unity, Formation, and Worship

16

The Centrality of the Nicene Creed in Liturgy and in Christian Belief

Antonios Kireopoulos

THE COUNCIL OF Nicaea (325 CE) was convened by the Byzantine Emperor Constantine I, with the aim of resolving various matters causing division, and even schism, within the Christian community. Such ecclesial resolution, through episcopal consensus, could also enhance social cohesion (and thereby help to consolidate Constantine's authority) in the empire, now comprised of its newly united eastern and western parts. The preeminent matter before the Council was the theological understanding of Jesus, in whose name people self-identified and gathered together as the Church, and under whose cross the emperor, a convert to Christianity himself, placed the well-being of his people and territories. The deliberations of this Council resulted in the first iteration of what became known as the Nicene Creed, the definitive statement of belief about the Trinitarian God that forms the centerpiece of the Christian faith.

The ongoing centrality of the Creed is most evident today in the Eastern Orthodox, Roman Catholic, and Anglican Churches, with its recitation prominent in the liturgical settings of these traditions, coming as it does in every celebration of the Divine Liturgy, or Mass, as well as in some Protestant Churches. While non-liturgical and non-creedal traditions may or may not include the recitation of the Nicene formulation in their worship services, the affirmations within the Creed still comprise a central tenet of these traditions. Indeed, calling on the name of Jesus, even in the least structured of communities, if they are to be considered Christian, still reflects the belief that Jesus is one of the persons in the Holy Trinity, whose divinity and humanity together enabled the salvation of the world.

This chapter, written from the perspective of my own Orthodox tradition,[1] though with reference to other Christian traditions, seeks to connect the centrality of the Creed in liturgical practice to its centrality in the life of the individual Christian, and in the life of the community of Christians. It will do this through a brief study of the liturgical texts, and the movement of these texts in eucharistic celebrations. That the Eucharist is the one unifying factor in the life of the Christian community writ large, at least as practiced in the early church, will be assumed. That the beliefs inherent in this assumption reflect the common conviction of those gathered in any and all particular contemporary Christian communities will further be assumed.

Liturgical Practice Following Nicaea

Formal liturgical worship is a hallmark of many Christian churches. Certainly, in more traditional communions, it acts as the connective tissue holding the body of Christ together. Baptism and Chrismation may initiate believers into the community, and other rites may mark certain moments in believers' lives, but it is the coming together in worship that ritually—in the moment, and over time—holds the body together. Indeed, when considering the primary worship experience of the community, namely the celebration of the Eucharist, not only does the Eucharist itself connect members gathered in that one place and time; symbolically it connects all members of the Church throughout the world and throughout the ages in a mystical community that is the Church that God has gathered.

Of course, the Creed begins with a rather simple declarative sentence that affirms belief in the Father as the Creator:

> I (We) believe in one God, Father Almighty, Creator of heaven and earth, and of all things visible and invisible.[2]

It is interesting to note that the liturgical use of the Creed originated in the early baptismal rite, where the person about to join the Church would declare that "I" believe. The use of the pronoun "I" continues in Orthodox corporate worship. The use of the pronoun "we" reflects the belief of all those assembled and hence maintains the original corporate reference as found in conciliar formulations. This use continues in Western Church traditions. This inclusion of the creed in corporate settings, specifically in eucharistic liturgies, began centuries later in both east and west.

In the eucharistic liturgy (Divine Liturgy in Eastern Christian Churches, Mass in Western Christian Churches), there is a movement in the text that is reflective of the life of Jesus, and of the individual and collective life of those who are called by his name. That movement includes the birth of Christ, his preaching and teaching, and his crucifixion and resurrection. Likewise, for our part, the movement includes the welcoming of Christ into our midst, our hearing of his word, and our participation in the mystical supper (emblematic of his death and resurrection) that gives life.

On the way toward this culminating moment, the Church stops to recall and affirm the belief about Christ that brings us to this point. It is no accident that the placement of this affirmation—the Creed—is in the middle of the movement. After hearing the Word, the people of God proclaim their belief in this Gospel, more so in the one about whom the Gospel is written, almost as a proof of why they are present in the congregation, and then they move toward the Eucharist.

These Nicene affirmations pertaining to Jesus are:

> And in one Lord Jesus Christ, the only-begotten Son of God, begotten of the Father before all ages; light of light, true God of true God, begotten, not made, of one essence

> with the Father, through whom all things were made. Who for us men [and women] and for our salvation came down from heaven, and was incarnate of the Holy Spirit and the Virgin Mary and became [hu]man. He was crucified for us under Pontius Pilate, and suffered [and died] and was buried; and He rose on the third day, according to the scriptures. And he ascended into heaven, and is seated at the right hand of the Father, and he will come again with glory to judge the living and dead. His kingdom shall have no end.

Ancient liturgical rites made this division in the service even more emphatic. In the liturgies of St. Basil the Great (fourth century) and St. John Chrysostom (fifth century), which are still used to this day in Eastern Christian traditions, the movement took into account of the presence of both catechumens, those learning about the faith but not yet a full member of the community, and baptized believers, those who were fully integrated into the Church. Together, the believers and the catechumens would listen to the reading of the Word and the celebrant's preaching about the Word immediately following, and then the catechumens would leave the room, separating themselves from the baptized believers who would then recite the Creed (and thereby reaffirm their belief) and move toward the eucharistic meal.

This division between the "liturgy of the catechumens" and the "liturgy of the faithful" was not meant to be exclusionary, as we might instinctively think today. The mystery of the Trinity explicated in the Creed was—and still is—considered the heart of the Christian faith, and those who have accepted the faith could then proceed to the celebration of the Eucharist. In a sense, the Church was providing a public opportunity to those outside the community to learn about Christ, and then offering a private opportunity to those in the community who had accepted the teaching to dive more deeply into their faith. Not incidentally, in a way this can be seen as building on the practice of the early church, particularly when communities were located in hostile geographic areas, where the privacy of ritual gatherings ensured the safety of the community at a time when Christians were persecuted. By the time of the fourth and fifth centuries, when Christianity was the religion of the

(Byzantine and later Roman) empire, such privacy enhanced the unity of the community of believers.

The latter were assured of their faith by the same Spirit that had moved upon the waters (Genesis 1:2), led the Israelites through the desert (Exodus 13:21-22) and accompanied them throughout history. The affirmation of the inclusion of the Spirit in the Trinity follows the affirmations about Jesus. As recited:

> And in the Holy Spirit, the Lord, the giver of life, who proceeds from the Father, who together with the Father and the Son is worshiped and glorified, who spoke through the prophets.[3]

Finally, in a seeming appendage to the affirmations of belief about God held by the faithful, the members of the congregation then profess who they are as renewed, and saved, people of God. To wit:

> In one, holy, catholic, and apostolic Church. I (We) confess one baptism for the forgiveness of sins. I (We) look for the resurrection of the dead, and the life of the age to come. Amen.

Yet, this is more than an appendage. In declaring the oneness of God, the believers expressed their unity as the body of Christ; in attesting to its holiness, they claimed their divinely-wrought transformation; in pointing to its universality and wholeness, they asserted their connection to all Christians across time and place; and in noting its apostolicity, they confirmed that their common belief was not a pipe-dream, but indeed based on the witness of the apostles, and on the ongoing testimony of the saints throughout history. It is this Church, with this belief rooted in history, that the community of Christians still proclaims when the Creed is recited today.

Liturgical Practice Today

Found again in ancient practice, it was at the Easter service, when the Eucharist was celebrated on the most sacred of ecclesial holidays, that catechumens were baptized into the Church and, after affirming their creedal belief, were then welcomed into the eucharistic part of the service. Today's Catholic Church retains a remnant of this practice; at Easter vigils, the newly baptized/chrismated members of the Church, those who have now accepted the faith, are welcomed to partake of the Eucharist with the rest of the body of communing believers. There is much intention in retaining this practice.

Likewise in Orthodox practice, there is a vestige of the ancient custom. This is more pronounced in Lenten liturgies, though it is still heard in typical Sunday liturgies, when the clergy, after praying for the catechumens and their enrichment in the faith, often seemingly shout out: "Those who are catechumens, depart; catechumens depart; all those who are catechumens, depart. Let none of the catechumens remain." Following this exhortation, the prayers resume with: "Again and again, in peace let all of us, the faithful, pray to the Lord."[4]

Of course, in today's Orthodox worship settings, those who are catechumens, or others present who are not baptized members of the church, are not expected to depart, but are welcome to remain worshipping with the congregation (though only those who are members of the church—and this largely goes for the Catholic Church as well—are welcome to partake of the Eucharist itself). This adaptation of the practice shows some evolution in thinking, including when it comes to the Creed: It is no longer solely a private testimony for those who have accepted it; it is rather a public proclamation of what those gathered hold most dear and essential. As a proclamation of the faith, it may also be understood as a testimony to those who are not officially part of the church but may one day still wish to accept the faith. Indeed, it connects our faith to our witness in the world: As noted by one of today's prominent Christian leaders, "the confession of the Faith that [is] made today is renewed in every Divine Liturgy and is essential to our ongoing witness to the love of God for each human being and the totality of His creation."[5]

In less formal traditions the components of worship still reflect the common affirmations made in the Creed. Whether in non-creedal communions or in communions that do not typically consider themselves liturgical, worship includes affirmations of the person of Jesus Christ and his role in salvation, the movement of the Spirit in the lives of those gathered, and in their collective presence in the community and the Lordship of God who created all. These affirmations, while not creedal in the strict sense, still conform with claims articulated in the Creed. As faith statements they therefore enable the inclusion of those particular congregations and denominations within the wider Christian community and provide for the recognition of such. In other words, the faith articulated in Nicaea holds for all who count themselves among Christians universally.

Conclusion

In short, acceptance of the creedal affirmations defines who is and who is not a Christian. Whether one's personal practice includes recitation of the credal formulation or does not include such practice, the Christian faith one claims to hold includes belief in the Trinity: the Father who created the world and all that is in it; the Son who became fully human while retaining full divinity, died for humanity's sins, and rose from the dead and thereby gave us eternal life; and the Spirit who enlivens us.

It must be recalled that this formulation came about in response to Christological controversies that challenged small-o orthodoxy regarding the person of Jesus. While some may see the application of this strict definition of Christian belief as an exclusion of subsequent historical and theological explorations in Christian thought, the reality is that it is maintained as a safeguard against other genuinely unorthodox challenges to the faith and as a way to keep the community whole.[6] If, in meeting some of these historical challenges, the Creed has been weaponized to exclude or injure other individuals and communities, the Church needs to repent. If it has been a matter of personal interpretation that causes, or perceives, rupture today, genuine ministry and pastoral care must be undertaken in order to reconcile diverging beliefs and to bring about healing.

Ironically, if there is one setting in which the understanding of the Creed as the sign of unity is not front and center, it is in the ecumenical movement, which by definition is an exercise in seeking ecclesial unity. While all churches to one degree or another individually affirm the creedal formulations or the beliefs behind them, nowhere do the conciliar bodies that give witness to the ecumenical search for unity specifically lift up a common belief in the trinitarian God. Indeed, it is as if the trinitarian understanding of God is merely a "loose" requirement for inclusion in such organizations. The NCC mission statement reads: "The mission of the NCC is to live as a community of communions called by Christ to visible unity and sent forth in the Spirit to promote God's justice, peace and healing of the world."[7] True enough, it mentions all three persons of the Trinity; nowhere does it explicitly affirm belief in the persons as comprising the one God.

The World Council of Churches organizational statements are similarly vague. This lack of specificity is an acknowledgment that churches come together with different beliefs. The glue holding them together is Jesus. While he is identified as "the divine head of the body" of the Church,[8] it is not clear, at least from the organizational documents, that this divinity is based on a trinitarian understanding of God. It could just as easily reflect belief in Jesus along the lines of one of the Christological controversies that prompted the composition of the Creed. We can presume a more small-o orthodox understanding, but one wonders if such a presumption would have held the Church together for 1700 years.

Notes

1 The author wishes to acknowledge his long-ago seminary professor and long-time Faith and Order member, Dr. Paul Meyendorff, from whom he learned much of what he knows about the history of the creed and its use in liturgical settings.

2 This essay will not enter into a conversation about the male naming of God, and of other possible formulations. That is left for another discussion at another time and place, as has been part of theological discourse for decades.

3 As with the naming of God cited above, this essay will also leave for another conversation the historic (and still-current) debate about the *filioque*, and whether the Spirit is written as proceeding from the Father only (as in the original formulation) or from the Father and the Son (as in the later Western interpolation in

response to the Muslim challenge regarding the oneness of God and the person of Jesus).

4 The Divine Liturgy of Saint John Chrysostom, The Small Litany, Greek Orthodox Archdiocese of America, website, accessed May 30, 2025, https://www.goarch.org/-/the-divine-liturgy-of-saint-john-chrysostom.

5 Archbishop Elpidophoros, Homily, 21 September 2024, Greek Orthodox Church in America, website, September 21, 2024, https://orthodoxyinamerica.org/2024/09/21/archbishop-elpidophoros-of-america-homily-at-the-outreach-adult-baptism-of-the-african-american-mission/.

6 One affirmation of this point is in a prayer following the recitation of the creed, wherein the believers pray that God save the Orthodox Christians from their adversaries. While sounding anachronistic, it nonetheless confirms the threat posed by, not only armed military assault, but the assault on the faith posed by heresies. With specific reference to the creed and its assertions, it is also affirmed at the end of the service, when those gathered state that "we have seen the true light, worshipping the undivided Trinity, who has saved us."

7 National Council of the Churches of Christ in the USA, website, accessed May 30, 2025, https://nationalcouncilofchurches.us/about-us/.

8 World Council of Churches, website, accessed May 30, 2025, https://oikoumene.org/about-the-wcc.

17

The Nicene Creed as Catechesis

James R. Thomas

THE CHURCH HAS historically used the Nicene Creed as pedagogy. Its formulation aimed to unify Christians and clarify orthodox beliefs in response to various heretical views of the time. The Creed, a concise summary of core Christian beliefs, is a significant part of the curriculum in many Christian denominations. An excellent means for teaching the essential doctrines of the faith, the Creed may be used as a teaching tool and as a method of catechesis. The Nicene Creed follows the same structure as the Apostles' Creed, and like the Apostles' Creed, it encapsulates the entire good news of the gospel in summary. Regrettably, for some, the Creed can seem somewhat rote, something taken for granted and something recited together in a monotonous tone. Yet, this profession of faith is far from routine or lifeless. Reciting the Creed helps congregants memorize the tenets of Christianity, reinforcing their understanding of the faith. Each phrase can be explored in detail, providing a framework for deeper theological study and discussion. Incorporating the Creed into worship emphasizes its importance in communal faith expression and encourages reflection on its meaning. The Creed may be used as a structured outline in catechism classes to guide discussions on the Trinity, the Church, and salvation. The Creed facilitates conversations between Christian denominations, highlighting shared beliefs while fostering mutual understanding. Educators and leaders can effectively impart foundational Christian teachings by utilizing the Nicene Creed in these ways.

The Nicene Creed was born of great faith and even significant controversies in the centuries of the early Church. It describes the triune God, who turns toward humanity in the person of Jesus, who suffered, died, rose again, and ascended. Christians profess their faith weekly, aiming for the words of the Nicene Creed to become woven into the essence of their identity. Additionally, the Creed expresses hope for the future and the purpose of living the Christian life. It mentions all three members of the Trinity in a similar order and retains the snapshot of the gospel story when it describes Jesus. It also expands the description of the life and work of Christ, explicitly stating that his mission was "for us and for our salvation." It serves as a renewal of baptismal promises each time the Church confesses it. Several texts from the fourth century use the Creed to present the faith in the context of catechesis. The Creed was not only the baptismal formula but, in many cases, served as the basis for catechetical instruction. For example, Cyril of Jerusalem[1] and Theodore of Mopsuestia[2] have catechetical lectures around the Creed. In a time when illiteracy was widespread, the Creed served as a concise and memorable expression of the faith. As an outline, the Creed provides structure but is often supplemented with whatever the catechist feels necessary for the catechumens to know. Each part of the Creed is a launching point into a doctrinal discussion.

The Nicene Creed has also been a unifying medium within the Christian community. Despite other theological divergences, its universal acceptance across Eastern and Western Christian traditions has functioned as an emblem of concord. In the Roman Catholic Church, the Creed is confessed during Mass, which is fundamental to Catholic doctrine and is used in faith formation for those preparing for baptism or confirmation. The candidate for baptism (or parents and godparents) responds to a series of questions, assenting to the teachings of the Catholic Church. In The Eastern Orthodox Churches, the Creed is central to Orthodox worship and is confessed during the Divine Liturgy, reinforcing its importance and helping congregants understand foundational Christian beliefs. The Anglican Communion includes the Creed in the *Book of Common Prayer* and recites it during the Sunday Liturgy. Every Sunday! In the Anglican Communion, standing up and reciting the creeds each week serves the important purposes of maintenance and training. Lutheran Christians often use the Nicene Creed at festivals like Easter and Christmas and during seasons of the year related to those festivals. The opening sentence of the chief Lutheran confession, the Augsburg Confession of 1530, reads:

> We unanimously hold and teach, in accordance with the decree of the Council of Nicaea, that there is one divine essence, which is called and which is truly God, and that there are three persons in this one divine essence, equal in power and alike eternal: God the Father, God the Son, God the Holy Spirit (AC I, 2-3).[3]

Methodist Churches frequently use the Nicene Creed to affirm faith in Methodist worship services. Affirmations help worshippers understand the Christian faith. They affirm unity in Christ with those followers who first wrote them, the many generations who have recited them, and those who will recite them.

Many Presbyterian congregations affirm the Nicene Creed as part of their worship and teaching. The Creed is significant in Presbyterian worship and doctrine, reflecting their commitment to the Church's historic faith. Various Reformed denominations also recognize the Nicene Creed as a part of their confessional standards, which are used in catechism classes to teach foundational Christian beliefs. In the United Church of Christ, many congregations utilize the Nicene Creed in their worship. In faith formation, the United Church of Christ congregations often encourage exploration and discussion of various creeds and confessions, including the Nicene Creed, to foster a deeper understanding of Christian beliefs. The focus is on inclusivity and the relevance of the Creed to contemporary faith life rather than strict adherence to specific doctrinal statements.

Seminaries and theological schools teach students about early Church history, doctrine, and the development of Christian theology using the Nicene Creed in their curricula. The Nicene Creed persists as a common denominator in ecumenical dialogues, nurturing discussions, and fostering cooperation among various Christian denominations. This idea of unity of belief is an essential insight into the development of the historical Christian creeds, their role in the fight against heresy and heterodoxy, and their role in catechesis.

Exploring the Nicene Creed

Paragraph 1: God the Father

> I believe in one God,
> the Father Almighty,
> maker of heaven and earth,
> of all things visible and invisible.

As the *Catechism of the Roman Catholic Church* states, "Whoever says 'I believe' says 'I pledge myself to what we believe.' Communion in faith needs a common language of faith, normative for all and uniting all in the same confession of faith."[4]

The faithful profess belief in God. The Creed speaks of God, human beings, and the world in relation to God. The Creed confesses God's oneness. It affirms the doctrine of the Holy Trinity. The Creed's articulation of the Father, Son, and Holy Spirit as "one in being" or "consubstantial" embodies the Church's response to the Arian heresy, a challenge to the divinity of Christ. This definitive affirmation laid the enduring foundation for the development of Trinitarian theology, shaping Christian understanding of the nature of God.

Paragraph 2: The Lord Jesus

> I believe in one Lord Jesus Christ,
> the Only Begotten Son of God,
> born of the Father before all ages.
> God from God, Light from Light,
> true God from true God,
> begotten, not made, consubstantial with the Father;

> through him all things were made.
> For us men and for our salvation
> he came down from heaven,

The Second Person of the Trinity is the Word of God, the Son. This Word of God, Jesus Christ, proceeds from the Father. He was "born" and "begotten" but not made. This mystery is challenging to comprehend. A great deal of discussion in theology has focused on how Jesus can be both God and man.

In other words, Jesus is fully God and eternal, just as the Father is eternal. This paragraph emphasizes that there is one God, but the Father is distinct from the Person of the Son.

The Council Delegates (Fathers) went to great lengths to combat the Arian heresy, which claimed that Jesus was created and was not truly God. We believe that Jesus is fully God and fully man. As the Word of God, He existed forever and will always exist. He proceeds from the Father as God from God and Light from Light, true God from true God.

There is also the realization that it is through the Word of God that all things were made. God reveals to us in Genesis that God speaks to create. God says, "Let there be light." And there was light. Jesus Christ, the Word of God, was sent on a mission by the Father to come down from heaven to redeem humanity and offer us salvation.

Paragraph 3: The Incarnation and The Virgin Mary

> and by the Holy Spirit was incarnate of the Virgin Mary
> and became man.

By the free choice of Mary and by the power of the Holy Spirit, the Word of God took on flesh. Jesus Christ, the uncreated Word through whom all things were made, condescended to share in our humanity. The almighty God emptied himself and took on the form of a servant, to use the language of St. Paul.

The Latin Rite has a tradition of bowing during this paragraph in honor of the Incarnation. The Incarnation is the "enfleshment" of Jesus, celebrated at Christmas. This paragraph marks one of the most critical moments in human history. Our God became one of us.

Paragraph 4: The Paschal Mystery

> For our sake he was crucified under Pontius Pilate,
> he suffered death and was buried,
> and rose again on the third day
> in accordance with the Scriptures.
> He ascended into heaven
> and is seated at the right hand of the Father.
> He will come again in glory
> to judge the living and the dead
> and his kingdom will have no end.

This paragraph is directly connected to the previous one. Jesus became man to accomplish the work of our salvation. It was for us that Jesus was crucified. The Council Fathers included "under Pontius Pilate" to show this was a historical reality. It happened. So, too, Jesus rose from the dead on the third day after being buried.

Many days after the Resurrection, Jesus rises into the air and is mysteriously lifted into heaven. The Ascension is one of several instances where early Christians, shaped by their first-century context, reflected theologically and sought to interpret their experience with Jesus of Nazareth. The second coming of Christ will result in the passing away of the old heaven and earth and the establishment of Jesus's everlasting kingdom.

Paragraph 5: The Holy Spirit

> I believe in the Holy Spirit, the Lord, the giver of life,
> who proceeds from the Father and the Son,[5]
> who with the Father and the Son is adored and glorified,
> who has spoken through the prophets.

The Creed's teaching about God, Jesus, and the Holy Spirit inspires ethical living, prompting Christians to embody love, justice, and compassion in their actions. We believe in one God in three Persons. The Third Person of the Trinity is the Holy Spirit, who we also rightly call the Lord and the giver of life. God breathed life into Adam. This holy breath of God is the Spirit, which gives life and sustains life. The Spirit is glorified and loved as God with the Father and the Son. We believe that the Holy Spirit preceded the Incarnation and inspired the prophets.

Paragraph 6: The Church

> I believe in one, holy, catholic and apostolic Church.
> I confess one Baptism for the forgiveness of sins
> and I look forward to the resurrection of the dead
> and the life of the world to come.

By proclaiming belief in eternal life and the Resurrection, the Creed encourages hope and purpose, motivating Christians to live with a focus on spiritual growth and service to others. By affirming belief in "one, holy, catholic, and apostolic Church," the Creed emphasizes the importance of community and fellowship among believers, encouraging them to support and uplift one another. The Church of Jesus Christ is Christ's mystical body. Therefore, the Church is holy, even if human beings who compromise it are not always holy. The Church is one because Christ is one. The Church is catholic because the Church is "universal." *Catholic* means universal. The Church is apostolic because Christ founded it upon the apostles.

We enter this Church through the one baptism of Christ, by which we are cleansed of sin, are grafted onto Christ, and become adopted sons and daughters of God.

The words of the Creed provide hope in the resurrection of the dead. Just as Christ is risen in a body that no longer suffers or is corruptible, we will also share in this glory.

We eagerly anticipate the life to come.

Conclusion: Amen

And with no going back . . . amen! *Amen* in Hebrew means "yes," "so be it," and "I believe." It signifies agreement and affirmation. Here, congregations and catechumens accept the beliefs articulated in the Creed, affirming the truth of the statements about God, Jesus Christ, the Holy Spirit, and the Church. This communal affirmation is a declaration of faith within the worship context, reinforcing unity among believers in their shared beliefs. God has revealed all God is and all that God has done for us, and our confident and faithful "Amen" is the response of our hearts.

Notes

1 Cyril of Jerusalem, *Catechetical Lectures of Cyril of Jerusalem*, Nicene and Post Nicene Fathers, second series, vol. 7, ed. Philip Schaff and Henry Wace (Buffalo: Christian Literature Publishing, 1894), Lectures 1- 23.

2 Daniel L. Schwartz, *Paideia and Cult: Christian Initiation in Theodore of Mopsuestia*, Hellenic Studies Series 57 (Washington, DC: Center for Hellenic, 2013), 8-297, https://chs.harvard.edu/read/schwartz-daniel-l-paideia-and-cult-christian-initiation-in-theodore-of-mopsuestia/.

3 R. Kolb, T. J. Wengert, and C. P. Arand, *The Book of Concord: The Confessions of the Evangelical Lutheran Church* (Minneapolis: Fortress Press, 2000), 27-29.

4 *Catechism of The Catholic Church* (New York: Crown Publishing Group, 1995), 185.

5 Or "who proceeds from the Father." The phrase "and the Son" is a later addition to the Creed.

18

A Bilingual Ecumenical Catechism of the Nicene Creed

Carmelo Santos-Rolón

A CREED IS a summary of the beliefs of a group. The Nicene Creed is a summary of the main beliefs that Christians hold in common. It was first adopted in the year 325 in the city of Nicaea (in what is today, İznik, Turkey), and then revised in the year 381 in the city of Constantinople (today, Istanbul, also in Turkey). That is why it is sometimes referred to as the Nicene-Constantinopolitan Creed. Even though there are some differences in interpretation across churches and matters of debate, nonetheless, in general for two millennia this Creed has been accepted as an overall accurate statement of the fundamental elements of the Christian faith.

The Creed is made of three sections called articles. The first article deals with God and creation, the second article deals with Jesus and salvation, and the third article is about the Holy Spirit, the church, and the last things, that is the things that we believe about life after death and the world to come (or the future of the world).

A key theme of the Creed is that God is One even as God is triune (tri / uno = Three in One / One in Three). The Creed is about who this triune God is, what is the relationship between the triune God and the world, and what is the relationship among the members of the triune God known historically by the biblical names of Father, Son, and Holy Spirit.

In this chapter we offer a brief explanation of the three articles of the Creed for those who are new to the faith or who are preparing for baptism, first Communion, confirmation, or for anyone interested in reviewing the basic elements of the Christian faith in general.

First Article: We believe in one God . . . maker of heaven and earth . . .

What does this mean?

The first article means that the world is not an accident; we are not an accident; you are not an accident. The world is God's poem, and God loves the world with the tenderness with which a loving parent loves their children. That is why God is called Father even though God has no sex or gender but includes them all. For the same reason some also call God Mother. To believe that God is our divine parent means to trust in God with our whole hearts, believing that God always wants what is best for all and each of us. It also means to treat all of creation with dignity, including all human beings, remembering that when we deal with them we are dealing with the Creator's beloved. We can also add, even though the Creed doesn't mention it, that science is a gift from God that allows us to understand the mysteries of God's beautiful creation and find ways to better care for it and make use of it in responsible ways for the well-being of all. "The earth is the LORD's and all that is in it, / the world, and those who live in it" (Psalm 24:1).

Second Article: We believe in one Lord, Jesus Christ, the only Son of God . . .

What does this mean?

The second article means that Jesus is "the [visible] image of the invisible God" (Colossians 1:15). More yet, Jesus is God in the flesh. For Christians this means that, if we want to know what God is like, then we look at Jesus. We pay attention to his teachings, to the way he treated others (especially those oppressed and marginalized by the community), and to the way he lived his life. In that sense, Jesus becomes the key for Christians to understand what the Bible has to teach.

The second article also means that God has experienced in person the pains, sorrows, and injustices of the world. That happened especially on the cross where Jesus was crucified. Christians also believe that on the cross Jesus bore the sins of all humanity. Because of the Resurrection, that means that the power of sin and of death has been destroyed. From the cross Jesus offers us all forgiveness and life even beyond death.

For all those reasons Jesus alone, the Christ, deserves our faith that is the absolute trust of our hearts and our allegiance above all else. That is why the Creed states that we believe "in one Lord, Jesus Christ." (In the Bible there is only one Lord, and that is God.) This is a warning against misplacing our trust and loyalty on things that are not God, such as money, power, fame, romantic love, or even things like race, ethnicity, gender, a political party, a country, or a leader, whether a king, an emperor, or a president. Only God is God! And it is to God that we must give an account of our lives at the end of times. That is what it means that "He will come again in glory to judge the living and the dead." That is not meant to scare us. It is simply meant to remind us that our actions have consequences on the well-being of others, and we are responsible for how we treat each other, especially the most vulnerable members of our world. We cannot earn salvation through good works, but we are accountable for how we live our lives. We are expected to "do justice and to love kindness / and to walk humbly with your God" (Micah 6:8).

Finally, the second article reminds us that Jesus had a history. He was born of Mary of Nazareth as a Palestinian Jew, living in a land that was under Roman occupation, ruled by proxy leaders like Pontius Pilate and Herod on behalf of the Roman Empire. His birth was a miracle because Mary was engaged to Joseph but was still a virgin. This fulfilled the prophecies of old. It also meant that Jesus was truly divine in his essence and not just adopted by God or spiritually possessed by God's Spirit: Jesus was fully human and fully God ("God from God, light from light, true God from true God"). As a human being he lived his life and conducted his ministry inspired and oriented by the traditions, practices, and sacred Scriptures of his people. And he was shaped by the social, economic, and political circumstances under which he and his people had to live, even to the point of facing a sham trial and being publicly humiliated and executed as a criminal even though he was innocent. But God vindicated him by raising him from the dead. He then assumed his place at the right hand of God, as God, which is not a physical location but a position of power and authority. All that is part of his history, and it is important in order to understand him, his teachings, and his significance.

Third Article: We believe in the Holy Spirit, the Lord, the giver of life. . . .

What does this mean?

The third article means that God is not far away. The Spirit of God is like breath, intimately close to all creation, as close as our own breath is to ourselves. It imbues creation with life and allows people to experience newness of life in Jesus Christ through the gifts of faith, hope, and love. The Holy Spirit is called holy because it is holy itself and because it works holiness in the hearts of people. She speaks through prophets who convey God's promises, denounce evil, and call people to repent, to live lives of loving-kindness, peace, justice, righteousness, and faithfulness, and to be of good courage, trusting in God's promises.

Throughout history and around the world, the Holy Spirit calls and gathers people into a community known as the Church. That community goes back to the early followers of Jesus, especially those whom he appointed as apostles, that is, "envoys," to spread the good news about God's love everywhere and with everybody. It is from them that we have received the foundational beliefs of the Christian faith summarized in the Nicene Creed, and it is thanks to their testimonies that we know about the teachings of Jesus and about his life, death, and resurrection. That is why the Church is called apostolic. It is catholic because it is universal, which is what the word *catholic* means. It is not meant to be an exclusive group but rather a radically inclusive spiritual community, including people of all languages, cultures, races, ethnicities, physical and mental abilities or disabilities, socioeconomic status, genders, and political ideologies. The Holy Spirit calls, gathers, heals, nurtures, empowers, and sends that community into the world to continue to spread God's love wherever they are. That is "the one, holy, catholic and apostolic church."

The Church, however, is not made of perfect people. That is why it is centered around baptism, which is the means by which the Holy Spirit cleanses people of sin and offers forgiveness. There is only one baptism because God's promises are trustworthy; if God says we are forgiven then we are truly forgiven, and there is no need to be baptized more than once. It is true that we continue to be sinful and have the need to repent daily. But in doing so we only need to remember the promises given to us in the waters of baptism and trust in those promises that have been sealed with the death and resurrection of Christ on the cross and with the Holy Spirit. God is faithful!

The Creed concludes with the bold affirmation: "We look for the resurrection of the dead, and the life of the world to come." What this means exactly is a mystery. One day we shall find out. For now, it is a promise that death does not have the last word, that in the end life wins. Resurrection means that whatever we are is not destroyed by death but ultimately reclaimed and transformed by the Holy Spirit so that it can participate in the life of the world to come. In God nothing is lost: Everything is saved; everything is healed; everything is redeemed. That includes the world itself as God's creation, that world that is God's beautiful poem, which God is still speaking into being. The "world to come" is not a different world than this one, but rather this world healed and fulfilled in its glorious plenitude at the end of times, on the other side of eternity. In the end all things work for good.

Thus, faith liberates us from the fear of death, from the anxiety of the future, and from the shame of guilt. It frees us to live fully, loving God, loving ourselves, loving our neighbors, and loving the rest of God's creation with the love with which the triune God has loved us. And that love is already a foretaste of the life of the world to come here and now.

19

Un Catecismo Ecuménico Bilingüe del Credo de Nicea

Carmelo Santos-Rolón

UN CREDO ES un resumen de las creencias de un grupo. El Credo de Nicea es un resumen de las creencias principales que la comunidad cristiana tiene en común. Dicho credo fue adoptado en el año 325 E.C. en la ciudad de Nicea (en lo que hoy día es İznik, Turquía). Luego fue revisado en el año 381 E.C. en Constantinopla (hoy día Estambul, también en Turquía); por eso se le conoce como el Credo Niceno-Constantinopolitano. A pesar de debates y diferencias de interpretación entre las iglesias, por casi dos milenios este credo ha sido aceptado por la mayoría del cristianismo como un resumen fiel de los elementos fundamentales de la fe cristiana.

El Credo consiste de tres partes llamadas artículos. El primer articulo trata sobre Dios y la creación, el segundo es sobre Jesus y la salvación, y el tercero es sobre el Espíritu Santo, la iglesia, y las ultimas cosas, es decir, lo que la iglesia cree sobre la vida más allá de la muerte y el mundo venidero (o el futuro del mundo).

Un tema clave del credo es que Dios es uno solo y a la misma vez que Dios es una trinidad (tri = tres en Uno / Uno en tres). El credo es sobre ¿quién es esta Trinidad que es Dios; cuál es su relación con el mundo; y cuál es la relación interna entre los miembros del Dios único y trino conocidos históricamente por los nombres bíblicos de Padre, Hijo y Espíritu Santo?

En este capítulo ofrecemos una breve explicación de los tres artículos del credo para aquellas personas que son nuevas a la fe cristiana y para quienes se están preparando para el bautismo, la primera comunión, o la confirmación, o para quienes simplemente quieren repasar los conceptos básicos de la fe cristiana en términos generales.

Primer artículo
Creemos en un solo Dios . . . creador de cielo y tierra, etc.

¿Qué quiere decir esto?

Quiere decir que el mundo no es un accidente; nosotros no somos un accidente; tu no eres un accidente. El mundo es el poema de Dios, y Dios ama al mundo con la ternura con la que una madre o un padre amorosos aman a sus crías. Esa es la razón por la que el credo se refiere a Dios como Padre a pesar de que Dios no tiene sexo ni género pero los incluye todos en su ser. Por la misma razón algunos llaman a Dios, Madre. Creer que Dios es nuestra Madre o Padre, significa confiar en Dios con todo nuestro corazón, confiando que Dios siempre quiere lo mejor para todas sus criaturas, incluyéndote a ti. También implica que debemos tratar a toda la creación con dignidad y respeto, recordando que lo que le hacemos a otras criaturas y a la creación se lo estamos haciendo a criaturas que Dios ama profundamente. Aunque el credo no lo dice, podemos añadir que la ciencia nos ayuda a entender los misterios de la creación de Dios y nos da herramientas para cuidarla mejor y saber cómo usarla responsablemente para el bienestar de todos. "Del SEÑOR es la tierra y todo lo que hay en ella; el mundo y los que lo habitan" (Salmo 24:1).

Segundo articulo
Creemos en un solo Señor, Jesucristo,
Hijo único de Dios, etc.

¿Qué quiere decir esto?

Quiere decir que Jesús es "es la imagen [visible] del Dios invisible" (Colosenses 1:15). Más aún, Jesús es Dios encarnado. Para los cristianos eso quiere decir que si queremos saber cómo Dios es entonces miramos a Jesús, prestamos atención a sus enseñanzas, a la manera en que trató a las otras personas (especialmente a los que la sociedad despreciaba y maltrataba), y cómo vivió su vida. En ese sentido Jesús se convierte para los cristianos en la clave para entender el mensaje de la Biblia.

También quiere decir que Dios ha experimentado en carne propia el dolor, el sufrimiento, y la injusticia del mundo; especialmente desde la cruz donde fue crucificado. Los cristianos también creemos que en la cruz Jesús cargó con los pecados de toda la humanidad. Gracias a la resurrección, eso quiere decir que el poder del pecado y de la muerte han sido destruidos. Desde la cruz Jesús le ofrece a toda la humanidad perdón y vida aún más allá de la muerte.

Por todas esas razones sólo Jesús, el Cristo (Jesucristo), se merece nuestra fe, es decir, la confianza total de nuestros corazones, así como nuestra lealtad absoluta. Por eso es que el credo dice que creemos "en un solo Señor, Jesucristo." (En la Biblia hay un solo Señor, únicamente Dios). Esta es una advertencia en contra de poner nuestra confianza y lealtad en cosas o personas que no son Dios, como por ejemplo en el dinero, el poder, la fama, el amor romántico, o aun en cosas como nuestra raza, etnia, genero, partido político, país, o líder, ya sea presidente, emperador o rey, hombre o mujer. ¡Solo Dios es Dios! Y es a Dios a quien le tendremos que rendir cuentas al final de nuestros días por cómo hemos vivido nuestra vida. Eso es lo que quiere decir que "vendrá con gloria para juzgar a vivos y muertos." El propósito no es meternos miedo sino más bien recordarnos que nuestras acciones tienen consecuencias y afectan el bienestar de otros. Somos responsables por cómo nos tratamos mutuamente y, especialmente, por el bienestar de los más vulnerables. No podemos ganarnos la salvación mediante obras (Dios no es así), pero somos responsables por como vivimos nuestra vida. Como dijo el profeta, "¿Qué requiere de ti el SEÑOR? Solamente hacer justicia, amar misericordia y caminar humildemente con tu Dios" (Miqueas 6:8 Versión RVA-2015).

Por último, el segundo artículo nos recuerda que Jesús tiene historia. Él nació de María de Nazaret como un palestino judío en un país bajo ocupación romana, gobernada por líderes como Pilatos y Herodes, vasallos del imperio romano. Su nacimiento fue un milagro porque Maria estaba comprometida con José, pero todavía era virgen. Así se cumplieron las profecías de antaño. También implica que Jesús era realmente divino y no meramente adoptado por Dios o poseído por el espíritu de Dios. Él era completamente humano y completamente Dios ("Dios de Dios, Luz de Luz, Dios verdadero de Dios verdadero"). Como ser humano él vivió su vida y condujo su ministerio inspirado y orientado por las tradiciones, practicas, y sagradas escrituras de su comunidad. Así mismo fue moldeado por las circunstancias sociales, económicas y políticas que aquejaban a su comunidad, incluso hasta el punto de haber sido condenado en un juicio corrupto, y haber sido humillado públicamente, y ejecutado como un criminal a pesar de que era inocente. Pero Dios lo vindicó, lo resucitó de entre los muertos, y lo restauró a la derecha del trono divino, que no es un lugar físico sino una posición de poder y autoridad. Todo eso es parte de su historia, y para poder entenderlo bien, sus enseñanzas, su vida, y su significado, hay que tomar todo eso en consideración.

Tercer artículo
Creemos en el Espíritu Santo, Señor y dador de vida, etc.

¿Qué quiere decir esto?

Quiere decir que Dios no está lejos. El Espíritu de Dios es como el aliento, íntimamente cerca a toda la creación, tan cerca como nuestro propio aliento lo está de nosotros. El Espíritu Santo permea la creación de vida y nos permite experimentar vida nueva en Jesucristo a través de los dones de la fe, el amor y la esperanza. Es santo porque lo es, pero también porque opera santidad en los corazones de la gente. Ella habla por medio de profetas que a su vez comunican las promesas de Dios, denuncian la maldad, y llaman al pueblo al arrepentimiento, a vivir vidas de misericordia, de paz, de justicia, de rectitud, y de fidelidad, y a que sean valientes confiando plenamente en las promesas de Dios.

A través de la historia y alrededor del mundo el Espíritu Santo llama y congrega a gente a ser parte de una comunidad llama la iglesia. Esa comunidad tiene sus raíces en los primeros seguidores de Jesús, especialmente los que él designó apóstoles, es decir, "enviados" o "embajadores," comisionados con la tarea de anunciar la buena noticia (el evangelio) del amor de Dios a toda la humanidad. De dichos apóstoles es que hemos recibido los fundamentos de la fe cristiana resumida en el Credo niceno, y es gracias a sus testimonios que sabemos sobre las enseñanzas de Jesús y sobre su vida, muerte y resurrección. Es por eso que la iglesia es apostólica. Es católica porque es universal, que es lo que la palabra *católica* significa. No debe ser un club de membresía exclusiva ni homogénea, sino una comunidad espiritual radicalmente inclusiva, abarcando gente de todas lenguas, culturas, razas, etnias, discapacidades, y diversidades mentales y físicas, estatus socio-económico, sexo, genero, y afiliaciones políticas. Es una porque es unificada por el amor, sin cancelar su diversidad, y fundada en Dios que es uno. El Espíritu Santo regularmente llama, congrega, sana, nutre, empodera, y envía a esa comunidad de regreso al mundo para sembrar y cultivar el amor de Dios dondequiera que estén. Esa es la una, santa católica y apostólica iglesia en la que creemos.

Pero la iglesia no está compuesta de gente perfecta. Es por eso que está centrada en el bautismo, que es el medio por el cual el Espíritu Santos limpia a la gente de su pecado y les ofrece perdón. Hay solo un bautismo porque la promesa de Dios es fiel; si Dios dice que somos perdonados entonces perdonados somos y no hace falta más de un bautismo. Ciertamente continuamos siendo pecadores y necesitamos arrepentirnos a diario, pero al hacerlo solo necesitamos recordar las promesas que recibimos en las aguas del bautismo y confiar en esas promesas que han sido selladas con la muerte y resurrección de Jesucristo en la cruz y con el Espíritu Santo. ¡Dios es fiel!

El credo concluye con la afirmación audaz: "Esperamos la resurrección de los muertos y la venida del mundo venidero.

Amén." Exactamente qué quiere decir eso es un misterio. Un día lo veremos. Por ahora, es una promesa, que la muerte no tiene la última palabra; que al final, la vida triunfa. La resurrección significa que lo que somos no será destruido por la muerte, sino que será reclamado y transformado por el Espíritu Santo para poder participar en la vida del mundo venidero. En Dios nada se pierde; todo es salvado, todo es sanado, todo es redimido. Eso incluye al mundo como creación de Dios, ese mundo que es poema cuya existencia Dios está declamando. El "mundo venidero" no es otro mundo distinto que este, sino que se trata de este mismo mundo, pero sanado y pleno en todo su glorioso esplendor, al final del tiempo, al otro lado de la eternidad. Al final, todo obra para bien.

Esa es la fe que confesamos con el Credo de Nicea. Es una fe que nos libera del temor de la muerte, de la ansiedad del futuro, y de la vergüenza de la culpa. Nos libera para vivir plenamente, amando a Dios, amándonos a nosotros mismos, amando a nuestros prójimos, y amando al resto de la creación de Dios con el mismo amor con que Dios, Uno y Trino, nos ha amado. Y ese amor es ya un anticipo de la vida en el mundo venidero aquí y ahora. Amen.

Apéndice: El Credo Niceno, Libro de Liturgia y Cántico (Minneapolis: Augsburg Fortress, 1998), 58.

Creemos en un solo Dios
Padre todopoderoso,
Creador de cielo y tierra,
De todo lo visible e invisible.
Creemos en un solo Señor, Jesucristo,
Hijo único de Dios,
Nacido del Padre antes de todos los siglos:
Dios de Dios, Luz de Luz,
Dios verdadero de Dios verdadero,
engendrado, no creado,
de la misma naturaleza que el Padre,
por quien todo fue hecho;
que por nosotros y por nuestra salvación

bajó del cielo,
y por obra del Espíritu Santo
se encarno de Maria, la Virgen, y se hizo hombre;
y por nuestra causa fue crucificado en tiempos de Poncio Pilato;
padeció y fue sepultado,
y resucitó al tercer día,
según las Escrituras,
y subió al cielo,
y está sentado a la derecha del Padre;
y de nuevo vendrá con gloria
para juzgar a vivos y muertos,
y su reino no tendrá fin.
Creemos en el Espíritu Santo,
Señor y dador de vida,
que procede del Padre y del Hijo,*
que con el Padre y el Hijo
recibe una misma adoración y gloria,
y que habló por medio de los profetas.
Creemos en la iglesia,
que es una, santa, católica y apostólica.
Reconocemos un solo bautismo
para el perdón de los pecados.
Esperamos la resurrección de los muertos
y la vida del mundo venidero. Amén.

*La frase "Y del Hijo" no era parte del Credo original; fue añadida luego.

20

Navigating Nicene Faith in Canada

Bishop Ali Tote and Sandra Beardsall

Coming to Faith

In about 1920, Rachel Uyarasuk was a small Inuit child living with her parents near Kangiqtugaapik (translated: "nice little inlet") on Baffin Island, Nunavut, when word reached the people of a religion called Christianity. Brought to southeastern Baffin Island by Uqammak (Edmund Peck, an Anglican missionary), who had left the Arctic fifteen years prior, the message had found its way slowly around the vast region by word of mouth as Inuit families traveled and interacted, and eventually it reached Rachel's people.

Rachel's parents decided to become Christians, so they went through a ritual: *siqqitirniq*. It took place in springtime at a windbreak, made of snow blocks to protect people working on seal skins. In this sheltered space, with the sun shining brightly, the people laid out a freshly caught seal, all of it cut into bite-sized pieces, including those parts forbidden by the *angakkuit* (shamans): intestines, heart, eyes, tongue. Each person, including Rachel, received a portion. Each one was asked, "Why are you doing this?" Rachel replied, as she had been instructed: "I want to be with Jesus."[1]

Rachel's brief creed, pronounced in Inuktitut sixteen hundred years after and oceans away from the site of the First Council of Nicaea, is but one of the countless ways people in what is now called Canada have professed their Christian faith over the centuries. Some Canadian Christians are intimately connected to the Creed of Nicaea; others rarely use it; yet others don't know of it or are opposed to reciting set creeds or prayers. Yet, we believe that all Christian faith professions can be traced by some thread, however thin, back to that Council that met by the shores of Lake Askania in 325 CE. We would like to see Canadian Christians discover some of those common threads and a special anniversary year offers that opportunity. In this brief essay, we will suggest ways that Nicaea might prompt Canadian Christians to explore their own faith, both within their own church communities and with other Christians, for the sake of a wider unity with their neighbours.

What Did It Take?

The First Council of Nicaea was a complex affair, and for all that we know of it, there is much we do not. Exactly who was there, when the Council started, and how the discussions unfolded are all matters of "calculated guesswork."[2] Scholars, fiction writers, and ordinary Christians debate Emperor Constantine's motives and contributions in calling the Council and sitting in its midst. What we do know is nonetheless astonishing: A humble religious sect, only a decade after the end of a brutal imperial persecution, found its leaders gathered from the ends of the Roman Empire to sit together and find common cause on matters of faith and practice. These bishops managed both to imagine a unified Christianity and to struggle to a fragile consensus. That moment unites Christians worldwide, despite all the ways they have divided themselves from one another.

What did it take for the bishops to reach that moment? Beyond significant physical resources, the Council demanded of the attending bishops skills we might now name as requirements for "ecumenical" dialogue, beginning with a compelling faith that the Church is the one body of Christ, "not because of what we have done, but because of what God has done in Christ."[3] The bishops needed the willingness to step outside their home environments, to listen to strangers with strange ideas, to seek a way through disagreement, and ultimately, for some, to accept a position not exactly their own as long as they could "live with" it. The search for consensus was strengthened by Constantine's determination that the Council would be a success.

While the Council made many decisions, the creed that emerged is of course the best-known accomplishment of Nicaea. Its most distinctive element was the Greek term *homoousias*, which declared the Son, Jesus Christ, to be "of one substance" with God the Father. It asserted that Jesus was truly God, not a secondary creation. The meaning of *homoousias* was not crystal clear even in the fourth century but perhaps was chosen as it was clear enough to reject the "Arian" position, yet potentially vague enough to allow for a range of understandings.[4] Some bishops accepted the term reluctantly, as it is not biblical. After the Council of Nicaea, acceptance of its Creed, and of the bishops who supported it, wavered according to the whim of the emperors who came after Constantine. For over fifty years bishops were deposed and reinstated according to imperial preference—a reminder of the fragility of group decisions, even when they are made through careful and lengthy processes.

What did it take, then, to produce a "unity statement" in 325 CE? It took perseverance, flexibility, the willingness to work toward consensus, and the desire that the Christian church, in all its diversity, would be a shining example of the oneness of the body of Christ.

What Will It Take?

Diversity has always been part of the Christian church, the body of Christ. As it brought about the Nicene Creed, it is an increasing reality in today's accelerated form of globalization. Like other nations around the world, the population of Canada is increasingly diverse. People from various parts of the world come to the country in large numbers and from more places than ever before. If the initial waves of migration to Canada, beginning in the sixteenth century, until the late twentieth century brought mostly immigrants from Britain, Europe, and the United States, today's immigrants come from all parts of the world, including West, East, and South Asia, Central and South America, the Caribbean, and Africa.[5,6]

The Canadian churches, much like the churches in Western Europe and in the West in general, are being de-centered, causing an identity crisis for Christian entities that have long been at the center of Canadian life, even helping to shape immigration and settlement policies. The churches contributed to the colonization of Indigenous people in Canada, through evangelization, but mostly through its enthusiastic partnership with the Canadian government in the "Indian Residential School" system, with a lasting negative and devastating impact on Canada's Indigenous population and culture.[7] The blowback of such a tragic legacy has contributed to the demise of the churches' status. The Christian church that was never meant to be at the center or hold and exert such power, embraced it, and in Canada claimed a handmaiden role to the powers that shaped the nation's identity and ethos.[8] Now, the tragic role of the Church in the colonization of Indigenous people is part of the reason the churches are being pushed to the margins.

Thus, the face of the Canadian church is slowly changing, with an accelerated change forecast for the next few decades as immigration combines with rapid attrition. Most mainstream Protestant denominations in Canada face a very different future than their forebears would have imagined. Immigrants from other parts of the world help offset low birth rates and human resource shortages. As migration helped establish the Church in North America, it is again being recognized as essential for the vitality and the survival of the Church.[9] It brings both blessings and challenges as the churches seek to identify what is core to preserve and what traditions, customs, and practices can make room for new ones.

We view the new identity the Canadian churches are struggling to accept as a blessing in disguise. The Church was never meant to be at the center! Being on the margins positions the churches to embrace Canada's increasing diversity. Most immigrants are coming from marginal and powerless places. Only a Church that understands marginalization can truly be a hospitable place for the marginalized. Being on the margins is going to help the churches focus on building up the body rather than maintaining what it has. Being on the margins can help the Church deconstruct the paradigm that has positioned individualism as a core value in Canada and in North America in general and led to a skewed understanding of faith as an individualistic reality as opposed to a communal experience.

Newcomers to Canada reinforce and bring to the Church, in its growing diversity, the notion of a shared identity that lies at the heart of the Nicene Creed and its origins. They remind Canadians that Christians are not isolated from one another in their faith and church life, but are full members of the body of Christ, who consciously acknowledge a common set of beliefs that bind them together. In the creeds, we exist together, share our faith and our faith life together, and we believe together. Faith is not an individualistic experience as it has been commodified to be in the Western paradigm and ethos. Rather, faith is lived out as a community of believers who depend on each other, rely on one another, and exist because others exist also. This is an *Ubuntu* approach to our shared Creed that is magnified and lived out more intentionally as the Church grows in its diversity in Canada.

This view presents a challenge to the mindset that has grown up around René Descartes's assertion, "I think, therefore I am," a mindset that suggests that human existence rests on the individual's capacity to think, and that life revolves around the individual.[10] With *Ubuntu*, on the other hand, we say, "I am because you are, because we all are." Here, the life of the individual is birthed out of our communal and interdependent relationships. It is a mutually supportive framework that carries through all the members of the community. *Ubuntu* does not negate the individual but rather places the individual always in the context of the relationship with others.[11]

The commemoration of the Nicene Creed in Canada cannot escape the multicultural and pluralistic context in which the Canadian churches carry out their ministry. However, we believe the Nicene Creed can in fact help Canadian Christians face the invitation to shift their paradigm from individualism to *Ubuntu*. At Nicaea the group of far-flung Christian leaders who came together to formulate the Creed required an understanding of the faith that relied on navigating the experiences and the understandings of others. It required setting some personal preferences aside for the sake of affirming that which was bigger than any individual and common to all.

Of course, we cannot simply assume, as we noted at the outset, that Canadian Christians will rally around the Creed. We need ways to encounter one another across our Christian differences. Those who love and use the Nicene Creed can teach those who never or rarely use it to see that it is a beautiful and uniting testimony to our faith. Those who use other creeds, or rely on other ways to proclaim their faith, can demonstrate how those ways of claiming Christ and the Gospel can enrich and deepen our spirituality, and can help us appreciate the gifts of Nicaea in new ways. We have seen a willingness to explore these differences in the Canadian Council of Churches and other ecumenical settings. Many church leaders recognize that finding our common faith will not only strengthen the church but challenge the winds of polarization and anti-immigration bigotry that blow through Canada as they do elsewhere.

What will it take for the Canadian churches to share the Nicene faith? As at Nicaea, it will take perseverance, flexibility, the willingness to work toward consensus, and the desire that the Christian church, in all its diversity, be a shining example of unity. From an Inuit family in an Arctic inlet to an immigrant African family navigating their first Canadian winter, Nicaea reminds us that our diversity is precious. We indeed face many challenges, but we can work with and through difference to speak together to the heart of our faith. As the Canadian churches join with churches worldwide to celebrate Nicaea, we seek to be aware of the gift of our reality and context: diverse people from all corners of the globe, flung across a vast land, yet knit together into one body through our union with Christ and God's good creation.

Notes

1 This story is told through interviews: Victor Tungilik and Rachel Uyarasuk, *Inuit Perspectives on the 20th Century: Volume 1: The Transition to Christianity*, ed. Jaich Oosten and Frédéric Laugrand (Iqaluit, Nunavut: Nunavut Arctic College, 1999), 12-24, 127.

2 David M. Gwynne, "Reconstructing the Council of Nicaea," *The Cambridge Companion to the Council of Nicaea*, ed. Young Richard Kim (Cambridge, UK: Cambridge University Press, 2021), 91.

3 Michael Kinnamon, *Can a Renewal Movement Be Renewed? Questions for the Future of Ecumenism* (Grand Rapids: Eerdmans, 2014), 160.

4 Wolfram Kinzig, "The Creed of Nicaea: Old Questions, New Answers," in *Ecumenical Review* 75, no. 2 (April 2023): 226-27.

5 See Valerie Knowles, *Strangers at Our Gates: Canadian Immigration and Immigration Policy, 1540-2006* (Toronto: Dundurn, 2007).

6 See Barrington Walker, *The History of Immigration and Racism in Canada: Essential Readings* (Toronto: Canadian Scholars' Press, 2008).

7 Peter G. Bush. "The Canadian Churches' Apologies for Colonialism and Residential Schools, 1986-1998," in *Peace Research* 47, no. 1/2 (2015): 47-70.

8 M. Chapman, R. Janzen, A. Stobbe, and J. Watson, "Canadian Christian Churches as Partners in Immigrant Settlement and Integration," in *Journal of Immigrant & Refugee Studies* 14, no. 4 (2016): 390-410.

9 Marian Nacpil, "The Church in the Twenty-First-Century Diaspora: The Local Church on Mission," *International Bulletin of Mission Research* 42, no. 1 (2018): 68-75.

10 See René Descartes, *Meditations on First Philosophy* (1673), trans. John Cottingham (Cambridge: Cambridge University Press, 1996), Med. 3.

11 C. Ewuoso and S. Hall, "Core aspects of *Ubuntu*: A Systematic Review," *South African Journal of Bioethics and Law* 12, no. 2 (2019): 93-103.

21

Christian Unity, Christian Healing, and Church Progress Today

Tessa E. B. Frost and Amanda Kiser

A SACRED PROMISE is found in the book of Acts. The vivid picture of spiritual unity among the first Christians, lit by the fires of the Holy Ghost, still speaks to us today of the viable hope of living as one "body of Christ" (1 Corinthians 12:27). In many ways, every church council, including Nicaea, has sought to bring this promise of unified Christianity to fruition, even as the complex theological, ecclesiastical, and imperial issues that mark so much of Christian history have, at times, seemed to impede it.[1] Yet, as the apostle Paul affirms, none of these things can "separate us from the love of God in Christ Jesus our Lord" (Romans 8:39). Christian Scientists see Paul as directing us to the fundamental *spiritual* reality—God's love for all—and the necessity of reflecting that love for one another in order to achieve genuine Christian unity. In being invited to write an essay reflecting on the 1700th anniversary of the Council of Nicaea, the Church of Christ, Scientist—a lay church without creeds, which holds "observer status" in the National Council of Churches (NCC)—recognizes and appreciates the embracing ecumenical spirit of fellow Christians in the NCC. From our perspective, it is Spirit, the reality and presence of God moving in the hearts of humanity, who binds us—in mutual love as God's children, if not in full doctrinal mutuality—as the body of Christ.

Known for its emphasis on Christ-healing, the Christian Science Church sees the pursuit of Christian healing as profoundly aligned with Jesus's own words when he charged those who would follow him and unite with his teachings: "Heal the sick, raise the dead, cleanse lepers, cast out demons" (Matthew 10:8).[2] So while we do not profess the Nicene Creed and hold a different sense of the meaning of the Trinity, it is precisely in our devotion to Jesus's command that we feel a sense of close fellowship with Trinitarian Christians of today. To Christian Scientists, the deepest expression of the Trinity is seen in how its aspects inform and empower Christian prayer for redemption from sin and the healing of human suffering in all its phases.

The individual seeking redemption and healing prays to God as the omnipotent Father who cares for each of his children with the infinite tenderness of a loving Parent who desires to keep them well, and has the power to do so. The individual seeking redemption and healing prays to realize the full measure of Sonship, evident in the life and example of God's Son, Jesus Christ, which unfolds the healing power that Christ gives to Christians to demonstrate their own wholeness as a child of God. The individual seeking redemption and healing prays for tangible evidence of the Holy Ghost to lift their lives beyond the mere words of worship, to experience the unmistakable presence of Spirit in practical, meaningful ways that bring restoration, healing, and transformation to their lives. For Christian Scientists, this is an expression of the Trinity coming alive in worship, of the Word made flesh today.

We revere and study the canonical writings of the Holy Bible and fully accept Jesus's role as Savior and Messiah. We take as historical fact his virgin birth, saving mission, teachings, healings, crucifixion, resurrection, and ascension. We acknowledge that the magnitude of Jesus's human life and love demonstrated with grace and truth the divine character of God who is Love. It is by Christ Jesus's singular "reflection of God's glory" (Hebrews 1:3) that we discover our own true, spiritual nature as children of God. It is here that the Pentecostal promise continues—that unity isn't merely found in sameness but in the richness and fullness of God's glory, which is wonderfully expansive yet individual, while rooted in and growing out from the living experience of Christ.

From those disciples first gathered at Antioch, to the faithful at Nicaea, and beyond, the followers of Jesus have wrestled with and sought to answer the crucial question of what it means to be a Christian. Turning to God to answer this question today offers great hope for the progress of the church. For Christian Scientists, this question continues to call us back to acknowledging the fullness of Christ Jesus's life and teachings as recounted in the Gospels—demonstrating in our lives, with heartfelt sincerity, all that he taught and lived. He showed the enduring relevance, vibrancy, and vitality of worship and demonstrated faith—that healing results from loving God with all one's heart and soul and loving our neighbors as ourselves. Christian Science teaches that being Christian centers on this relevance of the living Word—the aliveness of God's love within us found in daily communion with God through adherence to Christ's teachings. It involves the ongoing baptism of Spirit by which we not only repent but forsake sin and gain a wholly new view of ourselves and others as the eternal, spiritual expressions—offspring—of a God who is Life itself. As the apostle Paul emphasizes in his letter to the Romans, "The Spirit itself beareth witness with our spirit, that we are children of God" (8:16).[3] This Christian identity as children of the heavenly Father demands not a sort of gnostic "otherworldliness" that ignores the troubles of the flesh, but the genuine regeneration of soul (through salvation) and body (through spiritual healing)—Christ reaching humanity here and now. As our church's founder, Mary Baker Eddy, wrote, Christ is "the divine manifestation of God, which comes to the flesh to destroy incarnate error."[4]

The Church of Christ, Scientist, was established in 1879 to "commemorate the word and works of [Christ Jesus], which should reinstate primitive Christianity and its lost element of healing"[5]—this encourages followers of Christ Jesus to follow him in every way—in the "newness of life" (Romans 6:4) of those born again, as well as in the restoration of Christian healing as a reliable, Scripturally-sound practice. For us, it's the Spirit who reveals the soundness of any doctrine through the demonstration of God's love for humanity in the release of individuals from sin and suffering. As James said, "by works faith [is] brought to completion" (James 2:22).

For the earliest Christians, church was not a human institution, but a living power, and herein lies its permanent relevance today. When followers of Jesus come together to behold and express the power and presence of God, as did those early Christians in the book of Acts, lifting hearts in prayer and praise, healing follows. There are examples in every denomination of this healing power of the Spirit at work—of lives genuinely redeemed and transformed by the gospel of Christ as it's lived in love and self-sacrifice. Recognizing this is the beauty of Christian fellowship, and gives us the opportunity to see the universality of "the church of God" (Acts 20:28).

Christian Scientists continue to seek that fellowship with others as well as the communion with God that heals and saves. In one of our recent church periodicals, a man named Daniel Alexander shares his experience of coming to church for the first time just a few days after being released from prison, where he had served four decades for a crime he did not commit. It's an account that captures the essence of God's love that permeates Christian practice.

Daniel explains how he learned to discern through prayer in Christian Science his "God-given identity as a child of God, untouched by material elements such as environment, racial stereotypes, human history, and heredity."[6] He also tells how he found "complete freedom from terrible back pain that I had suffered from a sports injury as a young man, which had left me partially paralyzed on my left side."[7] For years he'd had to sleep in a wheelchair, leaning on a table every night. "But as my understanding of God grew, I found complete freedom from this disability."[8]

Daniel describes his experience growing in church as transformative and as finding true family. He says he is now "living a life free from crime and striving each day to bear witness to all the good that God has given me."[9] In the same issue of *The Christian Science Journal*, another member of that congregation, Julie Dunsire, shares her part in Daniel's story—how when ushering at the front door of the church one Sunday, she prayed specifically to embrace everyone in her community as a fellow child of God. She writes:

> I prayed to see that no one, whether a longtime church member or a community newcomer, could be separated from understanding their true being as God's loved and cherished child. Church was more than a building with a certain number of individuals participating in various activities; it is an emanation of God, divine Love, tangibly expressed and palpably felt by those in attendance.[10]

Daniel wasn't sure how he, a Black man and a stranger off the street, would be received. However, the congregation saw him as "our brother, the guest of God," Julie writes.[11] "The only difference between us was not the color of our skin or our cultural or racial backgrounds, but the unique and completely individual ways in which we each express the infinite qualities of God. God saw only His own precious children—loved, loving, and lovable—working together in cooperation."[12]

The commitment to seeing each other in the light of how God sees us is needed more than ever in our world today. As Rev. Dr. Renita Weems, a speaker at the NCC Christian Unity Gathering in 2023, put it, the end of the book of Acts hasn't been written yet.[13] The church of the future will surely consist of an even wider embrace of all as fellow children of God. It will call for more consecration and regeneration in each of us that allows such seeing to bring genuine, spiritual transformation to our society, where, as the textbook of Christian Science expresses it, "unselfishness, goodness, mercy, justice, health, holiness, love," the kingdom of heaven, reigns.[14] Then will the church be one in "demonstration of the Spirit and of power" (1 Corinthians 2:4).

A hymn, first published in 1885 by Mary Baker Eddy, and often sung by congregations across the world, expresses the joy we find in following Christ.

Communion Hymn
By Mary Baker Eddy

Saw ye my Saviour? Heard ye the glad sound?
Felt ye the power of the Word?
'Twas the Truth that made us free,
And was found by you and me
In the life and the love of our Lord.

Mourner, it calls you,—"Come to my bosom,
Love wipes your tears all away,
And will lift the shade of gloom,
And for you make radiant room
Midst the glories of one endless day."

Sinner, it calls you,—"Come to this fountain,
Cleanse the foul senses within;
'Tis the Spirit that makes pure,
That exalts thee, and will cure
All thy sorrow and sickness and sin."

Strongest deliverer, friend of the friendless,
Life of all being divine:
Thou the Christ, and not the creed;
Thou the Truth in thought and deed;
Thou the water, the bread, and the wine.[15]

Notes

1 See for example Philip Jenkins' 2024 book, *Kingdoms of this World: How Empires Have Made and Remade Religions* (Waco, TX: Baylor University Press, 2024). In referencing Jenkins, we acknowledge the paradox of respecting his scholarship, even while maintaining that his assessment of the teachings of Christian Science, particularly in his earlier work, draws almost entirely from polemical materials and differs sharply from more balanced academic appraisals of its essential Christianity and Christian practice. See for example, Amy B. Voorhees's 2021 study, *A New Christian Identity: Christian Science Origins and*

Experience in American Culture (Chapel Hill, NC: University of North Carolina Press, 2021).

2 Amplified Bible.

3 King James Version.

4 Mary Baker Eddy, *Science and Health with Key to the Scriptures* (Boston: Christian Science Board of Directors, Scientist, 1934), 583.

5 Mary Baker Eddy, *Manual of the Mother Church* (Boston: Christian Science Board of Directors, 1936), 17.

6 Daniel Alexander, "How I Found Church–and It Found Me," *The Christian Science Journal,* April 2024, https://journal.christianscience.com/issues/2024/4/142-04/how-i-found-the-church-and-it-found-me.

7 Alexander, "How I Found Church–and It Found Me."

8 Alexander, "How I Found Church–and It Found Me."

9 Alexander, "How I Found Church–and It Found Me."

10 Julie Dunsire, "We Saw Him as the Guest of God," *The Christian Science Journal*, April 2024, https://journal.christianscience.com/issues/2024/4/142-04/we-saw-him-as-the-guest-of-god.

11 Dunsire, "We Saw Him as the Guest of God."

12 Dunsire, "We Saw Him as the Guest of God."

13 Rev. Renita Weems, speech, National Council of Churches' Christian Unity Gathering, Nashville, TN, October 10, 2023.

14 Eddy, *Science and Health with Key to the Scriptures*, 248.

15 *Poems* (Boston: Christian Science Board of Directors, 1938), 75. Cf. *Christian Science Hymnal* (Boston: Christian Science Publishing Society, 1932), no. 298.

22

Word and Deed: Nicene Credal Perspectives and Covenantal Principles of Black Baptist Churches in Ancient and Contemporary Seasons

Angelique Walker-Smith

IN 2016, I was honored to author the article "African Christianity and Historic Afro-American Churches" in the groundbreaking book, *Anthology of African Christianity*, which is part of the Regnum Studies in Global Christianity series.[1] In this article, I argue that the independent and Indigenous historic Afro-American churches are not only expressions of American Christianity but also African Christianity by virtue of an integration of African identity in the development and evolution of such churches.

More specifically, I cite Orthodox scholars like Father Paisius Altschul and Father Jerome Sanderson in *An Unbroken Circle*, focusing on the ancient history of African churches as sources for the argument.[2] It is within this discussion that the Nicene Creed becomes a foundational source for deepening my discussion about the importance of this ancient history of African Christianity within the ecumenical family, then and now.

The Historic Black Baptist Churches in the USA is one of the ecclesial streams of the Historic Black Churches, within ancient African lineages and the wider ecumenical family. I have chosen the theme of word and deed in covenantal and credal expressions as a means of follow-up to my previous article in this moment of remembrance of the Nicene Council. While the Historic Black Baptist Churches represent a divergent Baptist stream from other Baptists who do not share an African lineage, regardless of their confessional relatedness, there is a distinctive converging stream with other Baptists concerning a focus on both word and deed. Both of these convergences and divergences contribute to these churches having complementary identities of being of African heritage—Baptist, ecumenical, and evangelical Christians. In this regard, the Baptist Covenant used by Historic Black Churches is a fundamental source to understanding the foundations for my discussion.

More specifically, the proposal of this paper is to probe critically the relatedness and distinctiveness of the covenant Black Baptist churches use and the Creed of the Nicene Council in such a way that brings more light to these convergences and divergences of each for this teachable moment in ecumenical life.

Ancient African Christianity Before, During, and After the Nicene Council

African theologians significantly shaped the Nicene and Athanasian Creeds.[3] Africans were at the Nicaea Council in 325. Indeed, African Christianity was present in Africa before the establishment of the Nicene Creed, the Roman Church, and the presence of white colonists who came centuries later to Africa. Contrary to many popular perceptions, Church Fathers were from Africa. Origen was from Alexandria, Egypt, and was Coptic Orthodox. Augustine of Hippo was from Annaba, Algeria. Athanasius, Clement, Ambrose, Pachomius, and Cyprian lived in Africa. Both Augustine and Cyprian were Berbers. Both Coptics and Berbers are Indigenous people groups native to northern Africa. Eusebius and Origen, both based in northern Africa, wrote of Christian preaching occurring in Ethiopia in the third and fourth centuries. Eusebius, Tertullian, and Cyprian wrote from Carthage (modern-day Tunisia).[4]

The African Presence in North America: Turtle Island and Its Influences on Faith and Spirituality of African Peoples and Their Descendants

Although Black Baptist churches share a Baptist lineage described in this writing, they also share a separate spiritual lineage and African lineage especially important to the discussion of this paper. The African lineage was carried from the earliest ancient days before, during, and after the colonial period. Scholars like Lerone Bennett and Garikai Chengu point this out. Chengu outlines this history and cites Black Egyptians, led by King Ramses III, sailing from Africa as early as 1292 BCE to North America. Indeed, Egyptian artifacts have also been discovered in North America. In 1920, a renowned American historian and linguist, Leo Weiner, of Harvard University, in his book, *Africa and the Discovery of America*, explains how Columbus noted in his journal that Native Americans had confirmed that "black skinned people had come from the southeast in boats, trading in gold-tipped spears."[5]

Following this earlier period, Harvard University scholar, Henry Louis Gates, points to the work of David Eltis and David Richardson and the Trans-Atlantic Slave Trade Database that shows the slave trade of 12.5 million African peoples from1525 to 1866 to the Americas. Approximately 450,000 came to what became the USA.

These correctives to popular notions and ideas about the scope of Africans to the history and design in sociopolitical life in North America-Turtle Island and the expressions of faith by African peoples are important contributions to the legacy of Black churches and, in this case, to Historic Black Baptist Churches. This Pan African regard is key to unlocking what Al Raboteau referred to in his writings as "Slave Religion"[6] and other spiritual expressions drawing from the period before enslavement of African peoples.

Both the specific ancient and colonial lineages are important to understanding Black church emergence and expression in North America-Turtle Island. At the same time, the colonial history has also resulted in a legacy of segregation and racialized sociopolitical histories affecting the expressions of these churches within church life and society. In the case of the Baptist lineage, these lineages contributed to the rise of Black churches that include Black Baptist churches and other Black churches.

African Christianity and Historic Black Church Heritage

These facts about ancient African Christianity raise a larger question of why the African presence and influence is not more visible in conventional teachings of ancient Christianity. This is an especially important question relative to this paper's discussion about Historic Black Churches and, in this case, Historic Black Baptist Churches in the USA, as well as Black churches in the African Diaspora in general. The occasion of the Nicene Creed, written in 325 CE, further raises this question. This oversight is significant given the argument in my earlier work that argues "that the independent and Indigenous historic Afro-American churches are not only expressions of American Christianity but also African Christianity by virtue of an integration of African identity in the development and evolution of such churches."[7] This is also an important question related to the basic design and presentation of the Nicene Creed itself. Although the Nicaea Council occurred in Türkiye, the influence of African theologians was quite important.

Although the focus of this writing is to probe critically the relatedness and distinctiveness of the substance of the Black Baptist covenant and the Creed of the Nicene Council, such a focus begs the question: How does this history apply to the convergences and divergences for this teachable moment in ecumenical life? A further discussion of the African influence in early Christianity before, during, and after the creation of the Nicene Council points to a larger discussion of Africa malignment in church history which deserves further consideration.

Scholars of African and African descent are doing this work of rewriting this narrative alongside others.[8]

The Nicene Creed and Black Baptists in the USA

For Baptists of African descent in the USA, perhaps three of the most distinctive and noticeable aspects of the Nicene Creed is that it is a Creed, has African relatedness and spiritual lineage, and was convened by the Roman Emperor Constantine I in 325 CE in Türkiye. In other words, it "is a Christian declaration of faith that is the sole ecumenical creed as it is affirmed as dogmatic by the Roman Catholic, Eastern Orthodox, Anglican, and some mainline Protestant churches."[9] At the same time, the Nicene Creed represents a legacy of African faith mentioned earlier and spirituality given the summations of my previous article, and critical engagement with the state. The idea of convenings by the state have historically been a challenge for people of African descent in and outside of their churches, especially since the colonial period in the USA. But this convening, in general, is also an important concern for Baptists as well.

The reference of "Creed" and of the state convening of the Nicene Council in Türkiye, inclusive of the Roman Empire, are points of concern generally for many Baptists, including some Baptists of African descendent. But the focus of this writing is not only about the divergences but convergences of word and deed for Baptists in the covenant, and the Creed for others regarding the Nicene Creed. Therefore, some discussion on the contextual framing of the Baptist covenant within the Articles of Faith and Baptist heritage may be helpful.

The Influence of Baptist Heritage and the Articles of Faith

In the classic and doctrinal book used in many Black Baptist churches in the USA, the *Standard Manual for Baptist Churches*, written by Edward Thurston Hiscox in 1903, Hiscox describes Baptists as being the present-day expression of the early Anabaptist movements (defense of adult baptism since the New Testament period), often referred to in Baptist confessional and denominational circles as well as ecumenically. Further, he refers to the disparate groups of Christians during the ancient period of the earliest days of the churches in the New Testament as foundational movements that grew into Baptist expressions today. Hiscox states: "As independent congregations, or small communities, with no other bond of union than a common faith, fellowship, and sympathy, often obscure and unobtrusive, taking the word of God as their guide, they sought to realize the idea, not of a temporal, but a spiritual kingdom in the gospel dispensation. "[10]

Kathleen M. Griffin spoke of these disparate groups and tensions of the state as convening authority of faith communities. She stated in her interview with the World Council of Churches concerning her research that Constantine employed Christianity as a tool for political unity, transforming it into an "imperial religion" to strengthen his hold on power. By convoking the Council of Nicaea, she argues, Constantine was able to formalize a version of Christianity that served the state's interests. This version of Christianity aligned religious leaders with imperial authority, effectively merging "creed, sword, and empire" to reinforce the emperor's agenda."[11] Hiscox states that the primary tenets of being Baptist have primarily emerged from the days of the New Testament period, vis-à-vis, the convening of the Nicaea Council. The first century became the focus of the Baptist Article of Faith with a strong emphasis for Baptists and for all churches to claim "covenantal relationship." These tenets include the following:

1) Declare and defend the rights of faith and conscience and freedom of worship.
2) Deny the authority of popes and the right of kings and states to interfere with the people in matters of religion.
3) Reject infant baptism.
4) Baptize by dipping.
5) Accept and hold the Bible to be the only rule and authority in concerns of religious faith and practice.
6) Admit none to the churches except such as professed to be regenerated and godly people.

The Supremacy of White Baptist Churches in North America-Turtle Island and the Black Baptist Experience Within and Outside of White Baptist Life

The North American context in the USA gave rise to a space that privileged white Christians who were fleeing persecution for their Anabaptist beliefs cited in the Articles of Faith of Baptist churches. The independent Baptist leadership of people like Roger Williams was an important Baptist example of this. The pioneering leadership of Williams for advocating for the separation of church and state during the colonial period in the USA led to the founding of the state of Rhode Island and the first Baptist church in the USA in 1683. His leadership included sojourning with the Indigenous community of the Wampanoag. He advocated for their rights and bought land from the Wampanoag to start the colony of Providence and the church which grew into the Colony of Rhode Island and Providence Plantations. This leadership played a key role in the First Amendment of the USA Constitution concerning the separation of church and state.

At the same time, these earliest Baptist expressions of freedom through Jesus Christ were limited when it came to the issues of enslavement of African peoples and their vision to be free. By 1770, Rhode Island controlled 70 percent of the slave trade. Although they started the slave trade in the 1720s, Rhode Island had no other serious American competitors after the American Revolution and thereby had a monopoly on the slave commerce despite the genesis of a Baptist leader founding the area. Although Williams established Providence Plantations as a haven for those seeking religious tolerance, he too participated in the recapture of enslaved Africans and their descendants, and Williams took enslaved captives for himself.[12] Their slaving made Williams, and other Baptist believers, participants in the fraternal and legal relationship of faith and state policies and merchant classes, like the Roman state during the reign of Constantine.

Black Baptist Churches and the Legacy of the Covenant

Despite these colonial horrors, the ecclesial polity framework of being Baptist invited Black Church independence and autonomy from captured polities and non-inclusive values that were directly connected to people in these churches being physically and spiritually free. While there were "connectional churches" that were still related to African peoples, there were also many African people who resonated with a polity that promoted autonomy and independence of local congregational expressions without connectional creeds and certain levels of accountability related to this. Very importantly and in any case of Historic Black Churches, whether "connectional" or not, they sought ecclesial freedom from their white enslavers.

The polity of independent Black Baptist churches offered some space for this to happen. Wayne E. Croft states in his book, *The Origin and Evolution of the Black Baptist Church*, "Black Baptists evolved from a need to address the inequities caused by racism and discrimination. They began to form their own congregations because they refused to accept second-class status within white Baptist churches."[13] The Baptist Covenant became and still is the center for this theological and congregational framework. The covenantal approach to church life together has given structure and space for creativity of ministry within Black Baptist communities.

Now and Forward: Word and Deed

The mixed lineage of African Christianity from the ancient periods, the troubled heritage of the colonial period of enslavement and eventually emancipation, and the troubled Baptist heritage in North America brings both present and future moments for creativity, lament, hope, and renewed faith. Today many Black Baptist churches recognize the importance of churches with credal legacies and are more concerned with the deeds of Christian faith, which is an important aspect of the Baptist covenant and ecumenical life. Since the earliest periods of the founding of Black Baptist churches, freedom from oppression has been a fundamental Christian principle and deed of these churches.

This is also true of Historic Black Churches that have credal statements. In both cases, however, word and deeds, including deeds that foster and lead to liberation spiritually, physically and mentally, are principles of faith and not just social actions.

This writing has sought to clarify the lineages and priorities distinctive of the Black Baptist churches with appreciation for both the credal and covenantal approaches of word and deed. The future holds promise for what this mutual regard can yet reveal for these churches and the ecumenical movement.

Notes

1 Angelique Walker-Smith, "African Christianity and Historic Afro-American Churches," in *Anthology of African Christianity*, ed. Isabel Apawo Phiri, Dietrich Werner, Chammah J. Kaunda, and Kennedy Owino, Regnum Studies in Global Christianity (previously Global Theological Voices)(Oxford: Regnum Books International, 2016), 114-122.

2 See Antonius Conner, Jerome Sanderson, et al, *An Unbroken Circle: Linking Ancient African Christianity to the African-American Experience* (n.p.: Brotherhood of St. Moses the Black, 1998).

3 See Andrew Butterworth, "African Christianity Thrived, Long Before White Men Arrived," The Gospel Coalition, website, November 16, 2022, https://africa.thegospelcoalition.org/article/african-christianity-thrived-long-before-white-men-arrived/.

4 See Butterworth, "African Christianity Thrived, Long Before White Men Arrived."

5 See Leo Weiner, *Africa and the Discovery of America* (Buffalo: EWorld, 2011).

6 Albert J. Raboteau, *Slave Religion: The "Invisible Institution" in the Antebellum South* (Oxford: Oxford University Press, 1978), 114.

7 See Walker-Smith, "African Christianity and Historic Afro-American Churches."

8 See Walker-Smith, "African Christianity and Historic Afro-American Churches."

9 "Nicene Creed," Britannica, website, May 19, 2025, https://www.britannica.com/topic/Nicene-Creed.

10 Edward T. Hiscox, *Standard Manual for Baptist Churches* (1890; Philadelphia: American Baptist Publication Society, 1903),

156. (See Internet Archive, accessed May 21, 2025, https://archive.org/details/standardmanualfo00hisc/page/10/mode/2up?view=theater.)

11 Kathleen M. Griffin, interview, World Council of Churches, website, November 7, 2024, https://www.oikoumene.org/news/why-did-the-emperor-constantine-convoke-the-council-in-nicaea.

12 See Kia Smith, "Roots of Resilience: History of Slavery in Providence," ArcGIS Online, website, June 20, 2024, https://storymaps.arcgis.com/stories/35b7603ad8ca45cda5888d236f72ce58.

13 Wayne E. Croft, Sr. *The Origin and Evolution of the Black Baptist Church*, quoted in The Christian Citizen, website, accessed May 21, 2025, https://christiancitizen.us/the-origin-and-evolution-of-the-black-baptist-church-book-excerpt/.

23

One Bishop in the City: A Reformed Reflection on Canon 8

Matthew J. van Maastricht

AS A CHILD I remember reciting the Nicene Creed: "We believe in one, holy, catholic, and apostolic Church." After learning that *catholic* means "universal," the term was always somewhat peculiar to me, living within the height of free market Protestant denominationalism. In my small town without a traffic light, there were five churches representing four different denominations. This number did not even include the churches on the outskirts of town or in nearby communities in the same zip code. So, the Church is one—except for all the divisions. This paper is going to reflect on the question of church unity, particularly through the lens of Canon 8 of the Council of Nicaea.

The presenting problem for convening the Council of Nicaea of 325 CE was to settle the Arian Controversy—in brief, Arianism posited that the second person of the Trinity was a creature and therefore subordinate and not equal to God. However, when one goes through the trouble of gathering bishops from all across the Christian world, it makes good sense to handle some other matters. Ecclesiological matters such as determining the common date for Easter and the initial canon law for the Church are laid out in the twenty canons of the council as well as the synodal letter to the Church in Alexandria. In this chapter, I will reflect on Canon 8 of the Council, or the canon that dealt with reintegrating separated clergy. I will first introduce Canon 8, offer a brief treatment of the Reformation of the sixteenth century, particularly through the lens of Calvin, and finally offer a Reformed[1] reflection on Canon 8. This canon is difficult for many today—Reformed folk included—however, I think that it remains an essential touchstone for future ecumenical work.

Canon 8 of the First Council of Nicea

> Concerning those who call themselves Cathari, if they come over to the Catholic and Apostolic Church, the great and holy Synod decrees that they who are ordained shall continue as they are in the clergy. But it is before all things necessary that they should profess in writing that they will observe and follow the dogmas of the Catholic and Apostolic Church; in particular that they will communicate with persons who have been twice married, and with those who having lapsed in persecution have had a period [of penance] laid upon them, and a time [of restoration] fixed so that in all things they will follow the dogmas of the Catholic Church. Wheresoever, then, whether in villages or in cities, all of the ordained are found to be of these only, let them remain in the clergy, and in the same rank in which they are found. But if they come over where there is a bishop or presbyter of the Catholic Church, it is manifest that the Bishop of the Church must have the bishop's dignity; and he who was named bishop by those who are called Cathari shall have the rank of presbyter, unless it shall seem fit to the Bishop to admit him to partake in the honour of the title. Or, if this should not be satisfactory, then shall the bishop provide for him a place as Chorepiscopus, or presbyter, in order that he may be evidently seen to be of the clergy, and that there may not be two bishops in the city.[2]

The context for canon 8 is the manner in which Novatian clergy might be restored to the fellowship of the Church. The story of Novatian and his followers is long and complex and is more aptly discussed elsewhere. For our purposes, though, what is of interest is the way the clergy are to be restored. Namely, those who have been ordained to holy orders should remain as such. A priest is to remain a priest, but the difficulty comes when a Novatian bishop enters into communion with the Catholic Church, and the main emphasis here is to ensure that there are not two bishops in a city.

This clarification makes good sense. There is one Church, and the *episkopos* is, among other things, the visible and tangible sign of ecclesiastical unity. In the return of the Novatians, it was important that the Church action be to incorporate them back into the one Church rather than establishing a second church alongside of it, and one does that by ensuring there is only one bishop, one *episkopos*.

Church, Unity, and Disunity Around the Time of the Sixteenth-Century Reformation

In the Middle Ages, the security of the clarity of apostolic succession of the Western Church was anything but certain. After the papal schism between Rome and Avignon, the Council of Basel split with a majority being moved to Ferrera and a minority remaining, and as Jaroslov Pelikan notes:

> There were not two heads with one body but, now, two bodies. It had become more than a rhetorical question to ask "Which is that church that knows a single origin [and hence a visible unity]?" or to ask, "How can we know and be certain who the vicar of Christ is when there are two, or even three men contending over the holy vicariate of Christ?" The massive fact of the schism made any attempt to define the church and its unity difficult without making the situation worse. . . . But in the face of the divisions that had appeared, which threatened to undermine the obedience to the church as such, the partisans of council over pope found it imperative to define the unity of the church

> primarily as its bond with "its one head, Christ," and only "secondarily" as its union with the pope as the vicar of Christ.[3]

While the schism in the Western Church was mended by the time of the sixteenth-century Protestant Reformation, this was the ecclesiological soil from which the Reformation grew.

Insofar as the veracity of the action is certainly debatable, the intent of the Swiss Reformation was not to split from the *Una Sancta,* but was rather to recover the teachings not only of the Bible but also of the Church Fathers. Indeed, the headship of Christ marks the Church. While visible institutional unity was incredibly important, consistent service to Christ was yet more important.

In his writing about the necessity of the visible unity of the Church, Calvin warns against jumping too quickly to disunity. He said: "We must not thoughtlessly forsake the church because of any petty dissension."[4] The unity of the visible Church was of great concern to Calvin. He continued: "The Lord esteems the communion of his church so highly that he counts as a traitor and apostate from Christianity anyone who arrogantly leaves any Christian society, provided it cherishes the true ministry of Word and sacraments."[5] And yet, at the same time, for Calvin, it was not simply the matter of right and wrong, or good and bad. We witness the important and operative clause at the end of the previous quotation. For Calvin, faithlessness and disunity were both sins, the latter of which Calvin did not take lightly. In fact, according to John Leith, "The denominational pattern of church life that was to develop in Protestantism could not have been imagined by Calvin. For the sake of Christian unity, he was willing to tolerate not only inconvenience but doctrinal errors. Yet it is also certain that for Calvin faithlessness is a greater sin than disunity."[6]

For Calvin, the existence of Protestantism was to be an emergency measure that would cease to exist when the emergency was resolved rather than being an enduring reality. Protestants existed only insofar as there was something essential to protest that made the sin of disunity worthy of temporary protest. In fact, Calvin himself was so concerned about the disunity or fracturing of the Church that he wrote, in visceral imagery, to Archbishop Thomas Cranmer about the importance of upholding unity as a key ecclesial virtue. Calvin said: "Thus it is that the members of the Church being severed, the body lies bleeding. So much does this concern me, that, could I be of any service, I would not grudge to cross even ten seas, if need were, on account of it."[7] Unfortunately, Protestantism has continued and is now assumed to be an enduring and self-evident reality, in large part due, in my estimation, to an overemphasis on the invisible Church, and an under emphasis on the unity of the visible Church.

Canon 8 of Nicaea from a Reformed Perspective

It might seem strange to reflect on Canon 8 from a Reformed perspective, particularly with the sheer number of Reformed denominations even within a single country. Yet, Canon 8 is important to consider given the significance of the Council of Nicaea for the foundations of the entire Church. John Meyendorff makes this strong observation about Canon 8: "No canonical regulation has ever been affirmed by the Tradition in the church with more firmness than the rule which forbids the existence of separate ecclesiastical structures in a single place."[8] The principle of the canon is the importance of a real and visible unity for the Church. This value was not discarded in the sixteenth-century Reformation.

Eventually, as the Protestant movement spread, the Holy Roman Empire allowed for the principle of *cuius regio, eius religio,* which meant that the ruler of the realm (such as a king or prince) set the religion for his region. Due to this arrangement, one region could be Roman Catholic whereas the next one might be Lutheran, but you wouldn't (rather, shouldn't) have both. Similarly, when the Reformation moved through France, Calvin was not supportive of setting up a church alongside the established Church, but preferred waiting for the state to come to the Reformed cause.[9] In the Netherlands (which is where my branch of the Reformed tradition developed its life), from the establishment of the Dutch Republic at the end of the sixteenth century to the French occupation at the close of the eighteenth century, the Reformed Church was the public church. That is, it was the only church that could present itself as a church to the public. While a degree of tolerance was tolerated (after all, Lutherans, Roman Catholics, and Jews all enjoyed distinct spaces for religious observance), these others could not publicly present themselves *as* churches. There was one Church by which the ministry of oversight (*episkopé*) did happen; and, whenever and wherever oversight did happen, all episcopacies were collegial, never personal. The churches were overseen by church councils, which were overseen by classical assemblies, which were overseen by synods. In this, the Reformed Church in the Netherlands was the single public church for the people.

In these first centuries after the sixteenth-century Reformation, we witness the importance of visible unity, even in the proliferation of churches. Not every church was united in a personal episcopacy, but the principle of one bishop in each city was still, in spirit at least, maintained, since the context was not the ecclesiastical free marketplace that characterizes American Christianity today. Not until the French years was the ecclesiastical landscape liberalized, and other churches were able to present themselves outwardly as churches, for the first time.

In the meantime, in the eighteenth-century United States, which was historically at least nominally Christian but of a variety of different traditions, churches all grew up alongside one another. While some colonies may have had an official church or a majority church, a great deal of Christian pluralism existed, particularly in the middle colonies. These colonies included the Reformed; the first church was established in the Americas in 1628. Indeed, it was the enlightenment principles of a liberal society that marked the Protestant landscape, with no church being granted the privilege of being "The Church." In many ways, the American colonial period expressed the further development of the enlightenment ideals of liberty, while still seeking to affirm an invisible unity with a visible plurality, a development which reached its peak in the post-denominational context.

Pluralism is not an ecclesial problem, but rather the actual divisions between them. The reason why no canonical Arian or Novatian bishops were allowed is because these did not present a consistent witness to Christ in the world. Without the ecclesiastical restriction of Canon 8, the universal Christian witness would be weakened. The magisterial reformers were also aware of this problem, which is why these leaders did not intend to produce an ecclesial free market. They still sought to maintain the principle of a single church for a single realm—showing to their people one church for one Christ. However, in a landscape like the American one, it is hard to say that there is one church for the one Christ, but rather, many churches which, if one squints a bit, might be able to see a meaningful unity—or not.

The task of church unity is now before us. One bishop in one city. A single church bearing witness to a single Christ. If the task of the first generation of ecumenical work was seeking to understand whether, and in what way, all of these other churches were Christian, the second generation of ecumenical work was seeking to work together with churches in mission and ministry (as far as was able for each). The next generation of ecumenical work will hopefully be working toward a clearer and more visible form of Christian unity. This is the hard work. The Confession of Belhar (1986) from South Africa was written in a context of imposed division of churches based on race. This confession speaks strongly of how divisions within the church confuse and harm the witness of the Gospel to the world and how unity, reconciliation, and justice are all tied together in a way in which they cannot be separated.

Canon 8 is difficult for most contemporary Reformed people to wrap their minds around, particularly in a post-Enlightenment context. Today, in overlapping ecclesial jurisdictions, living out Canon 8 is not presently a universal reality for any church. However, the principle that underlies it, that there is one Church to witness to one Christ, remains essential and indispensable, particularly for a fractured and fragmented world in which many of us live. While it may not seem, from a Reformed perspective, that Canon 8 bears much importance, there is, even in the history of the Reformed tradition, a deep awareness of the principle upon which the Reformed Church is built. Canon 8 is, in many ways, an eschatological vision of what the Church can be, and indeed, what we may all seek to be in the visible unity of the Church in the world.

Notes

1 "Reformed" here refers to the tradition of the Magisterial Reformation that grew from the Swiss regions in the sixteenth century from (but certainly not limited to) the work of Bucer, Zwingli, Calvin, and Beza, and rooted in the Reformation era confessions such as the Second Helvetic Confession, the Belgic Confession, the Heidelberg Catechism, and the Westminster Confession and Westminster Catechism.

2 "Canon 8 of the First Council of Nicaea," *The Nicene and Post Nicene Fathers*, 2nd series, ed. Philip Schaff and Henry Wace, 14 vols. 1890-1900. (Reprint; Peabody, MA: Hendrickson, 1994), 19-20.

3 Jaroslav Pelikan, *The Christian Tradition: A History of the Development of Doctrine, Vol. 4: Reformation of Church and Dogma (1300-1700)* (Chicago: University of Chicago Press, 1984), 73.

4 John Calvin, *Institutes of the Christian Religion*, ed. John T. McNeill, trans. Ford Lewis Battles, 2 vols. (Philadelphia: Westminster Press, 1960), IV.1.12.

5 Calvin, *Institutes*, IV.1.10.

6 John H. Leith, *Introduction to the Reformed Tradition* (Atlanta: John Knox Press, 1981), 54.

7 John Calvin, *Tracts and Letters*, ed. Jules Bonnet, trans. David Constable, vol. 5 (1858. Reprint; Carlisle, PA: Banner of Truth Trust, 2009), 348.

8 John Meyendorff, *Catholicity and the Church* (Crestwood, NY: St. Vladimir's Seminary Press, 1983), 111.

9 Herman A. Speelman, *Calvin and the Independence of the Church*, trans. Albert Gootjes (Gottingen: Vandenhoeck & Ruprecht, 2014), 156.; Robert McCune Kingdon, *Geneva and the Coming of the Wars of Religion in France: 1555-1563* (Geneva: Droz, 2007), 46.

Afterword

The First Council of Nicaea: Watershed or Threshold?

John Chryssavgis

THE FIRST REFERENCE to a celebration a hundred years ago of the 1600th anniversary of the First Ecumenical Council of Nicaea in 1925 was in an encyclical issued by the visionary Ecumenical Patriarch Meletios (Metaxakis) in February 1923, during the Pan-Orthodox Council. The patriarchal encyclical was addressed to the First Hierarchs of the Autocephalous Orthodox Churches, inviting them to select two representatives for the formation of an organizing committee for the celebration. The encyclical encouraged a pan-Orthodox celebration in addition to other local events. It also recommended inviting all communions that accept the Symbol of Faith or Nicaean Creed. Subsequently in an appeal to global Orthodox leaders on July 21, 1925, the newly elected Patriarch Basil of Constantinople expressed his hope "that the Lord may grant the Orthodox Church and the entire Christian world the consolation of once again witnessing that glory and beauty of the Church by restoring the divinely-mandated unity and charity among Christians."[1] The patriarch then proceeded to announce the celebration of Nicaea to eighty bishops of the Ecumenical Throne, including Archbishop Alexander of North and South America, Archbishop Germanos of Thyateira, and Archbishop Christophoros of Australia.

The celebration of an anniversary such as the 1700 years since the convocation of the First Ecumenical Council of Nicaea in 325CE provides, beyond a mere commemoration of a historical and formative event, a motivation to learn from the past in order to live more fully in the present. As Christians united in the proclamation of God and of Jesus of Nazareth, who assumed flesh and dwelt among people three centuries earlier, the gathering of bishops from all over the Roman Empire offered a unique opportunity. They deliberated on and formulated the fundamental principles of a creed professed with one heart and confessed with one voice throughout the centuries across the ecumenical spectrum.

Over the centuries, Christian churches may have differed in their interpretations and manifestations of that original statement or "Symbol of Faith,"[2] but they have nonetheless endured in their appreciation of and devotion to that earliest of convictions that they "believe in one God . . . and in one Lord Jesus Christ."[3] The unity and profundity of this doctrine should inspire us, even in our day, to imagine and illustrate the same faith in language that addresses the contemporary challenges of our age and our world. Indeed, our vocation as Christians is precisely to define and defend—to unravel and unveil—the same pristine principles in a way that embraces and heals every human being without discrimination and every aspect of God's creation without exception.

The question posed by Christ to his disciples is the same question addressed to every believer across generations. It is the question asked and answered by those in attendance at the Council of Nicaea: Is there a God? Who is God? How is God revealed to the world? These questions are answered clearly, concisely, and definitively by the articles of the Nicaean Creed that state unequivocally that there is "one almighty God, maker of heaven and earth, and of all things visible and invisible; and [there is] one Lord Jesus Christ—light from light and true God from true God, of the same essence as the Father—through whom all things came into being and who became human for our salvation."[4]

It is, furthermore, also the question explored by many of the participants in this volume published by the National Council of the Churches of Christ in the USA as a contribution of its Faith and Order Commission to the global celebration of this signature anniversary. The chapters here examine the divine incarnation in light of past controversies and modern dilemmas. They consider the scriptural and doctrinal perspectives of the articulation of the Creed, and they offer proposals about the significance of an ancient faith for the world today and in the future.

However, in pondering who exactly Christ is for humankind and the world, what we frequently overlook is the pre-Nicaean period of the early Christian church. In other words, do we conceive the historical convention and milestone of the First Council of Nicaea as a watershed or a threshold? Was it the definitive end of a tumultuous era, or the formative beginning of an imperial religion? For some reason, most of us believe—though historians know better—that the Nicaean Creed somehow magically was transmitted to us as a glossy, finished product carefully sculptured 1700 years ago in a city not too far from New Rome, the capital city of the Constantinian era. However, this is a rather romantic image of the Church as well as of its traditions and teachings that emerges from a mythological understanding of the early Church and Christian society. The truth is that this is an inaccurate, almost idolatrous concept or model of the Church during the fractured Nicaean era, from which we should disabuse ourselves in the modern era.

Instead, we should strive to consider and construct the importance of the pre-Nicaean era, which invariably and inevitably led to what emerged in the fourth century, especially after the "toleration"[5] of the Christian faith and "conversion" of the Roman Empire.[6] That is to say, we should perceive Nicaea—both the Nicaean Council and the Nicaean Creed—retrospectively through the lens of the period of persecution and martyrdom, the period that shaped the apostolic church and faith. After all, even the most vital institutional element of the Christian church, namely its synodal or conciliar dimension, was neither discovered nor established in the early fourth century. Rather, it occurred from the beginning of the second century, when synods or councils were convened universally—and especially on the African continent—to discuss and decide on doctrinal, canonical, and administrative dilemmas and disputes.

In this respect, Nicaea merely continued a long-standing tradition of bishops assembling and arguing over issues facing their congregations. More importantly, Nicaea was not the beginning but in many ways the end of a way of functioning ecclesiastically. In many ways, what occurred in Nicaea was not so much the creation of a new model for Church life, but the calcification of the essential way in which the Church had already functioned—with substantial success, even during the darkest of times—for three centuries. Nicaea marked the beginning of a new era, the imperial era; and for many, this was arguably the beginning of a decline, despite the fact that the Christian church and faith was now publicly favored and visible.

This means that, while it may be tempting to idealize the Nicaean period and decisions, we should be honest enough to admit that—at least for most of us living in post-Enlightenment, Western cultures—our age does not really reflect the post-Nicaean era as much as it recalls the pre-Nicaean era when there was no imperial support, i.e., a rather clear demarcation between Church and state. It is that period of time and model of Church that shaped what was ultimately determined and defined unilaterally in the Nicene Council of 325, where unity rather than uniformity in "faith and order" were affirmed once for all and enforced by imperial decree.

Just as in the Church of the apostolic and post-apostolic period, the Council of Nicaea formulated a statement or Symbol of Faith that could be expressed in different and diverse contexts. This is why this book assembles clerics, theologians, and laity from manifold and alternate backgrounds who approach the First Ecumenical Council in light of the modern ethical questions, such as immigration and warfare, oppression and power, as well as race and religion. However, unless we carefully study the developments of the early Church—before Emperor Constantine invited the bishops of the ecumenical Church at the time—then we cannot fully grasp the motivation, justification, and importance of that First Council of Nicaea.

I have a feeling that, with the social, economic, and political developments of our time—across the globe, but predominantly here in the United States—we will benefit greatly from discerning and discovering in this book how the first three centuries of uncertainty and disagreement among and within the early Christian communities led to the unequivocal and unprecedented unity-in-faith of the Nicaean Creed.

Notes

1 *Commemorative Pamphlet on the Festive Celebration of the 1600th Anniversary since the First Ecumenical Council of Nicaea* (Constantinople: Estia Publications, 1925), 13.
2 The "Symbol of Faith" signifies the theological definition of the Nicaean Creed.
3 Nicaean Creed.
4 Nicaean Creed.
5 The Edict of Milan, also known as a Decree of Toleration or religious freedom, was issued by Emperor Constantine in 313 CE.
6 Although it is almost certain that Emperor Constantine only converted on his deathbed, indeed if he converted at all, his religious experience on the battlefield of the Milvian Bridge marked a radical shift in the persecution of Christians.

About the National Council of the Churches of Christ in the USA

The purpose of the National Council of the Churches of Christ in the United States of America (NCC) shall be to live as a community of communions called by Christ to visible unity and sent forth in the Spirit to promote God's justice, peace and the healing of the world.

SINCE 1950, NCC has served as a leading ecumenical voice of witness to the living Christ in the public square, bringing together thirty-seven member communions representing approximately thirty million Christians and 100,000 congregations. NCC strives to embody a holy calling—that is, to live as a community grounded in the Gospel, committed to visible unity, and sent forth by the Spirit to promote justice, peace, and healing in the world.

The member communions of the NCC come from the Anglican, Orthodox, and Protestant traditions, the latter including Mainline, Historic Black, and Living Peace traditions. In addition, there are non-member communions that affiliate with the NCC as observers; these communions come from the Catholic, other Protestant, and still other traditions. Both member and non-member churches contribute to the common work of the NCC.

More Books from the Faith and Order Convening Table of the National Council of Churches

Confronting Racism and White Supremacy in the US: Twenty-First-Century Theological Perspectives (Friendship Press, 2024)

Thinking Theologically about Mass Incarceration: Biblical Foundations and Justice Imperatives (Paulist Press, 2017)

Unity in Mission: Theological Reflections on the Pilgrimage of Mission (Paulist Press, 2013)

Ecumenical Directions in the United States Today: Churches on a Theological Journey (Paulist Press, 2012)

Ancient Faith and American-Born Churches: Dialogues Between Christian Traditions (Paulist Press, 2006)

Love for the Poor: God's Love for the Poor and the Churches' Witness to It (2005)

The Fragmentation of the Church and its Unity in Peacemaking (Eerdmans, 2001)

Ending Racism in the Church (United Church Press, 1998)

Grounds for Understanding: Ecumenical Resources for Responses to Religious Pluralism (Eerdmans, 1998)

Telling the Churches' Stories: Ecumenical Perspectives on Writing Christian History (Eerdmans, 1995)

The Churches' Peace Witness (Eerdmans, 1994)

The Church in the Movement of the Spirit (Eerdmans, 1994)

Twelve Tales Untold: A Study Guide for Ecumenical Reception (Eerdmans, 1993)

Women and Church: The Challenge of Ecumenical Solidarity in an Age of Alienation (Eerdmans, 1991)

Faith to Creed: Ecumenical Perspectives on the Affirmation of the Apostolic Faith in the Fourth Century (Eerdmans, 1991)

The Church with AIDS: Renewal in the Midst of Crisis (Westminter/John Knox, 1990)

Apostolic Faith in America (Eerdmans, 1988)

Black Witness to Apostolic Faith (Eerdmans, 1988)

Christ in East and West (Mercer University Press, 1987)

Spirit of Truth: Ecumenical Perspectives on the Holy Spirit (Holy Cross Orthodox Press, 1986)

More Books from Friendship Press

A Call to Hope: Living as Christians in a Violent Society

A Legacy of Faith and Justice: Pan African Advocacy and Leadership for Ending Hunger

Behold, What Wonder: A 30-Day Advent Journal

Born of the Sun: A Namibian Novel

Confronting Racism and White Supremacy in the US: Twenty-First-Century Theological Perspectives

Ethics in the Present Tense: Readings from Christianity and Crisis

For Everything a Season: A 30-Day Ecclesiastes Journal

Free and Fearless: Life and Leadership Lessons from Women of the Bible

Hope and Justice for All in the Americas: Discerning God's Mission

Let Your Light Shine: Mobilizing for Justice with Children and Youth

Seeking to Be Christian in Race Relations

The Indian Affair

Through Faith and Flaws: A 30-Day Journal with Old Testament Women

United Against Racism: Churches for Change

United Against Racism Facilitator's Guide

Walking with Jesus in New Life: A 30-Day Easter Journal

Walking with Jesus in Suffering: A 30-Day Lenten Journal

Words of Wisdom: A 30-Day Proverbs Journal

Edited by Michael R. Fisher Jr.

CONFRONTING RACISM AND WHITE SUPREMACY IN THE US

TWENTY-FIRST-CENTURY THEOLOGICAL PERSPECTIVES

Confronting Racism and White Supremacy in the US: Twenty-First-Century Theological Perspectives

CONFRONTING RACISM AND White Supremacy in the US: Twenty-First-Century Theological Perspectives is a collection of essays considering contemporary issues in the ongoing fight against racial oppression and inequality in the United States. Edited by Michael R. Fisher Jr., it includes contributions from ecumenical leaders, religious scholars, and activists with insights about the role religion can and must play in advancing racial justice and equity.

Praise for Confronting Racism and White Supremacy in the US

Racism and all forms of discrimination continue to be pervasive in our society, disrupting human rights and diminishing human dignity. This book is timely and calls the church once again to find its way to being an active participant in the eradication of racism.
—Rev. Dr. Karen Georgia Thompson, General Minister and President/CEO, United Church of Christ, National Ministries

Confronting Racism and White Supremacy in the US: Twenty-First-Century Theological Perspectives is a powerful resource demonstrating the indispensable role of theological work in dismantling racism and white supremacy. Congregations and faith leaders will find enduring spiritual wisdom, innovative theological insights and urgent social analysis to respond to the 'fierce urgency of now.'
—Christophe D. Ringer, Author of *Necropolitics: The Religious Crisis of Mass Incarceration in America*

Elevating voices from the academy, the church, and activists' spaces, this volume is strongly recommended for those committed to building communities of sustainable resistance for the 21st century and beyond.
—Asa Lee, President and Professor of Theological Formation for Ministry, Pittsburgh Theological Seminary

An indispensable contribution and must-read for all people committed to fostering a more peaceable, loving, and just world.
—Lorena M. Parrish, Associate Professor of Urban Ministries and Director, Community Engagement Institute and Center for Public Theology, Wesley Theological Seminary

This volume is a must-read for those who see theological reflection and ecclesial participation as integral to the struggle for "another possible world" in which nation and race no longer limit love of neighbor.
—Rufus Burnett Jr., Assistant Professor of Systematic Theology, Fordham University